W9-BSE-308

A PRACTICAL GUIDE TO FEDERAL EVIDENCE:
Objections,
Responses,
Rules, and
Practice
Commentary

Revised Fourth Edition

This edition reflects changes to the
Federal Rules of Evidence
through December 1, 1998

NATIONAL INSTITUTE FOR TRIAL ADVOCACY
1999 Publications Committee

Kenneth S. Broun, Chair
Professor of Law
University of North Carolina
Chapel Hill, North Carolina

Joseph R. Bankoff
King & Spalding
Atlanta, Georgia

James J. Brosnahan
Morrison & Foerster
San Francisco, California

Jo Ann Harris
Pace University School of Law
White Plains, New York

Deanne C. Siemer
Attorney at Law
Washington, D.C.

A PRACTICAL GUIDE TO FEDERAL EVIDENCE:
Objections, Responses, Rules, and Practice Commentary

Anthony J. Bocchino
Jack E. Feinberg Professor of Litigation
Temple University School of Law

David A. Sonenshein
I. Herman Stern Professor of Law
Temple University School of Law

REVISED FOURTH EDITION

NATIONAL INSTITUTE FOR TRIAL ADVOCACY

© 1988, 1991, 1993, 1996, 1997, 1999

by

National Institute for Trial Advocacy

PRINTED IN THE UNITED STATES OF AMERICA
ALL RIGHTS RESERVED

No part of this work may be reproduced or transmitted in any form or by any means, electronic or mechanical, including photocopying and recording, or by any information storage or retrieval system without the prior written approval of the National Institute for Trial Advocacy unless such copying is expressly permitted by federal copyright law. Address inquiries to:

Reproduction Permission
National Institute for Trial Advocacy
Notre Dame Law School
Notre Dame, Indiana 46556
(800) 225-6482
Fax (219) 282-1263
E-mail: nita.1@nd.edu
www.nita.org

Bocchino, Anthony J. and David A. Sonenshein, *A Practical Guide to Federal Evidence: Objections, Responses, Rules, and Practice Commentary,* Revised Fourth Edition (NITA, 1999).

ISBN 1-55681-650-2

To my mentors, Joe Harbaugh, Ken Pye, and Ken Broun,
whose knowledge and wisdom are reflected on every page of this volume.
A.J.B.

To my parents
D.A.S.

TABLE OF CONTENTS

Section IX. Hearsay

FOREWORD

This book is designed for use by both practicing attorneys and law students. With respect to attorneys, the book provides a ready reference for the appropriate objection to proffered evidence and the appropriate response to such objection in support of admissibility. The book is divided into sections that group potential evidentiary objections by subject matter, making them easy to locate. Each section contains a definition of the evidentiary matter, the forms of objection and response, a reprint of the controlling rule, and a practice commentary that discusses the most common issues that must be confronted by the trial lawyer. The book also contains a delineation of the evidentiary foundations necessary for the admissibility of evidence. In short, a lawyer may refer to this book in order to quickly discover the appropriate way to offer evidence and oppose its offer both during the pretrial preparation stage and for quick reference at the time of trial.

With respect to the law student, this book is designed to be used either as the text for an evidence course or as a supplement to another text. This book not only provides students with a real understanding of the concepts that comprise the rules of evidence, but also provides a model of good practice which enables them to understand the rules in an advocacy setting. In this way the evidence student can see the applicability of the rules of evidence in an advocacy setting. The book is also designed for use as a supplementary text in both trial advocacy and clinical courses. By reference to this text, the student can readily solve potential evidentiary problems and move onto the more difficult tactical and advocacy issues presented by the case at hand.

The authors believe that this text can be of substantial assistance to lawyer and student alike in the improvement of the level of trial advocacy practice in our courts.

ACKNOWLEDGMENTS

The authors gratefully acknowledge the following people and institutions. The publication of this volume was supported by a research grant provided by the Temple University School of Law. We are grateful to Dean Carl Singley for providing us with the grant, and to the clerical staff at Temple, particularly David Bogan, who worked on numerous drafts of this book.

The authors also thank a decade of evidence and trial advocacy students as well as the participants in NITA programs around the nation whose questions and needs inspired this book.

Finally, the authors thank the able assistance of the National Institute for Trial Advocacy, its many fine instructors, and especially Robert Oliphant and Jim Seckinger for their particular assistance in this publication.

Section I. General Considerations

CHAPTER 1
OBJECTIONS

Definition

In order to challenge the admission of evidence, the opponent of the offer of the evidence must bring the challenge to the attention of the court by means of an objection. Generally, failure to object waives appellate consideration of any error in the admission of evidence at trial.

Forms of Objection and Response

Forms of Objection

> ➤ *I object on the ground that* _____.
> ➤ *I move to strike the witness' answer on the ground that* _____.

Form of Response

> ➤ *The evidence is admissible because* _____.

Federal Rule 103. Rulings on Evidence

(a) **Effect of erroneous ruling.** Error may not be predicated upon a ruling which admits or excludes evidence unless a substantial right of the party is affected, and

(1) **Objection.** In case the ruling is one admitting evidence, a timely objection or motion to strike appears of record, stating the specific ground of objection, if the specific ground was not apparent from the context; or

(2) **Offer of proof.** In case the ruling is one excluding evidence, the substance of the evidence was made known to the court by offer or was apparent from the context within which questions were asked.

(b) **Record of offer and ruling.** The court may add any other or further statement which shows the character of the evidence, the form in which it was offered, the objection made, and the ruling thereon. It may direct the making of an offer in question and answer form.

(c) **Hearing of jury.** In jury cases, proceedings shall be conducted, to the extent practicable, so as to prevent inadmissible evidence from being suggested to the jury by any means, such as making statements or offers of proof or asking questions in the hearing of the jury.

(d) **Plain error.** Nothing in this rule precludes taking notice of plain errors affecting substantial rights although they were not brought to the attention of the court.

Commentary

The Federal Rules of Evidence require that counsel object to an offer of evidence in order to seek its exclusion from the trial and the record. Thus, the court relies on counsel to call the inadmissibility of proffered evidence to its attention. Once the objection is lodged, the court should rule on the admissibility of the offered evidence by either sustaining (granting) or overruling (denying) the objection. Absent plain error, an appellate court will not review the erroneous admission of evidence to which no objection has been made. Furthermore, an appellate court will not reverse a judgment of a trial court "unless a substantial right of the party is affected." *Plain error* refers to errors in the admission of evidence which are clear and obvious, and which so substantially affect the rights of the complaining party as to fundamentally prejudice it.

Objections must state the specific ground for exclusion of evidence unless the ground for the objection is obvious. As a result, an objection or motion to strike based on the grounds of relevance, materiality, or competence will be insufficient to adequately preserve the matter for appeal unless the lack of relevance, materiality or competence is obvious. Objecting counsel must state, in specific terms, the reason why the evidence is not relevant, material, or competent. Furthermore, objections must be timely in that they must be stated as soon as the objectionable nature of the question or answer becomes apparent. This requirement is sometimes referred to as the contemporaneous objection rule. As a result, objections to the form of a question must be made at the time of the question. Similarly, where a question put to a witness calls for an inadmissible answer, the objection should be interposed before the answer. Where, however, the question on its face does not call for inadmissible information, but the witness' answer contains inadmissible information, then the objection takes the form of a motion to strike the answer.

The motion to strike must accompany any objection made to the testimony of a witness or the contents of a proposed exhibit. The failure to move to strike objected-to testimony by a witness makes that testimony available for consideration at the time of appeal to test the sufficiency of the evidence as to the matter to which it relates in the lawsuit.

CHAPTER 2
OFFERS OF PROOF

Definition

An offer of proof is a statement for the record of the substance of a witness' testimony which would have been given but for a ruling of a trial judge to exclude such testimony.

Forms of the Offer

- ➤ By asking the witness to state for the record, outside the hearing of the jury, what his testimony would have been if the judge had not excluded it; or
- ➤ By a statement by the counsel who had attempted to offer the witness' statement, which provides the substance of what the witness' testimony would have been, but for the adverse ruling; or
- ➤ By a prepared written statement of the witness' testimony which would have been given but for the adverse ruling.

Federal Rule 103. Rulings on Evidence

(a) Effect of erroneous ruling. Error may not be predicated upon a ruling which admits or excludes evidence unless a substantial right of the party is affected, and

(2) Offer of proof. In case the ruling is one excluding evidence, the substance of the evidence was made known to the court by offer or was apparent from the context within which questions were asked.

(b) Record of offer and ruling. The court may add any other or further statement which shows the character of the evidence, the form in which it was offered, the objection made, and the ruling thereon. It may direct the making of an offer in question and answer form.

Commentary

Where a question is posed to a witness at trial and the court sustains an objection that precludes the witness' answer, the correctness of the court's ruling is difficult, if not in some cases impossible, to review on appeal unless the trial record contains the witness' proposed answer. Only then can the appellate court ascertain if the information which would have been elicited but for the court's ruling, was truly inadmissible. The offer of proof provides the record with the witness' answer to the objected-to question. In the absence of the offer of proof, the appellate court may decline to review the trial court's ruling.

The offer of proof can be made in any of three ways, all outside the hearing of the jury. First, counsel may ask the witness to state what his testimony would have been. Second, counsel may state what the witness' testimony would have been. Third, counsel may submit a prepared, written statement of the excluded testimony. In addition, the offer of proof should contain a statement by counsel as to the admissible purpose for which the evidence is offered.

The offer of proof must be made at the time of the sustaining of an objection or it will be waived. The theory behind this rule is to provide the trial judge the most informed opportunity to make the proper ruling.

CHAPTER 3
COMPETENCE TO TESTIFY

Definition

A person is competent to be a witness if he possesses the ability to: (1) perceive the events about which he will testify; (2) to remember the events about which he will testify; (3) to communicate understandably to the trier of fact; and (4) to appreciate the obligation to tell the truth which is imposed by the oath or affirmation.

Forms of Objection and Response

Forms of Objection

> ➤ *I object to the calling of this witness on the ground that he is incompetent to testify because he lacks the ability to _____ which has been shown on the voir dire of the witness.*

> ➤ *I move to strike the witness' testimony and object to further testimony on the ground that the witness is incompetent in that his testimony shows he lacks the ability to _____.*

Forms of Response

> ➤ *The witness is presumed competent and there has been no showing of any inability on the part of the witness to perceive, remember, communicate, or appreciate the oath.*

> ➤ *The witness is competent to testify and any questions regarding the witness' testimonial capacities go to the weight of the evidence rather than the competency of the witness.*

Federal Rule 601. General Rule of Competency

Every person is competent to be a witness except as otherwise provided in these rules. However, in civil actions and proceedings, with respect to an element of a claim or defense as to which State law supplies the rule of decision, the competency of a witness shall be determined in accordance with the State law.

Federal Rule 602. Lack of Personal Knowledge

A witness may not testify to a matter unless evidence is introduced sufficient to support a finding that the witness has personal knowledge of the matter. Evidence to prove personal knowledge may, but need not, consist of the witness' own testimony. This rule is subject to the provisions of Rule 703, relating to opinion testimony by expert witnesses.

Federal Rule 603. Oath or Affirmation

Before testifying, every witness shall be required to declare that the witness will testify truthfully, by oath or affirmation administered in a form calculated to awaken the witness' conscience and impress the witness' mind with the duty to do so.

Federal Rule 604. Interpreters

An interpreter is subject to the provisions of these rules relating to qualification as an expert and the administration of an oath or affirmation to make a true translation.

Federal Rule 605. Competency of Judge as Witness

The judge presiding at the trial may not testify in that trial as a witness. No objection need be made in order to preserve the point.

Federal Rule 606. Competency of Juror as Witness

(a) At the trial. A member of the jury may not testify as a witness before that jury in the trial of the case in which the juror is sitting. If the juror is called so to testify, the opposing party shall be afforded an opportunity to object out of the presence of the jury.

(b) Inquiry into validity of verdict or indictment. Upon an inquiry into the validity of a verdict or indictment, a juror may not testify as to any matter or statement occurring during the course of the jury's deliberations or to the effect of anything upon the juror or any other juror's mind or emotions as influencing the juror to assent to or dissent from the verdict or indictment or concerning the juror's mental processes in connection therewith, except that a juror may testify on the question whether extraneous prejudicial information was improperly brought to the jury's attention or whether any outside influence was improperly brought to bear upon any juror. Nor may a juror's affidavit or evidence of any statement by the juror concerning a matter about which the juror would be precluded from testifying be received for these purposes.

Commentary

Competent is the term applied to a person who possesses the abilities to serve as a witness in a trial or hearing. Competence embodies four qualities: perception, recollection, communication, and appreciation of the oath or affirmation. Rule 601 states that a witness is generally presumed competent to testify in a federal court. Thus, unless challenged by the opponent or by the court on its own motion, a witness will be permitted to testify. Moreover, there is no affirmative duty on a proponent of a witness to lay a foundation of general competence for a witness. If, however, the opponent has reason to believe that a witness is deficient in one of the testimonial capacities such that he cannot serve as a witness, the opponent may move at or before the time the person is sworn as a witness to challenge competence on voir dire. Moreover, if the opponent learns of the alleged lack of competence in the course of the witness' testimony, the opponent may move to strike the witness' testimony based on a lack of competence.

The issue of competence is usually raised concerning child witnesses or witnesses who have some physical or mental deficiency. In these circumstances, either the age or condition of the witness potentially interferes with the abilities required of a competent witness. Upon objection or on the judge's own motion, a voir dire hearing will inquire into the ability of the witness, so-challenged, to meet the competence requirements. The hearing normally consists solely of an examination of the witness whose competence is questioned, but may include testimony of other witnesses who have information on the abilities of the proposed witness. The question of competence is a preliminary matter to be determined by the judge, and will only be overturned for an abuse of discretion.

Note that the rules make specific exceptions for judges and jurors who are considered *per se* incompetent to testify in cases in which they are serving in the role of judges or jurors respectively.

Finally, it is critical to appreciate the distinction between the competence of a witness to testify and the weight to be accorded a witness' testimony. Though a witness may possess sufficient testimonial abilities to survive the relatively low threshold of competence, the witness may well be subjected to impeachment with respect to the relatively unimpressive quality of those testimonial abilities, which will impact on the weight accorded the witness' testimony by the trier of fact.

CHAPTER 4
FIRSTHAND KNOWLEDGE

Definition

A witness may testify only as to matters about which he has personal or firsthand knowledge. In other words, a witness may testify only as to matters which the witness has perceived through one of the senses.

Forms of Objection and Response

Form of Objection

➤ *I object that there has been no foundation to show that the witness has personal knowledge of the matter about which he has been asked.*

Form of Response

➤ *The witness has shown that he had firsthand knowledge of the subject of his testimony. A foundation has been laid which demonstrates he was in a position to know the things about which he will testify.*

Federal Rule 602. Lack of Personal Knowledge

A witness may not testify to a matter unless evidence is introduced sufficient to support a finding that the witness has personal knowledge of the matter. Evidence to prove personal knowledge may, but need not, consist of the witness' own testimony. This rule is subject to the provisions of Rule 703, relating to opinion testimony by expert witnesses.

Commentary

A prerequisite of admissible testimony is the witness' possession of personal knowledge of the matter about which testimony is given. The requirement of firsthand knowledge underlies much of the law of evidence and explains generally the proscriptions against opinion testimony and hearsay. In a sense, lack of personal or firsthand knowledge demonstrates the incompetency of the witness to testify as to particular facts. Generally, the proponent of the witness must lay a foundation on the issue of personal knowledge by offering evidence sufficient to support a finding that the witness had firsthand knowledge of the subject matter of his testimony.

Note that an expert witness need not have firsthand knowledge of the subject of his expert opinion. The expert may rely on a hypothetical question drawn from facts proved by one with personal knowledge. In addition, though the proponent of an out-of-court statement must lay a foundation for the personal knowledge of an out-of-court declarant, the requirement of personal knowledge for the out-of-court declarant is suspended where the out-of-court statement is an admission of a party opponent under Rule 801.

CHAPTER 5
JUDICIAL NOTICE

Definition
A fact that is generally known in the jurisdiction where the case is being tried, or that is capable of ready and certain verification, may be proved by requesting the court to judicially notice the fact. Judicially noticed facts do not require proof by the presentation of evidence.

Forms of Objection and Response
Form of Objection

> ➤ *I object to the court judicially noticing* _____ (insert fact offered by opponent) *in that:*
>> (a) *it is not generally known in this jurisdiction,* and/or
>> (b) *it is open to dispute and not capable of ready and certain verification.*

Form of Response

> ➤ *Judicial notice of* _____ (insert fact) *is appropriate because:*
>> (a) *the fact is generally known by people in this local jurisdiction and to require other proof would waste the time of the court,* or
>> (b) *it is capable of ready and certain verification by resort to authoritative sources which have been provided to the court.*

Federal Rule 201. Judicial Notice of Adjudicative Facts

(a) Scope of rule. This rule governs only judicial notice of adjudicative facts.

(b) Kinds of facts. A judicially noticed fact must be one not subject to reasonable dispute in that it is either (1) generally known within the territorial jurisdiction of the trial court or (2) capable of accurate and ready determination by resort to sources whose accuracy cannot reasonably be questioned.

(c) When discretionary. A court may take judicial notice, whether requested or not.

(d) When mandatory. A court shall take judicial notice if requested by a party and supplied with the necessary information.

(e) Opportunity to be heard. A party is entitled upon timely request to an opportunity to be heard as to the propriety of taking judicial notice and the tenor of the matter noticed. In the absence of prior notification, the request may be made after judicial notice has been taken.

(f) Time of taking notice. Judicial notice may be taken at any stage of the proceeding.

(g) Instructing jury. In a civil action or proceeding, the court shall instruct the jury to accept as conclusive any fact judicially noticed. In a criminal case, the court shall instruct the jury that it may, but is not required to, accept as conclusive any fact judicially noticed.

Commentary

Judicial notice is an effective and timesaving method of proving facts that are generally known in the trial jurisdiction or that are capable of ready and certain verification by reference to authoritative sources. Judicial notice may be taken at any time during a proceeding, including at the appellate level. Rule 201 applies only to adjudicative facts, that is, facts that are in issue in the trial of a given case. For example, if it is important to a lawsuit that January 21 of a given year was a Monday, this fact would be an appropriate one for judicial notice. The federal rule excludes legislative facts from its scope, that is, facts that are not at issue in the particular lawsuit, but that form the policy basis for a particular statute or rule of law, (e.g., separate but equal educational systems established on the basis of race create a badge of inferiority for the minority race).

The first category of facts appropriate for judicial notice are those facts that are generally known in the trial jurisdiction. The fact must be generally known, not merely known by the judge. Facts in this category include such matters as the character of a particular neighborhood (e.g., business district, residential, rural) or other commonly known facts such as all police cars in the jurisdiction are blue and white in color.

The second category of facts appropriate for judicial notice are those capable of ready and certain verification by reference to authoritative sources. For this category of judicial notice, the proponent of the evidence must provide the court with the authoritative source. Typical facts in this category include geographical facts (e.g., Main Street runs north and south with a 30 m.p.h. speed limit), historical facts (a city was incorporated on July 1, 1970), calendar facts (May 29 of last year was a legal holiday), and scientific facts not open to dispute (e.g., gasoline vapor is heavier than air). The opponent of evidence proposed for judicial notice has the opportunity to be heard on the propriety of judicial notice, including the opportunity to produce contrary authoritative sources.

Where the court is provided with authoritative sources which prove the fact, judicial notice, on request, is mandatory. The court may, in addition, judicially notice an appropriate fact on its own motion. Judicially noticed facts are binding on the jury in civil cases, while in criminal cases the jury may accept the fact as true but is not required to do so.

Judicial notice is an effective and efficient way of proving facts in issue. A tactical advantage is gained when the court judicially notices a fact in that the jury is left with the impression that the judge is agreeing with the proponent of the evidence, an impression which may carry over to the rest of the proponent's case.

CHAPTER 6
PRESUMPTIONS

Definition

A presumption is a fact which is automatically proved by the proof of some other fact. In all federal-question civil cases, the creation of a presumption forces the opponent to come forward with sufficient evidence to rebut or meet the presumed fact. The presumption *does not*, however, shift the original burden of proof.

Forms of Motion and Response

Form of Motion

> ➤ *I move for a directed verdict on _____ (the fact presumed) because my opponent failed to come forward with sufficient evidence to rebut it.*

Form of Response

> ➤ *A directed verdict is inappropriate because we have produced sufficient evidence to rebut the presumption such that a reasonable juror could find for my client on this fact.*

Federal Rule 301. Presumptions in General in Civil Actions and Proceedings

In all civil actions and proceedings not otherwise provided for by Act of Congress or by these rules, a presumption imposes on the party against whom it is directed the burden of going forward with evidence to rebut or meet the presumption, but does not shift to such party the burden of proof in the sense of the risk of nonpersuasion, which remains throughout the trial upon the party on whom it was originally cast.

Federal Rule 302. Applicability of State Law in Civil Actions and Proceedings

In civil actions and proceedings, the effect of a presumption respecting a fact which is an element of a claim or defense as to which State law supplies the rule of decision is determined in accordance with State law.

Commentary

A presumption provides that where a party with the burden of proof establishes fact X by competent proof, fact Y is presumed or perforce established, unless the opponent comes forward with evidence to rebut the presumed fact Y such that a reasonable jury could find for the opponent on the issue of fact Y. In other words, a presumption is a substitute for proof of the presumed fact Y.

In the event that fact Y is established by the presumption, and the opponent fails to come forward with sufficient evidence to rebut it, the court will instruct the jury to find for the proponent on that issue or direct a finding on such point. At no time, however, will the presumption alter or shift the proponent's burden of proof or persuasion to the opponent. This burden always remains with the proponent throughout the lawsuit.

A classic and common example of a presumption is the so-called *mailbox rule*. This common law rule holds that where a party is charged with the burden of proving delivery of a letter to another person, then proof of addressing, stamping, mailing, and non-return (facts X) establish the delivery and receipt of the letter (facts Y). The opponent is free to offer evidence to rebut this presumption, which, if sufficient, creates a jury question on delivery and receipt. If the evidence is equally balanced in the jury's mind on delivery and receipt, then the jury should find for the opponent because the proponent has failed to carry its burden of proof. If, on the other hand, the opponent offers no rebuttal, or offers only insufficient evidence, then the jury will be instructed that it must find the letter was delivered and received.

Rule 302 adds the provision that in diversity of citizenship cases, state law governs the existence and effect of presumptions.

CHAPTER 7
PRIVILEGES

Definition

A privilege is a common law legal rule which requires the exclusion of otherwise rele-vant evidence to further some ulterior purpose and protect certain relationships.

Forms of Objection and Response

Form of Objection

> ➤ *I object to the admission of this evidence on the grounds that it is privileged pursuant to the _____ privilege.*

Form of Response

> ➤ *This evidence is admissible because:*

> (a) *it does not fall within the privilege,* or

> (b) *if privileged, such privilege has been waived.*

Federal Rule 501. Privileges

Except as otherwise required by the Constitution of the United States or provided by Act of Congress or in rules prescribed by the Supreme Court pursuant to statutory authority, the privilege of a witness, person, government, State, or political subdivision thereof shall be governed by the principles of the common law as they may be interpreted by the courts of the United States in the light of reason and experience. However, in civil actions and proceed-ings, with respect to an element of a claim or defense as to which State law supplies the rule of decision, the privilege of a witness, person, government, State, or political subdivision thereof shall be determined in accordance with State law.

Commentary

The federal rule makers attempted to codify many of the common law privileges in the proposed Article V Rules. This attempt was abandoned, however, in favor of the following approach:

(a) In federal-question cases, the federal court will apply the federal common law of privilege.

(b) In diversity cases, the federal court will apply the privilege applicable in the appropri-ate state court.

The two most commonly encountered privileged communications in the federal courts, though by no means the only ones, are the attorney-client privilege and the privileges applicable to spouses.

The attorney-client privilege generally protects (a) confidential communications (b) made to an attorney consulted for legal advice or representation (or a member of the legal representation team). The making of the communication in the presence of a third person who is not part of the legal representation team obviates its confidential character. The privilege holder is the client, who may waive the privilege or instruct counsel to do so. Ordinarily, the fact of representation is not privileged. The attorney-client privilege applies to statements made by the client and often will not cover attorney statements unless the statement of the attorney reveals statements made by the client.

The spousal privileges actually involve two distinct matters. First, either spouse may assert a privilege to preclude disclosure of confidential communications made between the spouses. Second, where one spouse is on trial in a criminal case, the other spouse retains the choice as to whether to testify at all as a witness against the defendant-spouse. Thus, this privilege is held by the witness-spouse who may testify at his/her election. If the testifying spouse does elect to testify, the privilege for spousal, confidential communication continues to preclude testimony regarding confidential communication between the spouses, though the witness-spouse is free to testify as to other matters as would any other witness. In interspousal litigation, neither form of the privilege is operative.

Section II. Forms of Questions

CHAPTER 8
AMBIGUOUS QUESTIONS

Definition

An ambiguous question is one that is susceptible to at least two interpretations, or so vague or unintelligible as to make it likely to confuse the jury or witness.

Forms of Objection and Response

Form of Objection

➤ *I object that the question is (ambiguous—vague—unintelligible).*

Form of Response

➤ In most circumstances it is better to rephrase the question unless counsel is certain the question is clear.

Federal Rule

There is no federal rule that specifically covers forms of questions. The court has discretion to sustain the objection pursuant to Rule 611(a) which provides:

Federal Rule 611. Mode and Order of Interrogation and Presentation

(a) Control by court. The court shall exercise reasonable control over the mode and order of interrogating witnesses and presenting evidence so as to (1) make the interrogation and presentation effective for the ascertainment of the truth, (2) avoid needless consumption of time, and (3) protect witnesses from harassment or undue embarrassment.

Commentary

This objection should only be made when, in the judgment of objecting counsel, the question will mislead the jury or witness to the detriment of counsel's client. The usual effect of such an objection is to make your opponent a better lawyer by forcing a more precise question.

If, however, the jury is obviously confused by the question of your opponent, the objection will communicate to the jury that objecting counsel is concerned with the ascertainment of truth in the trial process.

A likely response by a judge to this objection is to ask the witness if the witness understands the question. If the witness understands the question it will be allowed to stand. Otherwise questioning counsel will be required to rephrase the question.

CHAPTER 9
ARGUMENTATIVE QUESTIONS

Definition

An argumentative question is one that is asked not for the purpose of obtaining information from the witness but rather to make jury argument in the guise of a question. The objection to an argumentative question does not refer to a situation where the questioning counsel is arguing with the witness but rather the situation where counsel comments on the evidence or attempts to draw inferences from the evidence, seeking the witness' response to such comments.

Forms of Objection and Response

Forms of Objection

➤ *I object. The question is argumentative.*

➤ *I object. Counsel is arguing to the jury.*

Form of Response

➤ *I am trying to elicit evidence from the witness.*

Federal Rule

There is no federal rule that specifically covers forms of questions. The court has discretion to sustain the objection pursuant to Rule 611(a) which provides:

Federal Rule 611. Mode and Order of Interrogation and Presentation

(a) Control by court. The court shall exercise reasonable control over the mode and order of interrogating witnesses and presenting evidence so as to (1) make the interrogation and presentation effective for the ascertainment of the truth, (2) avoid needless consumption of time, and (3) protect witnesses from harassment or undue embarrassment.

Commentary

This objection applies to questions on both direct and cross examination. It is appropriate where counsel attempts, in question form, to (a) summarize the testimony of the witness, (b) comment on the evidence, or (c) draw inferences from the evidence. It is essentially jury argument during the questioning process. The objection is appropriate in the following circumstances:

a) When counsel repeats the previous answer in asking the next question, the question is argumentative. It is a mere repetition, for emphasis, of previous testimony.

Example: In a personal injury action involving a car accident, counsel might on direct examination of an eyewitness ask: "Now you just testified that at 1:00 p.m. you were standing on the corner of 5th and Pine and had an unobstructed view of the intersection. What did you then see?"

b) When counsel summarizes the testimony of a witness in question form and attempts to draw an inference from the testimony, the question is argumentative.

Example: In a personal injury action involving a car accident, the last question on direct examination of an eyewitness might be: "In light of your testimony that the defendant was looking to his left as he entered the intersection rather than straight ahead, can you say conclusively the defendant caused the accident?"

c) When counsel asks a question that essentially calls for a witness to testify as to his/her own credibility, the question is argumentative.

Example: In a civil case where a witness has admitted making a prior inconsistent statement and has admitted he/she is a friend of the plaintiff, defense counsel might ask on cross examination: "In light of your friendship with the plaintiff and your inconsistent statements, do you really expect the jury to believe you?"

Note that a question is not argumentative merely because it puts to the witness a fact that is contrary to what the witness has already testified. A witness may be contradicted on cross examination as a method of impeachment whereby counsel seeks to get the reaction of the witness to a view of the facts different than given by the witness on direct examination.

As a matter of tactics, this objection has the advantage of pointing out to the jury that the responses called for in testimony are really the summaries, comments, and inferences of counsel rather than of the witness. As such, these questions, if objected to, are useless for questioning counsel and may lead the jury to conclude that the evidence for questioning counsel cannot stand on its own because counsel "protests too much."

CHAPTER 10
ASKED AND ANSWERED

Definition

A question may be objected to as *asked and answered* when it calls for the repetition of testimony from a witness who has previously given the same testimony in response to a question asked by examining counsel. It is designed to prevent cumulative evidence by way of repetition of facts by witnesses.

Forms of Objection and Response

Forms of Objection

> ➤ *I object. The question has been asked and answered.*

> ➤ *I object. The witness has already answered that question.*

Forms of Response

> ➤ *The witness has not yet answered the question.*

> ➤ *The question has not been answered during my examination.*

Federal Rule

Because a question that has been asked and answered calls for cumulative evidence, it may be sustained pursuant to Rule 403 which provides:

Federal Rule 403. Exclusion of Relevant Evidence on Grounds of Prejudice, Confusion, or Waste of Time

Although relevant, evidence may be excluded if its probative value is substantially outweighed by the danger of unfair prejudice, confusion of the issues, or misleading the jury, or by considerations of undue delay, waste of time, or needless presentation of cumulative evidence.

The court has discretion to sustain the objection pursuant to Rule 611(a) which provides:

Federal Rule 611. Mode and Order of Interrogation and Presentation

(a) Control by court. The court shall exercise reasonable control over the mode and order of interrogating witnesses and presenting evidence so as to (1) make the interrogation and presentation effective for the ascertainment of the truth, (2) avoid needless consumption of time, and (3) protect witnesses from harassment or undue embarrassment.

Commentary

For the objection to be sustained, the question must have been asked and a response given during the examination of questioning counsel. The objection, therefore, will not lie where, on cross examination, counsel asks for testimony earlier elicited during direct examination. The objection is appropriate when on redirect examination a question is asked that was already asked and answered during direct examination. As such, the asked-and-answered objection would be properly sustained to the typical redirect examination which merely calls for a repetition of direct examination. The objection also applies when a witness is recalled to testify.

Most judges will usually not sustain this objection unless the testimony sought to be elicited is overly repetitive. In addition, greater latitude in repeating testimony is usually given on cross examination.

The objection is improper when it is made to a question calling for information from one witness merely because it has already been testified to by another witness. In that circumstance, the proper objection is that the testimony is cumulative. The appropriate response is that the testimony is corroborative.

CHAPTER 11
ASSUMING FACTS NOT IN EVIDENCE

Definition

A question is objectionable if it assumes, in the asking, facts that have not already been proved. These questions are a form of leading questions.

Forms of Objection and Response

Form of Objection

> ➤ *I object that the question assumes a fact not in evidence. There has been no testimony that* _____.

Forms of Response

> ➤ *I will elicit that fact from the witness in a separate question.*
> ➤ *That fact has been proved during the earlier testimony of this witness.*
> ➤ *That fact has been proved during the testimony of* _____ (insert name of another witness who has already testified).
> ➤ *This fact will be testified to during the testimony of* _____ (insert name of another witness who will testify later).

Federal Rule

Because a question that assumes a fact not in evidence is a subspecies of leading questions, the court may sustain the objection pursuant to Rule 611(c) which provides:

Federal Rule 611. Mode and Order of Interrogation and Presentation

(c) **Leading questions.** Leading questions should not be used on the direct examination of a witness except as may be necessary to develop the witness' testimony. Ordinarily leading questions should be permitted on cross-examination. When a party calls a hostile witness, an adverse party, or a witness identified with an adverse party, interrogation may be by leading questions.

The judge also has discretion to sustain the objection pursuant to Rule 611(a) which provides:

Federal Rule 611. Mode and Order of Interrogation and Presentation

(a) **Control by court.** The court shall exercise reasonable control over the mode and order of interrogating witnesses and presenting evidence so as to (1) make the interrogation and presentation effective for the ascertainment of the truth, (2) avoid needless consumption of time, and (3) protect witnesses from harassment or undue embarrassment.

In addition, if the assumed fact is not within the firsthand knowledge of the witness the court may sustain the objection pursuant to Rule 602 which provides:

Federal Rule 602. Lack of Personal Knowledge

A witness may not testify to a matter unless evidence is introduced sufficient to support a finding that the witness has personal knowledge of the matter. Evidence to prove personal knowledge may, but need not, consist of the witness' own testimony. This rule is subject to the provisions of Rule 703 relating to opinion testimony by expert witnesses.

Commentary

This objection should only be made when objecting counsel is confident that the witness cannot testify to the assumed fact. If the witness can testify to the assumed fact and questioning counsel knows how to ask the question, objecting counsel will be viewed by the jury as overly technical and attempting to hide the truth. In addition, by requiring questioning counsel to ask two questions instead of one, objecting counsel merely assists in making the opponent a better lawyer.

Even in circumstances where the witness cannot, for some reason, testify to the assumed fact, it might be wise to wait until cross examination to demonstrate this infirmity to the jury, thereby showing opposing counsel to be less than candid.

Although typically utilized in response to direct examination, the objection is also available to cross examination questions. On cross examination, a question that assumes a fact not in evidence will also typically misquote the witness and be argumentative. The objection to a cross examination question which assumes a fact not in evidence also has the tactical advantage of alerting the witness to an attempt by the cross examiner to obtain the assent of the witness to a fact, that either the witness does not know or does not agree with, by an unfair question. The witness is thereby alerted to the inappropriate tactics of the opposing counsel, and will be put on guard for the remainder of the cross examination.

CHAPTER 12
COMPOUND QUESTIONS

Definition

A question that asks for two or more items of information at the same time, so that it is impossible to understand the meaning of the answer to the question, is a compound question.

Forms of Objection and Response

Form of Objection

➤ *I object. The question is compound.*

Form of Response

➤ *I withdraw the question and will ask separate questions.*

Federal Rule

There is no federal rule that specifically covers forms of questions. The court has discretion to sustain the objection pursuant to Rule 611(a) which provides:

Federal Rule 611. Mode and Order of Interrogation and Presentation

(a) Control by court. The court shall exercise reasonable control over the mode and order of interrogating witnesses and presenting evidence so as to (1) make the interrogation and presentation effective for the ascertainment of the truth, (2) avoid needless consumption of time, and (3) protect witnesses from harassment or undue embarrassment.

Commentary

The vice of compound questions lies in their tendency to confuse the jury regarding the testimony of the witness of whom they are asked. When a witness answers yes to a question that asks about two items of information, it is impossible to know whether the witness is affirming the first query, the second, or both, and the potential for confusion is obvious.

As a rule, because compound questions are confusing, the making of the objection will usually result in making questioning counsel a more effective advocate by clearing up the confusion counsel has created by requiring the separation of the question into its component parts. Also, because the objection is easily met, the making of the objection often times gives the appearance that objecting counsel is being hyper-technical. The objection, then, is best made only when the compound question is likely to mislead the jury to the detriment of objecting counsel's client.

CHAPTER 13
LEADING QUESTIONS

Definition

A leading question is one which suggests the desired answer to the witness so that it puts the desired answer in the witness' mouth, or is unclear as to whether the witness or the lawyer is testifying. Leading questions are generally forbidden on direct examination and permitted on cross examination.

Forms of Objection and Response

Form of Objection

➤ *I object to the question as leading.*

Forms of Response

➤ *The question does not suggest the answer to the witness.*

➤ *Leading questions are permitted:*

    (a) *on preliminary matters,* or

    (b) *when necessary to develop the witness' testimony,* or

    (c) *because the witness is hostile, is an adverse party, or is identified with an adverse party.*

Federal Rule 611. Mode and Order of Interrogation and Presentation

(c) Leading questions. Leading questions should not be used on the direct examination of a witness except as may be necessary to develop the witness' testimony. Ordinarily leading questions should be permitted on cross-examination. When a party calls a hostile witness, an adverse party, or a witness identified with an adverse party, interrogation may be by leading questions.

Commentary

The vice of the leading question is that in suggesting the questioner's desired answer to the witness, the witness may be misled into giving inaccurate testimony. Though generally forbidden on direct examination, there are a number of situations where Rule 611(c) permits leading on direct.

Pursuant to the ability to develop the witness' testimony, courts will usually permit leading on preliminary matters dealing with the witness' educational, occupational, or other non-contentious background matters; agreed or stipulated matters; to put the witness in time and place about which inquiry will be made; or other relatively unimportant matters. Except for child or other witnesses who have difficulty understanding, courts will not generally permit leading to assist a forgetful witness. The better practice is to refresh recollection pursuant to Rule 612.

Leading is also permitted when necessary to develop testimony. As a result, counsel will typically be allowed to lead child witnesses and other witnesses who have difficulty in expressing themselves. On the other end of the spectrum, leading questions that explain technical testimony of an expert witness in terms understandable to lay persons will also typically be allowed.

Leading is permitted on direct examination where the witness is the adverse party or someone closely aligned with the adverse party, or where the witness is declared hostile by the court. A witness is "associated" with the adverse party if the witness and the party have a commonality in interest in the outcome of the lawsuit or if the association arises out of a relationship such as familial or employer/employee. A hostile witness is one whose demeanor, interest, bias, or general lack of cooperation shows that such witness is unfriendly (not merely neutral) to the questioner. Typically, hostility must be demonstrated during trial testimony by a difficulty in obtaining information from the witness. A witness may be declared hostile if the court feels that he is not forthcoming in responding to non-leading questions.

Leading questions are permitted on cross examination; but where the witness would ordinarily be expected to be called by the questioner, or was called on direct as an adverse party by the opponent, the examination of such witness, though technically cross examination, is treated like direct, and leading questions are precluded. Normally, if the witness can be examined by use of leading questions on direct examination because the witness is associated with the adverse party, leading questions will be impermissible on cross examination.

CHAPTER 14
MISQUOTING THE WITNESS

Definition

A question may be objected to as misquoting the witness when it includes as a factual premise that the witness had previously testified to certain information when in fact the witness had not.

Forms of Objection and Response

Form of Objection

➤ *I object. Counsel is misquoting the witness. The witness has testified to* _____.

Form of Response

➤ *The witness previously testified to* _____.

Federal Rule

There is no federal rule that specifically covers forms of questions. The court has discretion to sustain the objection pursuant to Rule 611(a) which provides:

Federal Rule 611. Mode and Order of Interrogation and Presentation

(a) Control by court. The courts shall exercise reasonable control over the mode and order of interrogating witnesses presenting evidence so as to (1) make the interrogation and presentation effective for the ascertainment of the truth, (2) avoid needless consumption of time, and (3) protect witnesses from harassment or undue embarrassment.

Commentary

This objection is frequently available when opposing counsel utilizes a form of cross examination that is structured in the terms of the direct examination (i.e., "you testified on direct that _____.") The objection is designed to prevent opposing counsel from shading the testimony of the witness as it had previously been given. The objection can serve as a reminder to the witness that the witness must listen carefully to opposing counsel's questions before answering.

The objection can also be interposed to direct examination but the circumstances for the making of the objection (i.e., reference to earlier testimony) are much less common.

The objection can be easily avoided by inquiring concerning the facts of the case as opposed to previous testimony concerning the facts of the case, although the question might still assume a fact not in evidence. In addition to avoiding the misquoting the witness objection, questioning concerning facts is obviously a preferable manner of proceeding in that it eliminates a potential level of quarrel between counsel and the witness, not about whether the fact exists, but whether testimony about the fact had already been given.

CHAPTER 15
NARRATIVES

Definition

A question can be objected to as calling for a narrative if it is unfocused as to particular information that is sought and calls for a mere recitation of what a witness knows without benefit of specific questions. Such question forms make it virtually impossible for opposing counsel to interpose objections concerning potential testimony before the jury has already heard the offending testimony.

Forms of Objection and Response

Forms of Objection

> ➤ *I object. The question calls for a narrative response.*

> ➤ *I object. The witness is testifying in the form of a narrative.*

Form of Response

> ➤ *The witness is testifying to relevant and admissible matters.*

Federal Rule

There is no federal rule that specifically covers forms of questions. The court has discretion to sustain the objection pursuant to Rule 611(a) which provides:

Federal Rule 611. Mode and Order of Interrogation and Presentation

(a) Control by court. The courts shall exercise reasonable control over the mode and order of interrogating witnesses presenting evidence so as to (1) make the interrogation and presentation effective for the ascertainment of the truth, (2) avoid needless consumption of time, and (3) protect witnesses from harassment or undue embarrassment.

Commentary

This objection seeks to prevent the situation where counsel is not provided with notice by the question as to potential objectionable testimony by a witness. When a witness testifies in a narrative form the only available method of excluding objectionable testimony is by making a motion to strike concerning the offending testimony. While the motion to strike protects the record, it cannot strike the testimony from the minds of the jurors. In fact, the offending testimony may very well be cemented in the jurors' minds by the making of the motion to strike.

If a question seeking specific information is asked, and the testimony sought is inadmissible, opposing counsel can object to the question and preclude the jury from hearing the testimony. As a practical matter, however, testimony in a narrative form is clear and easy to understand. It also is a faster way to present the testimony. As a result, it is unlikely that a judge will sustain an objection to a question that calls for narrative testimony. The best tactic for objecting counsel is to state, at the bench, the reasons for the objection; that is, to prevent inadmissible evidence from being heard by the jury and possibly cemented by a motion to strike. At the first instance that the witness testifies to inadmissible evidence during the narrative, opposing counsel should move to strike, approach the bench and ask the judge to reconsider the objection to testimony in a narrative form. At this juncture the judge is much more likely to require inquiry by way of more specific questions.

In rare circumstances where a witness has demonstrated a proclivity for providing run-on answers including inadmissible opinion or comments during deposition testimony, a pretrial motion to preclude questions calling for narratives may be successful. Even if the motion is then denied, the trial judge will be on notice of a potential trial problem with the witness.

CHAPTER 16
REFRESHING PRESENT RECOLLECTION

Definition

Where a witness has a failure of memory, the witness' memory may be refreshed by showing the witness a document or other item which revives the witness' memory. The witness may then testify from a refreshed or revived recollection.

Forms of Objection and Response

Forms of Objection

> *I object to the attempt to refresh the witness' recollection in the absence of a demonstrated failure of memory.*

> *I object to the witness' reading from the exhibit used to refresh his recollection because it is not in evidence and because it is hearsay.*

Forms of Response

> *The witness has shown a failure of memory and I am attempting to refresh his recollection pursuant to Rule 612.*

> *The exhibit used to refresh the witness' recollection is already in evidence and is either:*

> (a) *not hearsay,* or

> (b) *the exhibit meets an exception to the hearsay rule.*

Federal Rule 612. Writing Used to Refresh Memory

Except as otherwise provided in criminal proceedings by section 3500 of title 18, United States Code, if a witness uses a writing to refresh memory for the purpose of testifying, either

(1) while testifying, or

(2) before testifying, if the court in its discretion determines it is necessary in the interests of justice,

an adverse party is entitled to have the writing produced at the hearing, to inspect it, to cross examine the witness thereon, and to introduce in evidence those portions which relate to the testimony of the witness. If it is claimed that the writing contains matters not related to the subject matter of the testimony, the court shall examine the writing in camera, excise any portions not so related, and order delivery of the remainder to the party entitled thereto. Any portion withheld over objections shall be preserved and made available to the appellate court in the event of an appeal. If a writing is not produced or delivered pursuant to order under this rule, the court shall make any order justice requires, except that in criminal cases when the prosecution elects not to comply, the order shall be one striking the testimony or, if the court in its discretion determines that the interests of justice so require, declaring a mistrial.

Commentary

A forgetful witness' memory may be refreshed by showing the witness an item, usually a writing, which jogs the witness' memory. The steps in refreshing a witness' memory are as follows:

a. Establish the witness' failure of memory.

b. Mark the refreshing document for identification.

c. Show the witness the refreshing document and ask him to read it to himself.

d. Ask the witness if he has read it.

e. Ask the witness if his memory is now refreshed with respect to the forgotten fact.

f. Take the refreshing exhibit from the witness.

g. Re-ask the question which drew the original failure of memory.

Any document or thing used to refresh recollection must be made available to the opponent for use in the opponent's next examination of the witness. Though the proponent who uses the document to refresh may not offer the document into evidence unless it is otherwise admissible, the opponent may offer the pertinent parts of the refreshing document into evidence as it impacts the testimony of the witness. Finally, note that the trial court possesses the discretion to make available to the opponent any document used to refresh a witness' recollection in preparation for trial. Some courts have taken the position that even if a document used to refresh memory would be privileged or considered non-discoverable work product, that it still must be produced. Therefore, counsel should take care to avoid refreshing recollection either before or during trial with a document which contains damaging information that is not already in possession of the opponent.

CHAPTER 17
NON-RESPONSIVE ANSWERS

Definition

An answer that either exceeds the scope of the question or fails to respond to a question may be the subject of a motion to strike as non-responsive by questioning counsel. The objection is available only to questioning counsel.

Forms of Objection and Response

Form of Objection

> ➤ *I move to strike the answer of the witness as non-responsive.*

Forms of Response

> ➤ (If the objection is made by questioning counsel) *The answer of the witness is responsive to the question. The question put to the witness was _____.*

> ➤ (If the objection is made by opposing counsel) *I accept the answer.*

Federal Rule

There is no federal rule that specifically covers forms of questions. The court has discretion to sustain the objection pursuant to Rule 611(a) which provides:

Federal Rule 611. Mode and Order of Interrogation and Presentation

(a) Control by court. The courts shall exercise reasonable control over the mode and order of interrogating witnesses presenting evidence so as to (1) make the interrogation and presentation effective for the ascertainment of the truth, (2) avoid needless consumption of time, and (3) protect witnesses from harassment or undue embarrassment.

Commentary

Questioning counsel has the right to require a witness to respond to legitimate questions. If a witness fails to respond to the question or exceeds the scope of the question, a motion to strike the non-responsive portion of the question is permissible. Of course, control of the witness is the responsibility of questioning counsel. Tactically, questioning counsel may point out the failure of the witness to respond by repeating the same question in exactly the same words until the witness actually responds. This tactic not only elicits a response to the question but also informs the jury that the witness is being evasive.

The "non-responsive" objection belongs only to questioning counsel. Answers that exceed the scope of the question may be the subject of a motion to strike by opposing counsel on specific substantive grounds. Opposing counsel may also object to the testimony of a witness as testimony in a narrative form (see Narratives).

Section III. Relevance

CHAPTER 18
- RELEVANCE -
GENERALLY

Definition

Relevance is probative worth. That is, evidence is relevant in either a civil or criminal case if it has any tendency to establish a proposition or fact that is material to the lawsuit.

Forms of Objection and Response

Forms of Objection

> ➤ *I object on the ground that the question calls for an irrelevant answer.*

> ➤ *I move to strike the answer as irrelevant.*

Form of Response

> ➤ *The evidence is relevant because it has some tendency to make more likely a fact which is material to either a claim or defense in the lawsuit or bears on the weight or credibility of the evidence.*

Federal Rule 401. Definition of "Relevant Evidence"

"Relevant evidence" means evidence having any tendency to make the existence of any fact that is of consequence to the determination of the action more probable or less probable than it would be without the evidence.

Federal Rule 402. Relevant Evidence Generally Admissible; Irrelevant Evidence Inadmissible

All relevant evidence is admissible, except as otherwise provided by the Constitution of the United States, by Act of Congress, by these rules, or by other rules prescribed by the Supreme Court pursuant to statutory authority. Evidence which is not relevant is not admissible.

Commentary

Often the terms relevance and materiality are used interchangeably. This is incorrect. Materiality has a more precise meaning than relevance and can be seen as being a term which is within the meaning of relevance. Materiality is the relationship between the proposition on which the evidence is offered and the issues in the case. If the evidence is offered to prove a proposition which is not a matter in issue, the evidence is said to be immaterial. For example, assume an automobile collision case. If in the course of calling witnesses and asking questions, the plaintiff asks a witness a question about a contract which has no relationship to the collision involved, the objection on the part of the opponent would be immateriality. Very simply, a contract between the parties is not within the range of dispute as set forth in these pleadings. Bear in mind that it is the pleadings and the substantive law involved which define the range of issues within the lawsuit. When a party attempts to address evidence to a proposition which is not within these bounds, immateriality would be an appropriate objection.

Relevancy includes both the test of materiality and something more. Relevancy, as we use it in the law, is the tendency of the evidence in question to establish a material proposition. Thus, evidence of a proposition which is not provable in the case would be immaterial and by extension irrelevant. However, evidence which is not probative of the proposition to which it is directed, even if that proposition is material or provable in the case, would be irrelevant.

Rule 401 defines *relevant evidence* as having any tendency to make the existence of any fact that is of consequence to the determination of the action more probable or less probable than it would be without the evidence. In other words, relevancy refers to the logical relationship between the proposed evidence and a fact to be established, i.e., a tendency to establish a material proposition. The Rule 401 definition of relevance demonstrates the basic philosophy of the federal rules in favor of admitting evidence and allowing the fact-finder to determine the weight to be given the evidence.

Note that all the federal rules require is that relevant evidence have *some* tendency to make the existence of a material fact more or less likely. There is no requirement that the tendency to make the existence of the fact more or less probable need be the *most likely* tendency or the *best* tendency.

Direct and circumstantial evidence are included within the area of relevant evidence. Direct evidence is evidence which, if believed, establishes or resolves a matter in issue in a lawsuit. Circumstantial evidence is evidence which serves as a basis from which the fact-finder may make a reasonable inference about a matter in issue. An example of direct evidence would be eyewitness testimony to the effect that the witness saw a person break open a window in the victim's home on a snowy evening, enter the house, and leave the house carrying a stereo. Circumstantial evidence of the same crime might be the fact that on the morning after the alleged crime was committed, the victim looked outside his home and noticed snow had fallen overnight and there were footprints leading from the street up to the window in his home, the window was broken, and the stereo was missing. These are all items of circumstantial evidence which certainly have a tendency to prove that breaking and entering had occurred in the victim's home. Each piece of circumstantial evidence is direct evidence of some smaller fact which has a tendency in logic to infer the greater fact which is an element of a claim or defense.

An objection to the relevance of proposed evidence should normally be raised by way of a pretrial motion *in limine*. Should it be necessary to raise a relevance objection at trial, the making of the objection should be coupled with a request to approach the bench for argument on the objection. Otherwise, the jury will hear both the irrelevant evidence and the relevance argument from the proponent of the evidence. The judge may sustain the objection and strike the evidence from the record but will be unable to strike it from the minds of the jury.

CHAPTER 19

- RELEVANCE -
EXCLUSION OF RELEVANT EVIDENCE ON GROUNDS OF PREJUDICE, CONFUSION, OR WASTE OF TIME

Definition

Though evidence is logically relevant under Rule 401, it must be balanced against the considerations contained in Rule 403 to see if it will actually be admitted at trial. The considerations listed in Rule 403 include the dangers of *unfair* prejudice, confusion of the issues for the jury, misleading of the jury, unnecessary delay, wasting of time, or pointless presentation of repetitive or cumulative evidence.

Forms of Objection and Response

Forms of Objection

> ➤ *I object on the ground that this evidence is inadmissible because its probative value is substantially outweighed by the prejudicial effect of the evidence.*

> ➤ *The introduction of this evidence will confuse the issue before the jury.*

> ➤ *The evidence is merely cumulative.*

Form of Response

> ➤ *The evidence is admissible because it is logically relevant under Rule 401 and:*

>> (a) *its probative value is not substantially outweighed by the danger of unfair prejudice,* or

>> (b) *any potential for confusion of issues is easily cured by an instruction by the court,* or

>> (c) *the evidence is corroborative of an issue central to the case.*

Federal Rule 403. Exclusion of Relevant Evidence on Grounds of Prejudice, Confusion, or Waste of Time

Although relevant, evidence may be excluded if its probative value is substantially outweighed by the danger of unfair prejudice, confusion of the issues, or misleading the jury, or by considerations of undue delay, waste of time, or needless presentation of cumulative evidence.

Commentary

Although evidence may be logically relevant, that is, have probative value pursuant to Rule 401, it will only be admissible so long as its probative value is not substantially outweighed by the negative baggage described in Rule 403. Note that the balancing test of Rules 401 and 403 is tilted heavily in favor of the admissibility of logically relevant evidence or evidence with probative value, in that the prejudice must substantially outweigh the probative value in order to require exclusion.

However, where the probative value evidence is substantially outweighed by the dangers referred to in Rule 403, the trial judge will exclude otherwise relevant evidence. Of the Rule 403 considerations, the one that provides the most problems is the term *unfair prejudice*. Unfair prejudice does not refer to the fact that the evidence tends to make the opponent look guilty in a criminal case or liable in a civil case. Indeed, those qualities give the evidence its logical or probative value in the case. By unfair prejudice, the rules refer to evidence which will deflect the jury from actually deciding the case on its factual merits and lead or invite the jury to make its decision based on unfair considerations which do not relate to the issues in the case. Rule 403 balancing is appropriate to all offers of evidence with the exception of offers under Rules 412(c)(3), 609(a)(1), and 609(b) which contain their own balancing tests.

CHAPTER 20
- RELEVANCE -
CONDITIONAL ADMISSIBILITY

Definition

The relevance of a particular offer of evidence may be conditioned upon a proof of other facts. In these situations, the court may conditionally admit the proffered evidence subject to an offer of proof that the additional facts will be offered.

Forms of Objection and Response

Forms of Objection

➤ *I object. The proffered evidence is not relevant and admissible unless other facts are proved.*

➤ *I move to strike the conditionally admitted evidence of _____. Counsel has failed to prove additional facts that are necessary to show the relevance of that conditionally admitted evidence.*

Forms of Response

➤ *I will show the relevance of the proffered evidence by proof of the following additional facts through the testimony of _____* (insert name of witness).

➤ *The relevance of the conditionally admitted facts has been shown through the additional evidence given in the testimony of _____* (insert name of witness).

Federal Rule 104. Preliminary Questions

(b) Relevancy conditioned on fact. When the relevancy of evidence depends upon the fulfillment of a condition of fact, the court shall admit it upon, or subject to, the introduction of evidence sufficient to support a finding of the fulfillment of the condition.

Commentary

The judge is given a great deal of authority in making the preliminary findings necessary to determining the admissibility of evidence. Rule 104 sets out the procedures for making those determinations in a clear and concise way. There are two aspects to that rule.

First, the trial judge may, in making the initial decision on admissibility of evidence, consider evidence not otherwise admissible. The only rules of evidence that inhibit the judge are those pertaining to privilege (see Rule 104(a)).

Second, in making a determination on admissibility of a piece of evidence that depends for its proper admission on the proof of other facts, the judge may conditionally admit the proffered evidence subject to later proof of the foundational facts. This process is sometimes referred to as connecting up.

The quantum of proof necessary to fulfill the conditional admissibility requirement is sufficient evidence that a jury *could find*, by a preponderance of the evidence, the conditional facts exist. If proffering counsel fails to connect up, or fulfill the terms of the conditional admission, a motion to strike the conditionally admitted evidence must be made. In some circumstances, it will be appropriate to couple the motion to strike with a motion for mistrial.

CHAPTER 21
- RELEVANCE -
RULE OF COMPLETENESS

Definition

When a portion of a writing or recording is admitted in evidence, an adverse party has the right to have published to the jury other portions of the writing or recording, or related writings or recordings, which explain or put in context the originally admitted evidence.

Forms of Objection and Response

Forms of Objection

➤ *I object to the admissibility of the proffered writing (or recording) unless other portions of the writing (or recording) are also admitted. These other portions are necessary to explain or to put in context the proffered writing (or recording).*

➤ *I object to the admissibility of the proffered writing (or recording) unless other related writings (or recordings) are also admitted. These other writings (or recordings) are necessary to explain (or to put in context) the proffered writing (or recording).*

Form of Response

➤ *The proffered statement (or recording) does not need explanation or context. Other portions of the statement (or recording), or additional writings (or recordings), are not necessary to a fair understanding of the proffered statement (or recording).*

Federal Rule 106. Remainder of or Related Writings or Recorded Statements

When a writing or recorded statement or part thereof is introduced by a party, an adverse party may require the introduction at that time of any other part or any other writing or recorded statement which ought in fairness to be considered contemporaneously with it.

Commentary

The rule of completeness embodied in Rule 106 is essentially a rule of fairness. It provides that the jury be given evidence of writings or recordings in complete form when that complete form explains or gives context to that which is offered in evidence. The rule also applies to other writings or recordings that provide the same complete context in which the proffered writing or recording should be considered by the jury.

The judge has discretion to require the remainder of the writing or recording to be admitted by proffering counsel, or can allow the adverse party to admit the remainder of the writing or recording during the next opportunity to inquire of the witness through whom the writing or recording is admitted.

It is always appropriate for the adverse party to object on rule of completeness grounds at the time of the original proffer of the writing or recording even if the judge postpones the admissibility of the remainder of the writing or recording. In this way, the jury is put on notice of the claimed unfairness and will be waiting for the completion of the evidence. Because the appearance of unfairness can seriously damage the credibility of the proponent, the rule of completeness should be anticipated by proffering counsel, and every effort should be made to fairly show the appropriate context in which an offered statement or recording was made.

CHAPTER 22
- RELEVANCE -
LIMITED ADMISSIBILITY

Definition

Evidence that is relevant and admissible for one purpose may be irrelevant and inadmissible for another purpose. Similarly, evidence may be relevant and admissible against one party and irrelevant and inadmissible against another party.

Forms of Objection and Response

Forms of Objection

> ➤ *I object. The question calls for irrelevant information on the issue of _____ .*

> ➤ *I object. I move the court instruct the jury that the answer is irrelevant and inadmissible on the issue of _____ and I request a limiting instruction.*

> ➤ *I object. The question calls for irrelevant information as against my client.*

> ➤ *I object. I move that the court instruct the jury that the answer is irrelevant and inadmissible as to my client and I request a limiting instruction.*

Forms of Response

> ➤ *The evidence offered is relevant and admissible for all purposes and a limiting instruction is inappropriate.*

> ➤ *The evidence is relevant and admissible against all parties and a limiting instruction is inappropriate.*

Federal Rule 105. Limited Admissibility

When evidence which is admissible as to one party or for one purpose but not admissible as to another party or for another purpose is admitted, the court, upon request, shall restrict the evidence to its proper scope and instruct the jury accordingly.

Commentary

Rule 105 recognizes that evidence can be admissible for any number of purposes and allocates the responsibility to counsel to separate out the admissible from the inadmissible purpose. For example, evidence of a prior inconsistent statement is admissible in most situations solely for the fact it was said, as it may bear on the credibility of the witness. The prior inconsistent statement is not admissible for the truth of its contents unless it qualifies as non-hearsay pursuant to Rule 801(d) or as an exception to the hearsay rule pursuant to Rule 803 or Rule 804. It is incumbent upon opposing counsel to seek limitation of the evidence to its proper admissible purpose and to request a limiting instruction by the judge. Failure to do so allows consideration of the evidence for all purposes. Limited admissibility often is at issue when dealing with impeachment evidence pursuant to Rules 607, 608, and 609; evidence of limited relevance pursuant to Rules 404 to 412; and admissible, non-hearsay, out-of-court statements.

In cases involving multiple parties, the issue of limited admissibility arises when evidence is relevant and admissible against one party but not another. For example, in the situation where a plaintiff sues two defendants, the admissions of one defendant are not, except in Rule 802(d)(2)(C), (D), or (E) situations, admissible against the other defendant. Once again, the burden is on opposing counsel to appropriately limit the use of the evidence to appropriate parties by way of request for a limiting instruction.

CHAPTER 23
HABIT AND ROUTINE PRACTICE

Definition

Evidence of a personal habit or of the routine practice of an organization is admissible as relevant to show that on a specific occasion, such person or organization acted in conformity with the proffered habit or practice. For evidence to be admissible pursuant to Rule 406, personal habit or institutional routine evidence must rise to the level of a regular response to a repeated situation.

Forms of Objection and Response

Form of Objection

➤ *I object that this evidence is irrelevant in that it is such an isolated occurrence as to be insufficient to constitute a habit or routine practice.*

Form of Response

➤ *This evidence is relevant because it shows:*

(a) *a consistent habit or routine practice which*

(b) *raises a permissible inference that the party or organization likely acted in this case according to the habit or routine practice.*

Federal Rule 406. Habit; Routine Practice

Evidence of the habit of a person or of the routine practice of an organization, whether corroborated or not and regardless of the presence of eyewitnesses, is relevant to prove that the conduct of the person or organization on a particular occasion was in conformity with the habit or routine practice.

Commentary

By its nature, habit or routine practice testimony is circumstantial proof that certain conduct, or an act consistent therewith, occurred. Habit or practice evidence is only practically necessary in the absence of direct evidence of such conduct or act, but in those situations where the direct evidence is impeachable, the habit or routine practice can have substantial tactical value. Rule 406 represents a departure from the common law in two respects. First, Rule 406 allows habit and routine practice evidence even where there is first-hand or direct evidence of the event in question. Second, habit and routine practice evidence is admissible without corroborating evidence.

For example, if a party seeks to prove that a letter was mailed by an organization, but no witness is able to actually recall the act of mailing, the party may offer evidence of the organization's routine practice in the creation and mailing of letters. A typical foundation might be as follows:

Q. Does your firm have any kind of routine practice regarding the mailing of letters?

A. Yes, I created it three years ago.

Q. Describe such practice.

A. After I sign a final version of a letter, my secretary places it in a stamped envelope with an imprinted return address and puts it in an out box on her desk.

Q. What happens next?

A. Twice a day, the mail assistant comes by my secretary's desk, picks up all stamped mail and places it in a United States mailbox on the first floor of our office building.

Q. Who receives a letter that is returned by the post office?

A. My secretary, who will then give it to me.

If the witness recalls the writing and signing of a particular letter, the above foundation of habit or routine practice is relevant as proof that such letter was mailed. The presumption of the regularity of the delivery service of the United States mail provides *prima facie* evidence that such letter, if not returned, was, in fact, delivered to the addressee (the *mailbox rule*).

Thus, a party can show the mailing and delivery of a letter, despite no direct evidence of same, by the use of (a) habit or routine practice to show mailing and (b) the mailbox rule to show delivery.

In addition to being admissible to show an event occurred, habit or routine practice evidence is admissible to show an event did not occur. For example, in an automobile accident case where the claim is that the now deceased party failed to stop at a stop sign, a witness who had ridden to work with the party for many years and thereby knew the party's habit of always stopping at stop signs, can so testify to establish that the party did not run the stop sign in the situation at trial.

CHAPTER 24
SUBSEQUENT REMEDIAL MEASURES

Definition

A measure which is taken to repair or remedy a condition, after such condition has allegedly caused an event creating liability, and which, if done prior to the plaintiff suffering damage would have made such event less likely to occur, is a subsequent remedial measure. Evidence of such measures is inadmissible to prove negligence, a defect in a product, a defect in a product's design, or a need for a warning or instruction, but it is admissible for any other relevant purpose.

Forms of Objection and Response

Form of Objection

➤ *I object. This is evidence of a subsequent remedial measure.*

Forms of Response

➤ *This evidence is not offered on a prohibited issue, but is offered to show:*

    (a) *notice,*

    (b) *ownership,*

    (c) *control,*

    (d) *feasibility of precautionary measures,* or

    (e) *impeachment.*

➤ *My opponent has "opened the door" to this evidence by:*

    (a) *its pleadings,* or

    (b) *the questioning of* _____ (insert name of witness).

Federal Rule 407. Subsequent Remedial Measures

When, after an injury or harm allegedly caused by an event, measures are taken that, if taken previously, would have made the injury or harm less likely to occur, evidence of the subsequent measures is not admissible to prove negligence, culpable conduct, a defect in a product, a defect in a product's design, or a need for a warning or instruction. This rules does not require the exclusion of evidence of subsequent measures when offered for another purpose, such as proving ownership, control, or feasibility of precautionary measures, if controverted, or impeachment.

Commentary

Evidence of subsequent remedial measures is *per se* inadmissible on the issues of negligence, culpable conduct, defect, or a need for a warning or instruction *only*. The reason for such evidentiary bar is to remove any disincentive to the correction of dangerous or defective conditions. If admissible, the rule makers feared that owners of property or manufacturers would fail to correct dangerous conditions for fear of having such repairs offered to show the negligence or defect. After all, people do not fix things that are not broken.

However, the evidentiary bar is limited to the exclusion of such remedial measures when offered only on the explicitly prohibited issues. The rule clearly allows the offer of evidence which would otherwise amount to a subsequent remedial measure when offered for any other relevant purpose, including but not limited to, ownership or control of the repaired property, and the feasibility of precautionary measures, *if controverted.* Rule 407 also permits the offer of such evidence for impeachment where relevant, but note that, like virtually all other evidentiary offers, an otherwise admissible offer of a subsequent remedial measure is subject to exclusion by Rule 403.

The "if controverted" language applies to ownership, control, and feasibility, but limits the offer for such purposes to situations where the defendant *opens the door* by denying ownership, control, or feasibility of precautionary measures. Such denial could be found in defendant's answer or in trial evidence. Where the defendant admits ownership or control or fails to offer evidence on lack of feasibility of any precautionary measure, then evidence of subsequent remedial measures is inadmissible as irrelevant.

Prior to 1997, the federal courts of appeals were split on the issue of whether Rule 407 barred evidence of subsequent remedial measures in products liability actions. In a 1997 amendment, the rule makers adopted the majority rule and clearly applied Rule 407 to products liability actions.

CHAPTER 25
COMPROMISE AND OFFERS OF COMPROMISE

Definition

Evidence of settlement or of settlement negotiations in a disputed civil claim are inadmissible to prove liability or the amount of the claim. The preclusion of this evidence applies to all statements made during the course of compromise negotiations. Evidence of settlement, offers to settle or statements made during the course of settlement negotiations may, however, be admissible to show bias, to negate allegations of undue delay, or to show an effort to subvert a criminal investigation or prosecution.

Forms of Objection and Response

Form of Objection

➤ *I object that the proffered evidence is evidence of compromise negotiations offered on liability and/or damages.*

Form of Response

➤ *This evidence is admissible because:*

(a) *the claim was not in dispute at the time of the compromise discussions,* and/or

(b) *the evidence is not offered on liability or damages but to show:*

(1) *bias,*

(2) *no undue delay, or*

(3) *an effort to subvert a criminal investigation.*

Federal Rule 408. Compromise and Offers to Compromise

Evidence of (1) furnishing or offering or promising to furnish or (2) accepting or offering or promising to accept, a valuable consideration in compromising or attempting to compromise a claim which was disputed as to either validity or amount, is not admissible to prove liability for or invalidity of the claim or its amount. Evidence of conduct or statements made in compromise negotiations is likewise not admissible. This rule does not require the exclusion of any evidence otherwise discoverable merely because it is presented in the course of compromise negotiations. This rule also does not require exclusion when the evidence is offered for another purpose, such as proving bias or prejudice of a witness, negativing a contention of undue delay, or proving an effort to obstruct a criminal investigation or prosecution.

Commentary

Compromise or settlement discussions are deemed inadmissible in order to encourage parties to negotiate disputed settlements outside of court. Disclosure to the fact-finder by the admission of such evidence, in the eyes of the rule makers, would *chill* such compromise negotiations.

Note that the rule forbids the admission of negotiations regarding *disputed* claims only. Thus, for example, if one party to an automobile collision leaps from his car and offers the other driver a certain sum to cover the damage, such statements are admissible pursuant to Rule 408 because no one has yet disputed the claim. The term *disputed claim*, however, does not refer only to claims which are reduced to litigation. A claim which is asserted outside of court proceedings, or disputed originally as to liability or amount, is *disputed* for purposes of the rule. For example, a claim made to an insurance company for coverage in an automobile collision case may be sufficient to meet the disputed claim requirement of the rule, thereby, protecting the statements made during the process of the claim pursuant to Rule 408.

In addition, unlike the rule in most common law jurisdictions, statements of fact, and indeed, any statements at all (not merely offers and counter offers) made by the parties or their representatives in the course or context of compromise discussions, are inadmissible. For example, a statement by the defendant that he ran a red light, if made in the course of settlement or compromise negotiations (including the initial offer), is inadmissible at trial, even though the statement itself was not an offer of compromise. Such statements are protected because they are made as a precursor to compromise negotiations. Rule 408, thereby, does away with the need in many states to couch all factual discussions during compromise negotiations in hypothetical terms.

Of course, Rule 408 does not insulate from admission facts, which though mentioned in the compromise negotiations, are otherwise discovered. More important, the rule does not bar the admission of compromise negotiations or statements made where offered for *any relevant purpose* other than proof of liability or damages. For example, the rule provides that such evidence is admissible to impeach a witness for bias or prejudice, to deny the opponent's claim of undue delay, or to show an attempt or effort to obstruct a criminal prosecution.

An example of the offer of compromise negotiations to show bias would involve the impeachment of a servant-defendant who has agreed to testify on behalf of the plaintiff against his master in exchange for an agreement not to hold the servant personally liable. In such a case, the agreement between the servant-defendant, although in the nature of compromise, would be admissible to show that the defendant-servant has an interest in testifying in a manner favorable to the plaintiff.

CHAPTER 26
PAYMENT OF MEDICAL AND SIMILAR EXPENSES

Definition

Evidence of an offer to pay medical expenses to an injured person is not admissible to prove liability for such injury.

Forms of Objection and Response

Form of Objection

> ➤ *I object that this evidence is inadmissible as an offer to pay medical expenses.*

Form of Response

> ➤ *This statement is admissible because it is not offered on the issue of liability.*

Federal Rule 409. Payment of Medical and Similar Expenses

Evidence of furnishing or offering or promising to pay medical, hospital, or similar expenses occasioned by an injury is not admissible to prove liability for the injury.

Commentary

The rationale for this rule is similar to that of Rule 407 and Rule 408 relating to subsequent remedial measures and offers of compromise. The rule makers have excluded offers to pay medical expenses at trial so as to provide an incentive for those who believe themselves responsible to offer and/or pay the medical expenses of victims without resort to the courts. When medical bills are paid, the incentive to litigate is substantially lessened.

Evidence of such offers or payments are excluded only on the issue of liability and could be offered for any other relevant purpose. Note, too, there is no *disputed claim* requirement here (as in Rule 407), nor is there any explicit bar to the admission of statements of fact contained within or made in the context of the offer or payment of medical expenses. To the extent it has any weight, it would appear that a payment of, or offer to pay, medical expenses is admissible on the *amount* of damages since such an exclusion is not mentioned in this rule as it is in Rule 408 relating to compromise and offers to compromise. As a practical matter, however, it will be difficult to admit evidence as to the amount of damages without the jury also inferring that the party who paid your medical expenses is also liable, thereby making most unusual the admissibility of this evidence on the narrow issue of damages. Such a proffer would normally be excluded pursuant to Rule 403 as likely to cause a confusion of issues.

CHAPTER 27
GUILTY PLEAS, OFFERS OF PLEAS, AND RELATED STATEMENTS

Definition

Evidence of a later withdrawn guilty plea, a nolo contendere plea, or an offer of either, is generally inadmissible in any case, civil or criminal, against the person who made the offer or plea. Such evidence is admissible in a criminal proceeding for perjury or false statement, so long as the offer or plea was made under oath, in the presence of counsel, and on the record.

Forms of Objection and Response

Form of Objection

> ➤ *I object that this evidence is inadmissible as a withdrawn guilty plea, as a nolo plea, or as an offer to so plead.*

Form of Response

> ➤ *This evidence is admissible against the criminal defendant because the defendant is charged with perjury and the statement was made under oath, in the presence of counsel, and on the record.*

Federal Rule 410. Inadmissibility of Pleas, Plea Discussions, and Related Statements

Except as otherwise provided in this rule, evidence of the following is not, in any civil or criminal proceeding, admissible against the defendant who made the plea or was a participant in the plea discussions:

(1) a plea of guilty which was later withdrawn;

(2) a plea of nolo contendere;

(3) any statement made in the course of any proceedings under Rule 11 of the Federal Rules of Criminal Procedure or comparable state procedure regarding either of the foregoing pleas; or

(4) any statement made in the course of plea discussions with an attorney for the prosecuting authority which do not result in a plea of guilty or which result in a plea of guilty later withdrawn.

However, such a statement is admissible (i) in any proceeding wherein another statement made in the course of the same plea or plea discussions has been introduced and the statement ought in fairness be considered contemporaneously with it, or (ii) in a criminal proceeding for perjury or false statement if the statement was made by the defendant under oath, on the record, and in the presence of counsel.

Commentary

This rule is a criminal analogue to Rule 408 (Compromise and Offers to Compromise). Evidence of the plea *and statements connected therewith* are admissible against a criminal defendant, but only when charged with perjury or false statement, and if the statement is on the record, made under oath, and in the presence of counsel. Because of the inflammatory effect of this type of evidence, there is a flat bar for any purpose other than those specifically enumerated in the rule.

CHAPTER 28
INSURANCE AGAINST LIABILITY

Definition

Evidence that a person was (or was not) insured against liability is inadmissible as proof of negligence or other wrongful behavior or on the issue of the ability of a party to pay damages. The evidence is admissible on such issues as agency, ownership, or control, or for impeachment of the witness on bias or prejudice grounds.

Forms of Objection and Response

Form of Objection

> ➤ *I object that the proponent is offering evidence of liability insurance on the issue of negligence or other wrongful conduct. I move for a mistrial.*

Form of Response

> ➤ *This evidence of liability insurance is not offered on the issue of negligence, but to show:*
>
> (a) *ownership,*
>
> (b) *agency,*
>
> (c) *control,*
>
> (d) *bias,* or
>
> (e) *some other purpose other than liability.*

Federal Rule 411. Liability Insurance

Evidence that a person was or was not insured against liability is not admissible upon the issue of whether the person acted negligently or otherwise wrongfully. This rule does not require the exclusion of evidence of insurance against liability when offered for another purpose, such as proof of agency, ownership, or control, or bias or prejudice of a witness.

Commentary

Contrary to common belief, the mere mention of a defendant being insured against liability is not necessarily inadmissible, nor need it lead to a mistrial. Rule 411 forbids only the offer of proof of liability insurance on the issue of negligence or other wrongful conduct. Where evidence of liability insurance is offered for some other purpose, the rule does not bar its admission. For example, the rule mentions impeachment for bias as a relevant, non-negligence purpose.

As an illustration, assume an insurance investigator testifies in an automobile accident case on behalf of the defendant. The plaintiff may cross examine and impeach the investigator by showing that he is employed by the defendant-driver's insurer and is thus biased. Though the bias is established by evidence of liability insurance, the evidence is admissible for the impeachment purpose. It would be inadmissible to prove defendant's negligence.

In addition, evidence of insurance generally is not admissible on the issue of the ability of a party to pay damages. Although the rule does not specifically preclude the admissibility of evidence of insurance on the issue of ability to pay damages, such a preclusion is unnecessary because ability to pay is not relevant in any lawsuit except where punitive damages are alleged. In a case claiming punitive damages for intentional activity on the part of the defendant, the existence of insurance against such liability may be admissible so that the jury can properly assess the amount of punitive damages necessary to impress upon the defendant the seriousness of the acts underlying the lawsuit.

Section IV. Authentication and Original Documents

CHAPTER 29
AUTHENTICATION OF INSTRUMENTS

Definition

Authentication is the process of proving that a writing, document, photograph, handwriting, tape recording, or other instrument is genuine and that it is what the proponent of the instrument claims it to be. Before an instrument can be accepted in evidence the proponent must establish its identity and authorship by stipulation, by circumstantial evidence, or by the testimony of a witness with knowledge of its identity and authorship. In this context, *instrument* refers to any document, computer printout, photograph, or tape recording.

Forms of Objection and Response

Form of Objection

➤ *I object. This exhibit has not been authenticated.*

Forms of Response

➤ *The instrument has been authenticated by stipulation of counsel.*

➤ *The instrument has been authenticated through the testimony of _____* (insert name of witness) *who has testified that:*

    (a) *(s)he created the writing,* or

    (b) *(s)he was present at the creation of the writing and testified that it is in substantially the same condition as at the time of its creation,* or

    (c) *(s)he knows the handwriting because (s)he saw the author write or sign the instrument,* or

    (d) *(s)he knows the handwriting from having seen the author sign his signature at another time,* or

    (e) *(s)he knows the handwriting by circumstantial evidence that shows _____* (state circumstances), or

    (f) *(where proved by an expert witness) (s)he has compared the handwriting in question with an authentic handwriting exemplar and that her opinion to a reasonable degree of certainty is that the handwriting in question is that of _____* (name of purported author), or

    (g) *(s)he was present at the time the tape recording was made,* or

    (h) *(s)he saw the scene or items portrayed in the photograph at a relevant time and that the photograph is a fair and accurate representation of what was seen.*

➤ *Your Honor, I request that you compare the handwriting in question with an admittedly authentic handwriting exemplar and find that it is the handwriting of _____* (insert name of purported author).

Federal Rule 901. Requirement of Authentication or Identification

(a) General provision. The requirement of authentication or identification as a condition precedent to admissibility is satisfied by evidence sufficient to support a finding that the matter in question is what its proponent claims.

(b) Illustrations. By way of illustration only, and not by way of limitation, the following are examples of authentication or identification conforming with the requirements of this rule:

(1) Testimony of witness with knowledge. Testimony that a matter is what it is claimed to be.

(2) Nonexpert opinion on handwriting. Nonexpert opinion as to the genuineness of handwriting, based upon familiarity not acquired for purposes of litigation.

(3) Comparison by trier or expert witness. Comparison by the trier of fact or by expert witnesses with specimens which have been authenticated.

(4) Distinctive characteristics and the like. Appearance, contents, substance, internal patterns, or other distinctive characteristics, taken in conjunction with circumstances.

(5) Voice identification. Identification of a voice, whether heard firsthand or through mechanical or electronic transmission or recording, by opinion based upon hearing the voice at any time under circumstances connecting it with the alleged speaker.

(6) Telephone conversations. Telephone conversations, by evidence that a call was made to the number assigned at the time by the telephone company to a particular person or business, if (A) in the case of a person, circumstances including self-identification, show the person answering to be the one called, or (B) in the case of a business, the call was made to a place of business and the conversation related to business reasonably transacted over the telephone.

(7) Public records or reports. Evidence that a writing authorized by law to be recorded or filed and in fact recorded or filed in a public office, or a purported public record, report, statement, or data compilation, in any form, is from the public office where items of this nature are kept.

(8) Ancient documents or data compilation. Evidence that a document or data compilation, in any form, (A) is in such condition as to create no suspicion concerning its authenticity, (B) was in a place where it, if authentic, would likely be, and (C) has been in existence 20 years or more at the time it is offered.

(9) Process or system. Evidence describing a process or system used to produce a result and showing that the process or system produces an accurate result.

(10) Methods provided by statute or rule. Any method of authentication or identification provided by Act of Congress or by other rules prescribed by the Supreme Court pursuant to statutory authority.

Federal Rule 902. Self-Authentication

Extrinsic evidence of authenticity as a condition precedent to admissibility is not required with respect to the following:

(1) Domestic public documents under seal. A document bearing a seal purporting to be that of the United States, or of any State, district, Commonwealth, territory, or insular possession thereof, or the Panama Canal Zone, or the Trust Territory of the Pacific Islands, or of a political subdivision, department, officer, or agency thereof, and a signature purporting to be an attestation or execution.

(2) Domestic public documents not under seal. A document purporting to bear the signature in the official capacity of an officer or employee of any entity included in paragraph (1) hereof, having no seal, if a public officer having a seal and having official duties in the district or political subdivision of the officer or employee certifies under seal that the signer has the official capacity and that the signature is genuine.

(3) Foreign public documents. A document purporting to be executed or attested in an official capacity by a person authorized by the laws of a foreign country to make the execution or attestation, and accompanied by a final certification as to the genuineness of the signature and official position (A) of the executing or attesting person, or (B) of any foreign official whose certificate of genuineness of signature and official position relates to the execution or attestation or is in a chain of certificates of genuineness of signature and official position relating to the execution or attestation. A final certification may be made by a secretary of embassy or legation, consul general, consul, vice consul, or consular agent of the United States, or a diplomatic or consular official of the foreign country assigned or accredited to the United States. If reasonable opportunity has been given to all parties to investigate the authenticity and accuracy of official documents, the court may, for good cause shown, order that they be treated as presumptively authentic without final certification or permit them to be evidenced by an attested summary with or without final certification.

(4) Certified copies of public records. A copy of an official record or report or entry therein, or of a document authorized by law to be recorded or filed and actually recorded or filed in a public office, including data compilations in any form, certified as correct by the custodian or other person authorized to make the certification, by certificate, complying with paragraph (1), (2), or (3) of this rule or complying with any act of Congress or rule prescribed by the Supreme Court pursuant to statutory authority.

(5) Official publications. Books, pamphlets, or other publications purporting to be issued by public authority.

(6) Newspapers and periodicals. Printed materials purporting to be newspapers or periodicals.

(7) Trade inscriptions and the like. Inscriptions, signs, tags, or labels purporting to have been affixed in the course of business and indicating ownership, control, or origin.

(8) Acknowledged documents. Documents accompanied by a certificate of acknowledgment executed in the manner provided by law by a notary public or other officer authorized by law to take acknowledgments.

(9) Commercial paper and related documents. Commercial paper, signatures thereon, and documents relating thereto to the extent provided by general commercial law.

(10) Presumptions under Acts of Congress. Any signature, document, or other matter declared by Act of Congress to be presumptively or prima facie genuine or authentic.

Federal Rule 903. Subscribing Witness' Testimony Unnecessary

The testimony of a subscribing witness is not necessary to authenticate a writing unless required by the laws of the jurisdiction whose laws govern the validity of the writing.

Commentary

Authentication is a foundational requirement for the introduction of any instrument. Authentication, relevance, compliance with the original document rule, and avoidance of hearsay comprise the foundation for the introduction of any instrument. In most circumstances counsel should attempt to obtain a stipulation as to authenticity of instruments either informally or through a request for admissions. Most judges will assist in obtaining such a stipulation or admission unless there is a genuine issue on the question of authenticity. On the issue of authentication of handwriting, the federal rule presents a major departure from the common law by allowing authentication to be proved by a comparison by the court of the handwriting in question with an admittedly authentic exemplar.

Authentication is easily established in most situations. It is unusual that a witness will not be available who is capable of testifying that an instrument is what it purports to be. In those situations where a witness with direct knowledge of identity or authorship is not available, authentication can normally be proved by circumstantial evidence. For example, in many business situations the receiver of a letter will not have ever actually seen his correspondent sign his signature. However, if business has been conducted on the basis of that signature in the past, that circumstance alone will be sufficient for authentication purposes.

In circumstances where the basis for authentication by a witness is firsthand knowledge of the handwriting in question, such familiarity may not be obtained for the purpose of the litigation at hand. The witness must have gained knowledge of the handwriting and its author in some other way.

It is important to note that the question of authentication is preliminary and to be decided by the judge utilizing the standard of proof provided in Rule 104(b). A jury is not bound by this determination in weighing the evidence. For example, when a judge admits a letter purportedly signed by a party as authentic, the jury is not bound by that determination and may, by its verdict, find that the letter was actually signed by someone else. This is a product of the difference between the Rule 104(b) quantum of proof for admissibility and the preponderance of evidence or beyond a reasonable doubt quantum of proof required for a verdict in civil and criminal cases, respectively.

CHAPTER 30
AUTHENTICATION OF TELEPHONE CONVERSATIONS AND VOICES

Definition

Authentication of telephone conversations and voices is the process of proving the identity of the persons involved in the conversation. Before testimony can be had that a telephone conversation occurred, testimony must be elicited to prove the identity of the participants in the conversation.

Forms of Objection and Response

Forms of Objection

➤ *I object. The telephone conversation has not been authenticated.*

➤ *I object. The participants in the telephone conversation have not been properly identified.*

Form of Response

➤ *The identity of the participants in the telephone conversation has been established through the testimony of* _____ (insert name of witness) *who has testified that:*

    (a) *(s)he is familiar with and recognized the voice,* or

    (b) *(s)he called the number listed to* _____ (insert name of participant) *and the other party identified himself as* _____ (insert name of participant), or

    (c) *(s)he called the number listed to* _____ (insert name of participant) *and the content of the conversation showed* _____ (insert name of person) *to be the person who answered the call,* or

    (d) *(s)he called the number listed to* _____ (insert name of business) *and the conversation related to business conducted by* _____ (insert name of business) *over the telephone,* or

    (e) (where proved by a qualified expert witness) *(s)he has compared the voice in question with an authentic voice exemplar and that her opinion to a reasonable degree of certainty is that the voice in question is that of* _____ (insert name of purported speaker).

Federal Rule 901. Requirement of Authentication or Identification

(a) **General provision.** The requirement of authentication or identification as a condition precedent to admissibility is satisfied by evidence sufficient to support a finding that the matter in question is what its proponent claims.

(b) **Illustrations.** By way of illustration only, and not by way of limitation, the following are examples of authentication or identification conforming with the requirements of this rule:

(1) Testimony of witness with knowledge. Testimony that a matter is what it is claimed to be.

(3) Comparison of trier or expert witness. Comparison by the trier of fact or by expert witnesses with specimens which have been authenticated.

(4) Distinctive characteristics and the like. Appearance, contents, substance, internal patterns, or other distinctive characteristics, taken in conjunction with circumstances.

(5) Voice identification. Identification of a voice, whether heard firsthand or through mechanical or electronic transmission or recording, by opinion based upon hearing the voice at any time under circumstances connecting it with the alleged speaker.

(6) Telephone conversations. Telephone conversations, by evidence that a call was made to the number assigned at the time by the telephone company to a particular person or business, if (A) in the case of a person, circumstances, including self-identification, show the person answering to be the one called, or (B) in the case of a business, the call was made to a place of business and the conversation related to business reasonably transacted over the telephone.

Commentary

The authentication of telephone conversations is usually accomplished through the testimony of one of the participants, or any other person, who has gained familiarity with the voices of the participants and can give an opinion as to the identity of the persons whose voices (s)he recognizes. Familiarity may be obtained either before or after the telephone conversation in question so long as the circumstances of obtaining familiarity are sufficient to meet the quantum of proof required by Rule 104(b). In weighing the evidence and judging the credibility of the witness, the jury may of course decide that there is insufficient evidence of the identity of the participants on which to make a finding of fact.

When the authenticating witness is the person who placed the telephone call, testimony that the number called was listed to the other participant together with self-identification by the answering participant will be sufficient to meet the authentication requirement. It is not necessary to show voice familiarity as well.

When the authenticating witness is the witness who placed the telephone call to a business, testimony that the number called was listed to the business, together with a conversation that relates to the type of business normally conducted by that organization on the telephone will be sufficient to establish authenticity. It is not necessary to show voice familiarity as well.

When the authenticating witness is the receiver of a telephone call, self-identification by the alleged caller will not be sufficient, in and of itself, to authenticate the telephone call. Additional evidence, such as voice familiarity or the contents of the telephone call as it circumstantially shows identity of the caller, will be necessary.

Telephone conversations which have been recorded can be authenticated by expert testimony consisting of comparison of the taped conversations with a voice exemplar by utilizing voice spectrography or by any person who can demonstrate familiarity with the voice(s) in question.

CHAPTER 31
ORIGINAL DOCUMENT RULE
(BEST EVIDENCE RULE)

Definition

Where the proponent seeks to prove the contents of a writing, recording, or photograph, and the contents are directly in issue, the proponent must produce the original unless its production is excused.

Forms of Objection and Response

Form of Objection

> ➤ *I object to the proponent's offer to show the contents of a writing by the use of secondary evidence.*

Forms of Response

> ➤ *The terms of the writing are not directly in issue in the lawsuit and thus the original is not required. The writing is offered to prove _____.*

> ➤ *The original's absence has been sufficiently accounted for and thus secondary evidence is admissible because:*

>> (a) *the original has been shown to have been lost or destroyed,* or

>> (b) *the original cannot be obtained by any available judicial process or procedure,* or

>> (c) *the original is in the possession of an opposing party against whom the contents are offered, that party has failed to produce it, and that party has been put on notice, by the pleadings or otherwise, that the contents would be the subject of proof at trial.*

Federal Rule 1001. Definitions

For purposes of this article the following definitions are applicable:

(1) Writings and recordings. "Writings" and "recordings" consist of letters, words, or numbers, or their equivalent, set down by handwriting, typewriting, printing, photostating, photographing, magnetic impulse, mechanical or electronic recording, or other form of data compilation.

(2) Photographs. "Photographs" include still photographs, X-ray films, videotapes, and motion pictures.

(3) Original. An "original" of a writing or recording is the writing or recording itself or any counterpart intended to have the same effect by a person executing or issuing it. An "original" of a photograph includes the negative or any print therefrom. If data are stored in a computer or similar device, any printout or other output readable by sight, shown to reflect the data accurately, is an "original."

(4) Duplicate. A "duplicate" is a counterpart produced by the same impression as the original, or from the same matrix, or by means of photography, including enlargements and miniatures, or by mechanical or electronic re-recording, or by chemical reproduction, or by other equivalent techniques which accurately reproduces the original.

Federal Rule 1002. Requirement of Original

To prove the content of a writing, recording, or photograph, the original writing, recording, or photograph is required, except as otherwise provided in these rules or by Act of Congress.

Federal Rule 1003. Admissibility of Duplicates

A duplicate is admissible to the same extent as an original unless (1) a genuine question is raised as to the authenticity of the original or (2) in the circumstances it would be unfair to admit the duplicate in lieu of the original.

Federal Rule 1004. Admissibility of Other Evidence of Contents

The original is not required and other evidence of the contents of a writing, recording, or photograph is admissible if—

(1) Originals lost or destroyed. All originals are lost or have been destroyed, unless the proponent lost or destroyed them in bad faith; or

(2) Original not obtainable. No original can be obtained by any available judicial process or procedure; or

(3) Original in possession of opponent. At a time when an original was under the control of the party against whom offered, that party was put on notice, by the pleadings or otherwise, that the contents would be a subject of proof at the hearing, and that party does not produce the original at the hearing; or

(4) Collateral matters. The writing, recording, or photograph is not closely related to a controlling issue.

Federal Rule 1005. Public Records

The contents of an official record, or of a document authorized to be recorded or filed and actually recorded or filed, including data compilations in any form, if otherwise admissible, may be proved by copy, certified as correct in accordance with Rule 902 or testified to be correct by a witness who has compared it with the original. If a copy which complies with the foregoing cannot be obtained by the exercise of reasonable diligence, then other evidence of the contents may be given.

Federal Rule 1006. Summaries

The contents of voluminous writings, recordings, or photographs which cannot conveniently be examined in court may be presented in the form of a chart, summary, or calculation. The originals, or duplicates, shall be made available for examination or copying, or both, by other parties at reasonable time and place. The court may order that they be produced in court.

Federal Rule 1007. Testimony or Written Admission of Party

Contents of writings, recordings, or photographs may be proved by the testimony or deposition of the party against whom offered or by that party's written admission, without accounting for the nonproduction of the original.

Federal Rule 1008. Functions of Court and Jury

When the admissibility of other evidence of contents of writings, recordings, or photographs under these rules depends upon the fulfillment of a condition of fact, the question whether the condition has been fulfilled is ordinarily for the court to determine in accordance with the provisions of rule 104. However, when an issue is raised (a) whether the asserted writing ever existed, or (b) whether another writing, recording, or photograph produced at the trial is the original, or (c) whether other evidence of contents correctly reflects the contents, the issue is for the trier of fact to determine as in the case of other issues of fact.

Commentary

The original document rule requires the proponent to offer the original of a document, photograph, or recording in evidence where the proponent seeks to prove its contents and the contents are directly in issue, unless production is excused under the terms of the rule.

The original document rule is only, however, a rule of preference. There are numerous qualifications to this rule. First, an *original* includes a counterpart intended by the executing persons to have the same effect as the original. Second, a duplicate, e.g., a photocopy, is generally considered the equivalent of an original. Third, the original document rule has no application if the writing, recording, or photograph is *collateral,* i.e., does not deal with a controlling issue in the lawsuit.

Because the original document rule is merely a rule of preference for the original, the original need not be produced where:

(a) the original is lost or destroyed (not at the behest of the proponent of the document), or

(b) the original cannot be obtained by judicial process, or

(c) the original is in the control of the opponent and the opponent has been put on notice, by the pleadings or otherwise, that the contents of the document, recording, or photograph would be the subject of proof at trial.

The proponent of secondary evidence (i.e., something other than the original) bears the burden of persuading the trial judge, pursuant to Rule 104, that the excuse for nonproduction is met. For example, the proponent can lay a foundation for the loss of the original by offering evidence of a diligent, but unavailing, search for the document.

The key to understanding the original document rule is the following. The rule applies where the facts contained in the document are directly in issue in the case and the facts do not exist independent of the document. For example, the bequests in a will are clearly in issue in a will contest and such bequests only exist because they are contained in the will. In other words, the facts are embodied in the writing, and have no existence independent of the writing. If the writing, the will, does not exist, then the operative facts, the bequests, do not exist. Contrarily, where a proponent seeks to prove the fact of payment for which he has a receipt, the proponent need not offer the original receipt (or any receipt). This is because the fact of payment exists irrespective of whether a writing, a receipt, has been created to evidence it. In other words, the fact of payment exists, whether or not a receipt was made to memorialize payment. The receipt is merely evidence of payment, not the payment itself. Therefore, secondary evidence of payment, including oral testimony, would be admissible.

Thus, when deciding whether the original document rule applies to a particular proffer, the ultimate question is whether the writing is more like a will as opposed to a receipt, i.e., whether the facts to be proved have an existence independent from the writing. Note that if the proponent chooses to use a writing as the sole method of proof of its terms, e.g., chooses to prove payment solely by way of a receipt, then the proponent must normally offer the original of the writing unless excused.

Finally, the federal rules create no hierarchy of secondary evidence to be offered (except with regard to Rule 1005, public records) if production of the original is excused. Thus, once production of the original is excused, the proponent may offer any sort of otherwise admissible evidence of the contents of the writing, including oral testimony.

Section V. Exhibits

CHAPTER 32
- EXHIBITS -
WRITINGS

Definition

In order to introduce a writing in evidence, four foundational requirements must be met. The writing must be shown to be relevant, authentic, meet the requirements of the original document rule, and either qualify as non-hearsay or meet an exception to the hearsay rule.

Forms of Objection and Response

Form of Objection

➤ *I object to the introduction of the exhibit in that there is an improper foundation because:*

    (a) *it is not relevant,* or

    (b) *authenticity has not been shown,* or

    (c) *the original document rule has not been met,* or

    (d) *the writing is hearsay.*

Form of Response

➤ *The foundational requirements regarding relevance, authentication, the original document rule, and hearsay have been met through the testimony of* _____ (insert names of witnesses) *who have testified that* _____ .

Federal Rule

Relevance is governed by Article IV, authenticity by Article IX, original documents by Article X, and hearsay by Article VIII. Each of these rules receive specific treatment in this book.

Commentary

A writing may not be received in evidence until potential objections as to relevance, authentication, original documents, and hearsay are met. In addition, because documents are capable of alteration, the judge will normally require some testimony that the document is in the same or similar condition as it was at a relevant time. Thus, in order to ensure successful introduction of a writing, the proponent should keep a checklist as to the means for establishing each foundational matter, and the testimonial source of each. This is especially important when dealing with writings that require the testimony of several witnesses for introduction.

It is important to note that testimony as to the contents of the writing should not be elicited until the document has been accepted in evidence. It is usually best, as a tactical matter, therefore, to elicit foundational information about the writing before presenting the writing for identification to the witness. This avoids the natural tendency of the witness to read from the writing in describing or identifying it. As a matter of form, many lawyers, in asking for authentication testimony, will frame the identification question to the witness in the following way: "Without disclosing the contents of Exhibit 24 for Identification, tell me whether or not you recognize it."

Opposing counsel should also keep a checklist as to foundational requirements so that specific objections can be framed to the introduction of the exhibit. As with any exhibit, opposing counsel has the right at the time of the offer of the exhibit to question on voir dire as to the admissibility of the writing. Many writings will contain both admissible and inadmissible material, or be admissible for one purpose and not for another. Opposing counsel has the duty to separate the admissible from the inadmissible pursuant to Rule 105. In some cases it is appropriate to request portions of a writing be redacted before publication to the jury.

In modern day civil practice, the admissibility of writings will ordinarily be determined at the pretrial conference. For example, the admissibility of a document can be shown by reference to discovery such as depositions, document production, and requests for admission. The issue of redaction is also typically handled at the pretrial conference by way of pretrial rulings on motions in limine.

CHAPTER 33
- EXHIBITS -
ILLUSTRATIVE

Definition

Illustrative exhibits are exhibits that assist a witness in the giving of testimony. They are utilized to clarify the testimony of witnesses and as an aid in explaining testimony. Typical illustrative exhibits are diagrams, charts, and graphs.

Forms of Objection and Response

Forms of Objection

> *I object. The proffered illustrative exhibit has not been properly authenticated.*

> *I object. The proffered illustrative exhibit is confusing and/or misleading.*

> *I object. The proffered illustrative exhibit contains markings that will lead the witness in the giving of testimony.*

Forms of Response

> *The illustrative exhibit has been authenticated by the testimony of* _____ (insert name of witness). *The witness has testified that:*

>> (a) *(s)he recognizes what the exhibit, that has been marked for identification, portrays,* and

>> (b) *the exhibit will aid in the illustration and/or explanation of the witness' testimony.*

> *The exhibit is not offered as a to-scale diagram; it is merely an aid to the explaining of testimony. Any problems with the illustrative exhibit can be demonstrated during cross examination.*

> _____ (insert name of witness) *has already testified as to what the markings contained on the exhibit portray. The exhibit is offered merely to illustrate that testimony.*

Federal Rule

There is no specific rule on illustrative exhibits. They must merely be authenticated pursuant to Rule 901(a) which provides:

Federal Rule 901. Requirement of Authentication or Identification

(a) General provision. The requirement of authentication or identification as a condition precedent to admissibility is satisfied by evidence sufficient to support a finding that the matter in question is what its proponent claims.

Further, the judge has discretion to allow the use of illustrative exhibits pursuant to Rule 611(a) which provides:

Federal Rule 611. Mode and Order of Interrogation and Presentation

(a) Control by court. The court shall exercise reasonable control over the mode and order of interrogating witnesses and presenting evidence so as to (1) make the interrogation and presentation effective for the ascertainment of the truth, . . .

Commentary

The foundation for an illustrative exhibit is as follows:

(1) the witness must testify as to firsthand knowledge of the thing which the exhibit illustrates;

(2) mark the exhibit for identification;

(3) direct the witness' attention to the exhibit;

(4) elicit testimony from the witness that (s)he recognizes what the exhibit shows;

(5) elicit testimony from the witness that (s)he can utilize the exhibit to either illustrate or explain her/his testimony.

The illustrative exhibit is one of the most important tools of the trial lawyer. It is especially helpful in cases where a physical scene is important to the case. For example, it would be a most unusual automobile accident case where the testimony of a witness would not be better presented utilizing a diagram of the accident scene as an illustrative exhibit. Care must be taken to make markings on the illustrative exhibit as the witness utilizes it so that the transcribed record is clear for potential appellate purposes. For example, the path of the defendant's car in an automobile accident case may be shown on an illustrative diagram by numbers 1, 2, 3, etc.

All markings should be made on the illustrative exhibit before it is introduced in evidence. (Note that illustrative exhibits may or may not be admitted as a matter of judicial discretion). Once an illustrative exhibit has been introduced, no further markings may be made on it. In a case where more than one witness will testify concerning the scene of an incident, the basic diagram can be prepared on poster board, and the particular illustrations of each witness' testimony can be made with a grease pencil on plastic overlays.

Illustrative exhibits are also very helpful as an aid to expert testimony. Charts, graphs, and calculation sheets can be enlarged and utilized in giving the trier of fact a clear picture of the expert's testimony. In addition, with the aid of readily available computer technology, illustrative exhibits can be created in the courtroom as a witness testifies. For example, an economist can actually perform the calculations necessary for his/her expert opinion in the courtroom and display them on an enlarged computer screen.

Illustrative exhibits, including diagrams, charts, graphs, etc., may also be utilized during opening statements and closing arguments as an aid to persuasion. No formal foundation is necessary as long as the exhibit utilized in the opening statement illustrates the testimony of a witness to be called. It is a good idea to raise the issue of utilizing illustrative exhibits during opening statements during the pretrial conference. Similarly, there is no foundation necessary for utilization of illustrative exhibits during closing argument as long as the exhibit illustrates either the testimony of a witness or a fair inference from the testimony of witnesses during the trial. The illustrative exhibit thereby becomes an effective device for essentially outlining either the opening or closing speech, which obviates the need for the use of notes that can distract from effective presentation to the jury.

CHAPTER 34
- EXHIBITS -
DEMONSTRATIVE

Definition

Demonstrative exhibits are exhibits that depict a particular thing in issue at a trial. They are not the thing itself, but a representation of the thing that is in issue. These exhibits are utilized to demonstrate to the jury, in a visual way, what was seen by a witness, utilized by a witness, or a relevant object in the events that are at issue at trial. Typical demonstrative exhibits are photographs and to-scale models.

Forms of Objection and Response

Forms of Objection

➤ *I object. The proffered exhibit has not been properly authenticated.*

➤ *I object. The proffered exhibit has not been shown to be:*

    (a) (photographs) *a fair and accurate depiction of a relevant scene,* or

    (b) (to-scale models) *a fair and accurate representation of an object in issue.*

Forms of Response

➤ *The demonstrative exhibit has been authenticated by the testimony of* _____ (insert name of witness). *The witness has testified that:*

    (a) (photographs) *the exhibit looks like an object in issue,* or

    (b) (to-scale models) *the exhibit is a fair and accurate representation of a scene in issue.*

➤ (Photographs) *The witness has testified that the photograph shows a relevant scene as it appeared at a relevant time and the exhibit is a fair and accurate depiction of that scene.*

➤ (To-scale models) *The witness has testified that the exhibit is a to-scale model and a fair and accurate representation of an object that is in issue.*

Federal Rule

There is no specific rule on demonstrative exhibits. They must be authenticated pursuant to Rule 901(a) which provides:

Federal Rule 901. Requirement of Authentication or Identification

(a) General provision. The requirement of authentication or identification as a condition precedent to admissibility is satisfied by evidence sufficient to support a finding that the matter in question is what its proponent claims.

The judge has discretion to allow the use of demonstrative exhibits pursuant to Rule 611(a) which provides:

Federal Rule 611. Mode and Order of Interrogation and Presentation

(a) Control by court. The court shall exercise reasonable control over the mode and order of interrogating witnesses and presenting evidence so as to (1) make the interrogation and presentation effective for the ascertainment of the truth, . . .

Commentary

The foundation for a demonstrative exhibit is as follows:

(1) the witness must testify as to firsthand knowledge of the thing or place that the exhibit demonstrates;

(2) mark the exhibit for identification;

(3) direct the witness' attention to the exhibit;

(4) elicit testimony from the witness that (s)he recognizes the exhibit or what the exhibit depicts;

(5) elicit testimony from the witness that the exhibit is a fair and accurate depiction or representation of a scene or object that is in issue in the case.

Demonstrative exhibits are important tools of the effective trial lawyer in that they bring alive for the jury scenes and things that are in issue in a particular case. Demonstrative exhibits take two basic forms—photographs and tangible objects such as models.

Photographs

In modern day practice, photographs are typical demonstrative exhibits in any case that involves a physical scene. The basic requirements for introduction of a photograph are that a witness with firsthand knowledge of the scene in issue testify that the photograph shows a relevant view of a scene at a relevant time, and that it is a fair and accurate depiction of that scene. This foundation requires only the testimony of a witness who was present and familiar with the scene in issue. There is no requirement that the photographer be called as a witness. In addition, the photograph need not be taken at the time of the event in question so long as the photograph fairly and accurately depicts that scene at the time of the event in question.

As a matter of tactics counsel should elicit the testimony of the witness about the relevant scene before showing the photograph to the witness. For example, in a case where a traffic accident took place at the intersection of 5th and Main at 3:00 p.m. on July 31, YR-1, and was witnessed by Joan Jones, the foundation for the introduction of a photograph is as follows:

(1) Elicit the testimony of Ms. Jones about how the intersection appeared to her at the time of the accident.

(2) Mark the photograph as Exhibit 1.

(3) Show the exhibit to opposing counsel.

(4) Approach the witness.

(5) Ask the following question: "Showing you what has been marked as Exhibit 1, do you recognize what it shows?"

(6) Ask the qualifying question: "Is what has been marked as Exhibit 1 a fair and accurate depiction of the intersection of 5th and Main as it appeared to you on July 31, YR-1 at 3:00 p.m.?"

(7) Move the exhibit in evidence.

(8) Show the exhibit to the jury and have the witness use the photograph to further testify about what the photograph shows.

Differences between what the witness saw at the relevant time and what the photograph shows will not usually mandate exclusion of the exhibit so long as the differences are acknowledged and the differences do not render the exhibit misleading.

Models

In any litigation where the physical characteristics of a thing are in issue, such as product liability cases, a to-scale model of the thing in question will be most helpful to the jury's understanding of the case. The foundation for admissibility of a model will typically be laid by use of expert testimony. The expert must testify that the essential physical characteristics of the thing in question are demonstrated by the model so that it fairly and accurately represents the thing in issue. The foundation should proceed in much the same way as the foundation for photographs outlined above.

The foundation for the use of computer models of events in question in a lawsuit is essentially the same as outlined above. It is necessary, however, to also show that the program used to generate the computer model is an accepted one, that is it produces accurate models, and to show the competence of the operator of the computer who created the model. Computer-generated models, based on the testimony of witnesses with firsthand knowledge of an event, can be powerful persuasive tools. They have the effect of bringing to life for the jury the events in question in a graphic way. By use of computer models, a jury can be shown how an operation in a medical negligence case allegedly went wrong, or how an alleged hit-and-run driver ran down an innocent pedestrian. The model allows the jury to easily visualize the events in question from the perspective of the proponent of the model, and thereby imprints that version of the facts on their minds.

CHAPTER 35
- EXHIBITS -
TANGIBLE OBJECTS

Definition

In order to introduce a tangible object in evidence, the proponent must show that it can be identified by a witness who had knowledge of the tangible object at a relevant time and who can testify that the tangible object is in the same or substantially the same condition as it was at the relevant time.

Forms of Objection and Response

Form of Objection

➤ *I object. The proffered exhibit is incompetent for lack of proper foundation.*

Form of Response

➤ *I have shown through the testimony of _____ (insert name of witness) that:*

    (a) *he perceived the exhibit at a relevant time,* and

    (b) *the exhibit is the one perceived,* and

    (c) *the exhibit is in substantially the same condition as it was at a relevant time.*

Federal Rule 901. Requirement of Authentication or Identification

(a) General provision. The requirement of authentication or identification as a condition precedent to admissibility is satisfied by evidence sufficient to support a finding that the matter in question is what its proponent claims.

Commentary

The process of admitting a tangible object in evidence is essentially a process of authentication. Counsel must show that the tangible object is the same tangible object observed by a witness at a relevant time and that it is in the same or similar condition as it was at the relevant time. For example, in a murder case, in order to introduce the gun allegedly used to kill the victim, the government must show how the gun is admissible by showing the method of obtaining the gun by the police, that the exhibit is the gun actually obtained, and that it is in the same or similar condition as when it was obtained. The foundation for the introduction of the gun through an eyewitness, Ms. Smith, would be as follows:

(1) Elicit the testimony of Ms. Smith as to what she saw at the murder scene. For example, she could testify that she saw a person who she now identifies as the defendant shoot the victim, drop a gun, and flee the scene. After the defendant fled, she picked up the gun and gave it to a police officer who investigated the shooting. The police officer took the gun and placed a sticker on the gun with the date, time, and place of the investigation and the witness' name.

(2) Mark the gun as Exhibit 1.

(3) Show the exhibit to opposing counsel.

(4) Approach the witness.

(5) Ask the following question: "Showing you what has been marked as Exhibit 1, do you recognize it?"

(6) Ask the following question: "How do you recognize Exhibit 1?"

(7) Ask the qualifying question: "Is what has been marked as Exhibit 1 in the same or substantially the same condition as when you gave it to the police?"

(8) Move the exhibit in evidence.

(9) Show the exhibit to the jury or have the witness use the exhibit to show how the defendant used it in shooting the victim.

In cases where there has been testing of the exhibit for some physical observations such as ballistics testing, fingerprint analysis, or chemical analysis, a chain of custody must be shown from the time of the obtaining of the exhibit until the time of testing to ensure admissibility. Counsel must account for the exhibit as it passed from person to person to show that there has been no tampering with the exhibit. The process will obviously require the testimony of a number of witnesses, and in order to show that a chain of custody has been maintained, the proponent should keep a checklist as to proof of the chain of custody as it has been shown by the testimony of the various witnesses involved for argument to the court at the time of offering the exhibit.

Section VI. Opinions

CHAPTER 36
LAY OPINION EVIDENCE

Definition

Generally, lay witnesses must testify in the language of perception rather than in the language of characterization or opinion. A lay witness may, however, testify in the form of an opinion or inference where such opinion or inference is (a) rationally based on the perception of the witness, and (b) helpful to a clear understanding of his testimony or the determination of a fact in issue.

Forms of Objection and Response

Forms of Objection

➤ *I object. The question calls for an opinion.*

➤ *I move to strike the answer because it is stated in the form of an opinion.*

Form of Response

➤ *This is permissible opinion from a lay witness because it is rationally based on the perception of the witness and would help the trier of fact to understand his testimony and determine a fact in issue in this lawsuit.*

Federal Rule 701. Opinion Testimony by Lay Witnesses

If the witness is not testifying as an expert, the witness' testimony in the form of opinions or inferences is limited to those opinions or inferences which are (a) rationally based on the perception of the witness and (b) helpful to a clear understanding of the witness' testimony or the determination of a fact in issue.

Federal Rule 704. Opinion on Ultimate Issue

(a) Except as provided in subdivision (b), testimony in the form of an opinion or inference otherwise admissible is not objectionable because it embraces an ultimate issue to be decided by the trier of fact.

Commentary

Generally, the determination of factual conclusions is within the province of the jury or other trier of fact. Therefore, witnesses ordinarily are permitted to testify as to what they have perceived, e.g., seen, heard, felt, tasted, or smelled, without testifying as to their opinions derived or inferred from perception.

There are many situations, however, where a witness' inference, when based on perception, would be helpful to the members of the jury because it would give them a more accurate picture of the witness' perception.

Lay opinion is generally allowed where its admission makes the jury's fact-finding easier and more accurate, and where a witness provides an inference to the jury which takes the place of describing a series of perceptions which in common experience add up to a rather ordinary inference or characterization. In these situations, the lay person ordinarily describes his or her observations in terms of opinion. For example, witnesses will be allowed to testify that they observed a person who appeared happy, sad, nervous, excited, depressed, etc. Witnesses would be hard pressed to break down what they observed into the component parts of the observation that led to a conclusion. They are, however, capable of understanding what was observed and to preclude such testimony would be to deprive the jury of reliable evidence by operation of a hyper-technical rule. Other opinions of lay witnesses that are typically allowed when based on observation are opinions as to sobriety or intoxication, speed of moving objects, value of personal property, authenticity of handwriting, size, color, and weight of objects, and time and distance.

There is one other typical situation where lay witnesses are allowed, pursuant to Rule 701, to testify in the form of opinion. Commonly this situation is described as the *collective fact doctrine.* In collective fact situations, a witness forms an instantaneous opinion as to matters that are observed, even though there is an inability to express the component observations that gave rise to the instantaneous opinion.

The typical example is where a pedestrian claims that he was struck by a car and a witness is prepared to testify that she observed the accident and, based on that observation, reached the instantaneous conclusion that the pedestrian could have gotten out of the way of the car. Obviously, the witness could not describe the physics of body movement that led to the opinion nor give a clear, factual statement as to facts that led to the opinion. That is, the observation of the witness and the witness' opinion are so intertwined as to make separation impossible. To preclude the witness from testifying as to this sort of opinion would preclude the jury from hearing any account of what the witness actually saw, and make the eyewitness testimony inadmissible. The federal rules do not compel such an anomalous result.

Finally, it should be noted that pursuant to Rule 704(a), lay opinions that are otherwise admissible are not precluded merely because they embrace the ultimate issue in the lawsuit. For example, if a plaintiff in an automobile accident case claims negligence on the basis of the defendant's drunk driving at a rate of speed that exceeds the speed limit, lay witnesses will not be precluded, on ultimate issue grounds, from giving opinions as to both the drunkenness of the defendant and the rate of speed of the defendant's car.

CHAPTER 37
EXPERT OPINION

Definition

Where the proponent seeks to offer opinions, conclusions, or inferences to assist the fact-finder in determining a fact in issue, and such opinions are beyond the ability of the fact-finder, the proponent may offer such opinions, conclusions, or inferences from a witness qualified as an expert in the relevant field of experience, training, or knowledge.

Forms of Objection and Response

Forms of Objection

> ➤ *I object to the qualification of the witness as an expert.*

> ➤ *I object to the admission of expert testimony because the discipline in which the witness purports to qualify will not provide information that is helpful to jury determination or understanding of any fact in issue.*

> ➤ *I object to the admission of the witness' opinion because it is beyond the area of expertise in which he has been qualified.*

Forms of Response

> ➤ *I have shown that the witness is qualified as an expert in* _____ (insert field) *through his knowledge, skill, experience, training, or education.*

> ➤ *I have shown that the area of expertise in which the witness is qualified is one that will be helpful to the jury in determining* _____ (insert fact or conclusion in issue).

> ➤ *The court has qualified the expert in the area of* _____ (insert field) *and his opinion is within that area.*

Federal Rule 702. Testimony by Experts

If scientific, technical, or other specialized knowledge will assist the trier of fact to understand the evidence or to determine a fact in issue, a witness qualified as an expert by knowledge, skill, experience, training, or education may testify thereto in the form of an opinion or otherwise.

Federal Rule 703. Bases of Opinion Testimony by Experts

The facts or data in the particular case upon which an expert bases an opinion or inference may be those perceived by or made known to the expert at or before the hearing. If of a type reasonably relied upon by such experts in the particular field in forming opinions or inferences upon the subject, the facts or data need not be admissible in evidence.

Federal Rule 704. Opinion on Ultimate Issue

(a) Except as provided in subdivision (b), testimony in the form of an opinion or inference otherwise admissible is not objectionable because it embraces an ultimate issue to be decided by the trier of fact.

(b) No expert witness testifying with respect to the mental state or condition of a defendant in a criminal case may state an opinion or inference as to whether the defendant did or did not have the mental state or condition constituting an element of the crime charged or of a defense thereto. Such ultimate issues are matters for the trier of fact alone.

Federal Rule 705. Disclosure of Facts or Data Underlying Expert Opinion

The expert may testify in terms of opinion or inference and give reasons therefor without first testifying to the underlying facts or data, unless the court requires otherwise. The expert may in any event be required to disclose the underlying facts or data on cross-examination.

Federal Rule 706. Court Appointed Experts

(a) Appointment. The court may on its own motion or on the motion of any party enter an order to show cause why expert witnesses should not be appointed, and may request the parties to submit nominations. The court may appoint any expert witnesses agreed upon by the parties, and may appoint expert witnesses of its own selection. An expert witness shall not be appointed by the court unless the witness consents to act. A witness so appointed shall be informed of the witness' duties by the court in writing, a copy of which shall be filed with the clerk, or at a conference in which the parties shall have an opportunity to participate. A witness so appointed shall advise the parties of the witness' findings, if any; the witness' deposition may be taken by any party; and the witness may be called to testify by the court or any party. The witness shall be subject to cross-examination by each party, including a party calling the witness.

(b) Compensation. Expert witnesses so appointed are entitled to reasonable compensation in whatever sum the court may allow. The compensation thus fixed is payable from funds which may be provided by law in criminal cases and civil actions and proceedings involving just compensation under the fifth amendment. In other civil actions and proceedings the compensation shall be paid by the parties in such proportion and at such time as the court directs, and thereafter charged in like manner as other costs.

(c) Disclosure of appointment. In the exercise of its discretion, the court may authorize disclosure to the jury of the fact that the court appointed the expert witness.

(d) Parties' experts of own selection. Nothing in this rule limits parties in calling expert witnesses of their own selection.

Commentary

Expert opinion is required to provide conclusions or inferences from facts which a lay person is unqualified to make. When an issue in the case requires for its resolution an inference regarding some area of technical or specialized knowledge, the lay witness is in no better position than the average juror to assist in the making of that inference. If, however, the proponent is able to provide an expert witness who possesses the appropriate specialized education, knowledge, training, or experience, then that expert witness will be permitted to testify as to an inference from facts presented in the lawsuit which the jury, because of its lack of specialized training or experience, would otherwise be unable to make. Thus, the expert witness, assuming (s)he has been qualified as such, will be permitted to testify as to his or her opinion or inference from such facts.

There are no particular requirements under the federal rules for the qualification of an expert. The rules do require, however, that the trial judge be persuaded that the purported expert have knowledge or training in an area of specialized knowledge which is beyond the abilities of the ordinary juror. The expert may be qualified because of education, training, professional experience, and/or knowledge gained in some other way.

A question often arises as to whether or not a particular area of expertise is sufficiently established as reliable in order for the court to entertain expert opinion. In 1993, the United States Supreme Court in *Daubert v. Merrell Dow Pharmaceuticals, Inc.*, set the standard for whether an area of expertise is sufficiently well developed to allow the jury to consider the testimony of an expert in that area. The court made clear that the test pursuant to Rule 702 is whether the testimony will in fact assist the jury in determining a matter at issue in a case. In making that determination, the court suggested four areas of inquiry (with no one of these areas controlling) concerning the reliability of the scientific theory or technique in issue: (1) whether the theory or technique can or has been tested; (2) whether the theory or technique has been subjected to peer review and/or publication; (3) whether, in the case of a technique, (a) is there a known or potential rate of error, or (b) do standards controlling the technique exist and how are they maintained; and (4) whether the theory or technique has gained substantial acceptance in the relevant scientific community. The court emphasized that the standard pursuant to Rule 702 is a flexible one, with the key being whether the theory or technique about which expert testimony is proffered has scientific reliability. Finally, the court provides that the responsibility for applying the Daubert test rests with the trial judge. In making the determination as to the admissibility of proffered expert testimony, the court can rely on either the expert herself, other experts, or a learned treatise (see Rule 803(18)).

Pursuant to Rule 703, an expert is permitted to rely on otherwise inadmissible evidence reaching an expert opinion so long as such evidence is the type of evidence reasonably relied upon by experts in that particular field in forming opinions upon that subject. There is some controversy, however, as to whether the expert is allowed to share that basis with the jury. Some courts have taken the position that allowing the jury to hear otherwise inadmissible evidence solely as the basis of an expert opinion, invites jury use of that information for other purposes. Other courts have taken the contrary position, that the jury is entitled to hear whatever basis that experts relies on in forming an opinion, and that the potential problem of inappropriate jury use for other purposes is handled by way of a Rule 105 limiting instruction. Both sides of the controversy agree, however, that such evidence, offered merely to show the basis of the expert's opinion, is not admissible for substantive purposes, and cannot, in and of itself, support a verdict.

In addition, pursuant to Rule 704, a federal court will permit an expert to form an opinion for the trier of fact which embraces an ultimate issue to be decided by the fact-finder in the case. For example, a medical expert in a medical malpractice case will be permitted to testify in a federal court that a particular act on the part of the defendant doctor would be considered malpractice. Note, however, that Rule 704 has been amended to exclude testimony on the ultimate issue of the legal sanity or insanity of a criminal defendant in a criminal case. In practice, the federal courts, in response to this recent amendment to Rule 704, have permitted the psychiatrist testifying in a criminal case to testify in the terms of the etiology of the mental disease or defect as they may involve the mental condition of the defendant at the time of the commission of the act in question. For example, a psychiatric expert could testify in a criminal case in federal court that a particular defendant suffered from a mental disease or defect, opine as to his diagnosis, and describe the symptoms, characteristics, and treatment of the diagnosed mental disease or defect.

Pursuant to Rule 705, an expert in a federal court will be permitted to testify as to his opinion whether or not he first testifies or indeed ever testifies as to the basis, supporting information, or data from which he reached that opinion, unless required to do so by the judge. If the expert does testify without stating his basis, the opponent is, of course, permitted to attempt to elucidate that basis on cross examination. In other words, the proponent of an expert, after qualifying an expert witness, may simply ask the expert witness whether or not (s)he has an opinion on a particular relevant matter. After answering that question in the affirmative, the expert could then be asked to state the opinion, thereby completing the testimony. Although theoretically permissible, this formula for the direct examination of an expert witness is inadvisable because it allows the opponent to waive cross examination and argue that the expert's opinion, without any basis, is inherently unreliable.

The practical impact of Rule 705 permits the proponent of the expert witness to obtain relevant opinions first and then elicit the bases that support the proffered opinion. This system provides a tactical advantage in that an expert witness can provide relevant opinions immediately after being qualified as an expert witness when jury attention is highest. This is especially true before judges who require that the expert be proffered as an expert before eliciting opinion testimony. The ability to elicit the opinion immediately after the witness has been "certified" as an expert witness by the judge gives heightened credibility to the opinion.

Another significant impact of the federal rules is the abandonment of the common law requirement of utilizing hypothetical questions in the examination of experts. Though no longer required, hypothetical questions remain a permissible method for eliciting expert opinions.

The federal rules, through the operation of Rule 803(18) which relates to learned treatises, make these authoritative texts admissible as substantive evidence of the technical information and conclusions contained therein so long as they were relied upon by the expert in coming to relevant opinions. In addition, the federal rules allow the traditional common law use of authoritative texts for impeachment purposes.

Finally, Rule 706 provides for the appointment by the court of an expert witness, either after the parties agree to such *neutral* expert or in the absence of such agreement. If an expert is appointed by the court and testifies, such witness will be subject to cross examination by each party irrespective of whether one party or the other calls him as a witness.

Section VII. Cross Examination and Impeachment

CHAPTER 38
- CROSS EXAMINATION -
GENERALLY

Definition

As to every witness presented by a party, the adverse party has the right to a full and fair cross examination. If a full and fair cross examination is not afforded to the adverse party, the remedy generally is to strike the direct testimony.

Forms of Objection and Response

Form of Objection

> ➤ *I move to strike the direct testimony of the witness because I have not had the opportunity to conduct a full and fair cross examination of the witness. I ask that the jury be instructed to disregard the testimony of the witness.*

Forms of Response

> ➤ *The purposes of cross examination have been substantially completed.*

> ➤ *Counsel has waived the right to a full and complete cross examination by _____.*

Federal Rule

There is no federal rule that specifically addresses the issue of the right to a full and fair cross examination. The trial judge has the authority to strike direct examination of a witness who has not been fully and fairly cross examined pursuant to Rule 611(a)(1) which provides:

Federal Rule 611. Mode and Order of Interrogation and Presentation

(a) Control by court. The court shall exercise reasonable control over the mode and order of interrogating witnesses and presenting evidence so as to (1) make the interrogation and presentation effective for the ascertainment of the truth, (2) avoid needless consumption of time, and (3) protect witnesses from harassment or undue embarrassment.

Commentary

There are several situations where a party will not be afforded a full and fair opportunity to cross examine a witness as a result of which the direct examination of that witness must be excluded from evidence. Typical of these situations are: (1) where a witness becomes ill or otherwise incapacitated before cross examination has been fully and fairly completed; (2) where a witness claims a valid privilege as to matters properly within the scope of cross examination; and (3) where a witness persists in a refusal to answer proper cross examination questions despite an order by the judge to do so.

Counsel may waive the right to a full and fair cross examination by voluntarily deciding not to cross examine the witness for tactical reasons, e.g., deciding not to cross examine a visibly ill witness, even though the witness is able to answer questions, in order to avoid potential jury disfavor that might result from questioning a witness in such a condition. Waiver of the right to cross examine may also result from failure to agree to a suspension of the trial, during which time an incapacitated witness may recover.

When a witness becomes incapacitated during cross examination, the judge may still allow the direct examination to stand if a determination is made that the purposes of cross examination have been substantially completed. To avoid such a ruling, cross examining counsel must make an offer of proof to demonstrate what additional areas of inquiry have not been covered with the witness and what counsel expects inquiry in those areas to accomplish.

CHAPTER 39
- CROSS EXAMINATION -
SCOPE

Definition

Cross examination is limited to the scope of the subject matter of direct examination plus matters affecting the credibility of the witness.

Forms of Objection and Response

Form of Objection

> ➤ *I object. The question on cross examination exceeds the scope of direct examination.*

Forms of Response

> ➤ *The subject matter of the question was raised when the witness testified on direct examination that _____.*

> ➤ *The question seeks to elicit information that is relevant to the credibility of the witness.*

> ➤ *I request that the court allow inquiry outside the scope of the direct examination. I will inquire of the witness as if on direct examination.*

Federal Rule 611. Mode and Order of Interrogation and Presentation

(b) Scope of cross-examination. Cross-examination should be limited to the subject matter of the direct examination and matters affecting the credibility of the witness. The court may, in the exercise of discretion, permit inquiry into additional matters as if on direct examination.

Commentary

The federal courts follow a limited scope of cross examination rule. On cross examination, counsel may inquire into the subject matter of the direct examination as well as matters affecting credibility. The rule, of course, does not limit questioning on cross examination to the answers elicited on direct examination, but rather to the subject matter raised or implicated by the direct examination. If, for example, a defendant in a criminal case testified to an alibi, on cross examination the government may properly inquire of the defendant concerning acts of the defendant that took place at the same time as the alleged alibi behavior, i.e., the charged offense as well as other matters that would tend to disprove the alibi.

The federal rules also provide that the trial judge may allow, upon request, inquiry that exceeds the scope of direct examination. The inquiry must, however, be conducted as if on direct examination. The practical impact of the rule is that a non-party witness must be interrogated by use of non-leading questions. As to adverse parties, witnesses associated with adverse parties or hostile witnesses, however, if the judge allows inquiry beyond the scope of direct examination, the effect is to allow a wide open cross examination of these witnesses. Such witnesses, if called on direct examination, could be interrogated by use of leading questions pursuant to Rule 611(c). If the judge exercises discretion to not allow questioning outside the scope of direct examination, the remedy is to recall the witness during the next opportunity for counsel to present affirmative evidence.

Note, in some jurisdictions, if the defendant, on cross examination of a witness called by the plaintiff, requests and is allowed to exceed the scope of the direct, the legal effect might be to technically open the defendant's case. As a result, the defendant may waive its mid-trial motion for judgment as a matter of law (formerly denominated a directed verdict).

CHAPTER 40
- IMPEACHMENT -
GENERALLY

Definition

Impeachment is the process whereby a lawyer attacks the credibility of (generally) opposing witnesses. Impeachment can occur on cross examination or in more limited circumstances as part of the opponent's extrinsic evidence presented either by testimony of other witnesses or by the introduction of exhibits. There are nine basic areas of impeachment: bias, prejudice, interest, improper motive, prior inconsistent statements, prior convictions, character evidence as it affects credibility, prior acts that relate to truthfulness and veracity, and attacks on the witness' perception or memory. A witness who has been impeached can be rehabilitated on redirect examination or in more limited circumstances through extrinsic evidence presented either by the testimony of other witnesses or by the introduction of exhibits.

Who May Impeach

Any person who has been called as a witness places his credibility in issue and may be impeached.

Federal Rule 607. Who May Impeach

The credibility of a witness may be attacked by any party, including the party calling the witness.

Commentary

Rule 607 presents a major departure from the common law. Rule 607 does away with the common law view that when a party calls a witness, such party vouches for the witness' credibility. The federal rules recognize the fact that most witnesses in a trial have something favorable and something unfavorable to say for each party. Thus, a witness may be impeached by any party including the party who calls him as a witness.

The rule also recognizes and specifically allows the proponent of a witness to attempt to take the sting out of potential impeachment by raising the impeaching material during the direct examination of the witness. If, for example, a witness has a financial interest in the outcome of the case, that interest can be raised during direct examination and put in appropriate context. The witness, and the party that called the witness, show themselves, thereby, to be forthcoming. Also, by raising the impeaching material on direct examination, it tends to blunt its impact by allowing the jury to infer from its presentation that the potential impeaching value of the evidence is not considered great by the proponent of the witness because there is no attempt to hide its existence.

What follows is a chart that shows the various forms of impeachment, the rule that governs its use, whether it may be accomplished during cross examination and/or with extrinsic evidence, the evidentiary foundation for the use of extrinsic evidence, and the available means of rehabilitation.

IMPEACHMENT CHART

A. FORM OF IMPEACHMENT	B. FEDERAL RULE	C. CROSS EXAMINATION	D. EXTRINSIC EVIDENCE ALLOWED	E. FOUNDATION FOR EXTRINSIC EVIDENCE	F. REHABILITATION
1. Bias, Prejudice, Interest, and Improper Motive	607 & 611(a)	Yes	Yes	Confront on cross & denial	Prior Consistent Statements FRE 801(D)(1)(B) for improper motive; Inquiry re: effect of bias, prejudice, interest, and improper motive
2. Perception	607 & 611(a)	Yes	Yes	None required	Show reasons to focus on events in question
3. Memory	607 & 611(a)	Yes	Yes	None required	Show reasons to remember event in question
4. Inconsistent Conduct	607 & 611(a)	Yes	Yes	None required	Show circumstances of conduct and explain
5. Prior Inconsistent Statement	613	Yes	Yes, if not collateral	Opportunity of witness to explain or deny	Circumstance of giving the statement; FRE 106–Rule of Completeness
6. Acts Relating to Honesty	608(b)	Yes	No		Circumstances of Act; Reputation or opinion evidence re: honesty
7. Reputation or Opinion re: Dishonesty	608(a)	No	Yes	Witness to be impeached has testified; Reputation–knowledge of reputation in some community; Opinion–firsthand knowledge of witness to be impeached	Reputation or opinion re: honesty–FRE 608(a)
8. Prior Conviction	609	Yes	Yes	Witness to be impeached has testified	Circumstances of Conviction; fact of appeal–FRE 609(e) Reputation or opinion re: honesty–FRE 608(a)

A Practical Guide to Federal Evidence

CHAPTER 41
IMPEACHMENT BY BIAS, PREJUDICE, INTEREST, AND IMPROPER MOTIVE

Definition

A witness may be impeached by showing that the witness is biased in favor of a party, that the witness is prejudiced against a party, that the witness has an interest (usually pecuniary) in the outcome of the case, or that the witness has an improper motive for giving testimony.

Forms of Objection and Response

Forms of Objection

➤ (To questions posed on cross examination) *I object. Counsel is attempting to impeach the witness on improper grounds. The testimony attempted to be elicited is irrelevant.*

➤ (To extrinsic evidence) *I object. Counsel has not laid the proper foundation for use of extrinsic evidence to impeach. The witness whom counsel is attempting to impeach:*

    (a) *has not yet been called as a witness,* or

    (b) *was not confronted with the alleged bias, prejudice, interest, or improper motive on cross examination,* or

    (c) *was confronted with the alleged bias, prejudice, interest or improper motive, but did not deny its existence.*

Forms of Response

➤ (To an objection posed to cross examination) *I am attempting to show that the witness:*

    (a) *is biased,* or

    (b) *is prejudiced,* or

    (c) *has an interest in the outcome of the case,* or

    (d) *has an improper motive for giving testimony.*

➤ (To an objection posed to extrinsic evidence)

    (a) (Where the witness with the alleged bias, prejudice, interest or improper motive has not already testified) *The witness has been listed as a witness by my opponent and I offer this evidence conditionally to avoid recalling the witness presently on the stand at a later time.*

    (b) (Where the witness with the alleged bias, prejudice, interest, or improper motive has already testified) *I confronted* _____ (insert name of witness) *with his* (bias, prejudice, interest, or improper motive) *during cross examination when I asked him* _____, *and he has denied it.*

Federal Rule

There is no federal rule that specifically deals with bias, interest, or improper motive. These are traditional areas of impeachment that fall within the general impeachment provision of Rule 607 which provides:

Federal Rule 607. Who May Impeach

The credibility of a witness may be attacked by any party, including the party calling the witness.

The judge has discretion to admit this evidence pursuant to Rule 611(a) which provides:

Federal Rule 611. Mode and Order of Interrogation and Presentation

(a) Control by court. The court shall exercise reasonable control over the mode and order of interrogating witnesses and presenting evidence so as to (1) make the interrogation and presentation effective for the ascertainment of the truth, (2) avoid needless consumption of time, and (3) protect witnesses from harassment or undue embarrassment.

Commentary

Bias, prejudice, interest, and improper motive are particularly fertile areas for impeachment, and are probably the most typical areas of impeachment with most witnesses. Because these impeachment categories often tend to overlap, they are grouped together in this chapter. With this caveat, the categories are treated separately.

Bias

a) A witness can be biased for as many reasons as there are for one person to be associated with another. Typical associations that form the basis for showing bias are: family relationships (e.g., mother, father, siblings, cousins, aunts, uncles, family relationships by marriage); friendships (e.g., schoolmates, workmates, members of the same organization); and similar economic, social, or occupational positions (e.g., same neighborhood, same ethnic group, same occupation).

b) Use of Extrinsic Evidence. The general rule is that before extrinsic evidence of bias can be introduced through either the testimony of another witness or by use of a document, the witness with the alleged bias must be confronted with that alleged bias on cross examination and deny the alleged bias. The determination of whether extrinsic evidence of bias is admissible for impeachment or excluded as time wasting or cumulative evidence is vested in the discretion of the trial judge pursuant to Rule 611(a) applying Rule 403.

Prejudice

a) A witness may be prejudiced against a party for many reasons. Prejudice is merely the opposite of bias in that it involves a showing as to why a witness has negative feelings or a negative inclination toward a party. Prejudice can be general in form such as prejudice against persons of a certain race, religion, or ethnic group, or it can be case specific. For example, a former employee of a party who has been fired by that party can have a prejudice against that party.

b) Use of Extrinsic Evidence. The general rule is that before extrinsic evidence of prejudice can be introduced through either the testimony of another witness or by use of a document, the witness with the alleged prejudice must be confronted with the alleged prejudice on cross examination and deny the alleged prejudice. The determination of whether or not extrinsic evidence of prejudice is admissible for impeachment excluded as time wasting or cumulative is vested in the discretion of the trial judge pursuant to Rule 611(a), applying Rule 403.

Interest in the outcome

a) Civil Cases. Interest in the outcome of the case usually results from a pecuniary interest of the witness in the verdict sought by the party who calls the witness to testify. In civil cases, the parties always have a pecuniary or economic interest in the outcome. Likewise, family members of the party and employees of the party may also have a pecuniary interest in the outcome of the lawsuit. For example, an employee has an economic interest, both in terms of continued employment and job advancement, to testify in favor of his or her employer. An interest in the outcome may result from a promise or expectation on the part of the witness that (s)he will benefit as a result of favorable testimony.

b) Criminal Cases. The defendant in a criminal case obviously has a liberty interest in testifying favorably to himself. Family members and others dependent on the defendant for economic well-being have an economic interest attached to the liberty interest of the defendant.

Government witnesses who testify pursuant to a negotiated agreement with the government often will also have a liberty interest in testifying in favor of the government. It is for this reason that plea agreements with government witnesses must be disclosed to the criminal defendant because of the potential exculpatory nature of this evidence.

c) Use of Extrinsic Evidence. The general rule as to the use of extrinsic evidence of interest is the same as that relating to bias and prejudice. The witness must normally be confronted with the alleged interest on cross examination and deny or attempt to explain away the alleged interest before extrinsic evidence of the alleged interest may be introduced. The admissibility of extrinsic evidence of the alleged interest is within the discretion of the court pursuant to Rule 611(a), applying Rule 403.

Improper motive or influence

a) The classic case of improper motive or influence arises where a witness' testimony has been purchased by money or threats to the well-being of the witness or those persons close to the witness by the party who calls the witness to testify. Improper motive or influence impeachment often is intertwined with impeachment by way of showing interest in the outcome. For example, improper influence can be claimed where a witness has an economic interest created by current or prospective employment or advancement. Likewise, a witness who testifies for the government pursuant to a negotiated agreement is subject to attack on the grounds of interest in the outcome as well as on a charge that he has been improperly influenced to give his testimony by the agreement.

With regard to impeachment as to improper influence, the focus is on the mind of the witness and not on the party that calls him. Therefore, a belief or a hope on the part of the witness that he will receive favorable economic treatment, or in the case of a government witness testifying pursuant to a negotiated agreement that he will receive favorable treatment by the government in current or future (potential) personal criminal problems, will be sufficient to allow admissibility of this sort of evidence.

b) Use of Extrinsic Evidence. The general rule with regard to the use of extrinsic evidence of improper influence or motive is the same as for bias, prejudice, and interest. The witness who has an improper motive or allegedly has been improperly influenced must normally be confronted with the alleged improper motive or influence or cross examination and either deny it or attempt to explain it away before extrinsic evidence can be utilized. The admissibility of extrinsic evidence of alleged improper motive or influence is within the discretion of the trial court pursuant to Rule 611(a), applying Rule 403.

Rehabilitation

A witness who has been impeached by a showing of alleged bias, prejudice, interest, or improper motive or influence can normally be rehabilitated by the party that called him in a number of ways. The proponent of the witness may show that the alleged bias, prejudice, interest, or improper motive or influence does not, in fact, exist. Secondly, the proponent of the witness may show that the witness would not be influenced to the point of perjury by any such relationship with the party.

The rehabilitation of a witness thus impeached can be accomplished by redirect examination or by the use of extrinsic evidence. It is often wise for the proponent of a witness who will be attacked by an alleged bias, interest, or improper influence or motive to confront these items on direct examination in anticipation of cross examination, and thereby steal the thunder of the cross examiner.

Finally, a witness who has been impeached during cross examination with a claim of improper influence or motive may be rehabilitated by introduction of prior consistent statements pursuant to Rule 801(d)(1)(B). The consistent statement must have been made at a time when the alleged improper motive or influence did not exist. For example, if it is claimed during cross examination that a witness for a criminal defendant was threatened by the criminal defendant two week before the trial, a consistent statement made before the alleged threat would be admissible to rehabilitate the witness. A consistent statement made after the alleged threat, would not be admissible, because the same motive claimed to infect the witness' testimony at trial existed at the time of the making of the consistent statement. The rule presents a major departure from the common law in an important way. At common law, prior consistent statements were only admissible to rehabilitate a witness impeached by a claim of improper influence or motive. Under the federal rule, the prior consistent statement is allowed in evidence for both its rehabilitative purpose and the truth of its contents.

CHAPTER 42
IMPEACHMENT BY CHARACTER EVIDENCE

Definition

A witness may be impeached by the offer of either reputation or opinion evidence from a character witness concerning the witness' character trait of dishonesty.

Forms of Objection and Response

Forms of Objection

- ➤ *I object. The character witness has insufficient knowledge of the witness' character to give an opinion.*
- ➤ *I object. The character witness has insufficient knowledge of the witness' reputation for dishonesty to report that opinion to the court.*

Form of Response

- ➤ *A sufficient foundation has been laid to demonstrate the character witness' sufficient familiarity with:*
    - a) *the witness' character for dishonesty, or*
    - b) *the witness' reputation for honesty in the community.*

Federal Rule 608. Evidence of Character and Conduct of Witness

(a) Opinion and reputation evidence of character. The credibility of a witness may be attacked or supported by evidence in the form of opinion or reputation, but subject to these limitations: (1) the evidence may refer only to character for truthfulness or untruthfulness, and (2) evidence of truthful character is admissible only after the character of the witness for truthfulness has been attacked by opinion or reputation evidence or otherwise.

(b) Specific instances of conduct. Specific instances of the conduct of a witness, for the purpose of attacking or supporting the witness' credibility, other than conviction of a crime as provided by rule 609, may not be proved by extrinsic evidence. They may, however, in the discretion of the court, if probative of truthfulness or untruthfulness, be inquired into on cross examination of the witness (1) concerning the witness' character for truthfulness or untruthfulness, or (2) concerning the character for truthfulness or untruthfulness of another witness as to which character the witness being cross examined has testified.

The giving of testimony, whether by an accused or by any other witness, does not operate as a waiver of the accused's or the witness' privilege against self-incrimination when examined with respect to matters which relate only to credibility.

Commentary

A witness' credibility may be attacked by an extrinsic offer concerning the witness' character for honesty, i.e., the testimony of a character witness. A character witness is limited in a number of ways in the giving of testimony. First, the character witness may only testify as to the character trait for dishonesty of the witness being impeached. Second, the character witness is limited to testimony as to an opinion of the impeached witness' character for truthfulness or testimony with regard to the witness' reputation for truthfulness. The character witness may not testify to specific instances of conduct that form the basis of the witness' opinion or reputation testimony.

Once a witness has been impeached by evidence of dishonest character, such witness may be rehabilitated by the calling of a character witness who will testify as to the witness' character for honesty or truthfulness by way of opinion or reputation evidence.

Once a character witness has testified by way of either opinion or reputation concerning another witness' truthfulness, such witness may be impeached by use of specific instances of conduct by the witness about whom such character evidence has been given. Such inquiry is allowed to impeach the character witness as it may show either: (1) incomplete information concerning the witness about whom character evidence has been given, or (2) a faulty notion of what constitutes good or bad character for truthfulness. Inquiry of reputation witnesses as to specific instances or conduct takes the form of, "Have you heard _____?" Inquiry of opinion witnesses as to specific instances of conduct takes the form of, "Do you know _____?" Of course, inquiring counsel must have a good-faith basis for believing that the specific instances of conduct occurred.

Once a witness has been impeached by the testimony of a character witness for bad character for honesty, that witness may be rehabilitated by the testimony of a character witness for good character for honesty. Good character for honesty witnesses may be presented at the next time the proponent of the witness who has been impeached has the opportunity to present evidence.

CHAPTER 43
IMPEACHMENT OF MEMORY

Definition

A witness may be impeached by showing that the witness has an impaired ability to remember the events in question or by showing the unlikelihood that the witness can actually remember those items about which testimony is given.

Forms of Objection and Response

Form of Objection

> ➤ *I object. The question seeks to elicit irrelevant information; the question involves improper impeachment.*

Form of Response

> ➤ *The question calls for an answer that will show the witness' inability to remember the events about which he has testified. This is proper cross examination.*

Federal Rule

There is no federal rule that specifically deals with impeachment with regard to faulty memory. This is a traditional area of impeachment that falls within the general impeachment provision of Rule 607 which provides:

Federal Rule 607. Who May Impeach

The credibility of a witness may be attacked by any party, including the party calling the witness.

Commentary

Impeachment on the basis of faulty memory is a typical form of impeachment in most cases. Obviously, memory fades with the passage of time. The objective of the cross examiner is to show that the witness has no particular reason to remember the events about which testimony is given. For example, this form of impeachment is especially forceful where a witness has testified about an event that was mundane at the time of its occurrence but has since obtained significance by virtue of a dispute between the parties to the litigation. A critical element, then, is the passage of time between the occurrence of the event and the date when the event gained importance (e.g., the arising of a dispute between the parties).

Impeachment by showing faulty memory is often coupled with impeachment by showing bias, prejudice, interest, or improper motive, which provides a reason for the witness' testimony. In addition, impeachment by showing faulty memory is also often coupled with impeachment by prior inconsistent statements. (See Rule 613)

Rehabilitation of witnesses impeached by an attack on memory is typically accomplished by showing the reasons why the event sticks in the mind of the witness. The more unusual the event or the greater its impact on the witness, the more likely it is that it has been recalled correctly by the witness.

CHAPTER 44

IMPEACHMENT OF PERCEPTION

Definition

A witness may be impeached by showing that the witness had an impaired ability to perceive the events in question.

Forms of Objection and Response

Form of Objection

➤ *I object. The question seeks to elicit irrelevant information. The question involves improper impeachment.*

Form of Response

➤ *The question calls for an answer which will show the witness' inability to perceive. This is proper cross examination.*

Federal Rule

There is no federal rule that specifically deals with impeachment with regard to ability to perceive. This is a traditional area of impeachment that falls within the general impeachment provision of Rule 607 which provides:

Federal Rule 607. Who May Impeach

The credibility of a witness may be attacked by any party, including the party calling the witness.

Commentary

Impeachment on the basis of faulty perception is a typical form of impeachment in cases that involve physical activity of the parties. Matters of perception include the ability to see, hear, smell, or feel some particular item in question. Typical of cases in which sensory or perception impeachment is critical are cases involving automobile accidents and most criminal cases. Impeachment by showing faulty perception typically involves showing distraction on the part of the witness, a showing of some sort of physical impairment to perception, a state of excitement on the part of the witness which interferes with an ability to perceive, and obstructions to vision, impediments to hearing, etc.

Impeachment of a witness' perception is typically accomplished by showing the time, place, and circumstances in which the perception occurs, from which the lawyer can argue and the jury can infer that the witness is not worthy of belief. As in most areas of cross examination, the ultimate conclusion as to ability to perceive must be left to closing argument.

Rehabilitation of a witness who has been impeached by an attack on ability to perceive is typically accomplished by either demonstrating the reasons the witness focused on the event in question or denigrating the significance of the alleged obstruction or impediment to perception.

CHAPTER 45

IMPEACHMENT BY PRIOR CONVICTION
(Civil Cases)

Definition

A witness in a civil case may be impeached by (a) any conviction for a crime which carries a potential sentence of either death or imprisonment for more than a year subject to the provisions of Rule 403, or (b) any conviction, irrespective of the potential punishment which involves dishonesty or false statement. Both types of impeaching convictions are subject to the time limit restrictions of Rule 609(b) and the pardon, annulment, or certificate of rehabilitation restrictions of Rule 609(c).

Forms of Objection and Response

Forms of Objection

> ➤ *I object. The proffered conviction is neither for a crime which carries a potential sentence of at least one year in prison nor is it a conviction for a crime involving dishonesty or false statement.*

> ➤ *I object. The date of the conviction and the witness' release date from sentence for the conviction occurred more than ten years ago **and** written notice has not been given **and/or** the probative value of the conviction on the issue of credibility does not substantially outweigh the prejudice to a party of admitting such conviction.*

> ➤ *I object. (For Rule 609(a)(1) crimes) The prejudicial effect of the conviction substantially outweighs the probative value of the evidence on the issue of credibility **and/or** the admission of the evidence will lead to confusion of the issues or will mislead the jury.*

Forms of Response

> ➤ *The proffered conviction is a felony conviction **or** a crime involving dishonesty or false statement.*

> ➤ *Though the proffered conviction and the witness' release date occurred longer than ten years ago, written notice has been given **and** the probative value of the conviction on the issue of credibility substantially outweighs the prejudice to the opposing party.*

> ➤ *The prejudice to the opposing party does not substantially outweigh the probative value of the conviction on the issue of the witness' credibility. The jury will not be misled or confused as to the import of the evidence of conviction as it is limited solely to the issue of the witness' credibility.*

Federal Rule 609. Impeachment by Evidence of Conviction of Crime

(a) General Rule. For the purpose of attacking the credibility of a witness, (1) evidence that a witness other than an accused has been convicted of a crime shall be admitted subject to Rule 403, if the crime was punishable by death or imprisonment in excess of one year under the law under which the witness was convicted, and evidence that an accused has been convicted of such a crime shall be admitted if the court determines that the probative value of admitting this evidence outweighs its prejudicial effect to the accused; and (2) evidence that any witness has been convicted of a crime shall be admitted if it involved dishonesty or false statement, regardless of the punishment.

(b) Time limit. Evidence of a conviction under this rule is not admissible if a period of more than ten years has elapsed since the date of the conviction or of the release of the witness from confinement imposed for that conviction, whichever is the later date, unless the court determines, in the interests of justice, that the probative value of the conviction supported by specific facts and circumstances substantially outweighs its prejudicial effect. However, evidence of a conviction more than 10 years old as calculated herein, is not admissible unless the proponent gives to the adverse party sufficient advance written notice of intent to use such evidence to provide the adverse party with a fair opportunity to contest the use of such evidence.

(c) Effect of pardon, annulment, or certificate of rehabilitation. Evidence of a conviction is not admissible under this rule if (1) the conviction has been the subject of a pardon, annulment, certificate of rehabilitation, or other equivalent procedure based on a finding of the rehabilitation of the person convicted, and that person has not been convicted of a subsequent crime which was punishable by death or imprisonment in excess of one year, or (2) the conviction has been the subject of a pardon, annulment, or other equivalent procedure based on a finding of innocence.

(d) Juvenile adjudications. Evidence of juvenile adjudications is generally not admissible under this rule. The court may, however, in a criminal case allow evidence of a juvenile adjudication of a witness other than the accused if conviction of the offense would be admissible to attack the credibility of an adult and the court is satisfied that admission in evidence is necessary for a fair determination of the issue of guilt or innocence.

(e) Pendency of appeal. The pendency of an appeal therefrom does not render evidence of a conviction inadmissible. Evidence of the pendency of an appeal is admissible.

Commentary

Rule 609(a)(1) allows impeachment of a witness by showing conviction for a crime with a potential penalty in excess of one year imprisonment or death. It essentially draws a line between felony and misdemeanor convictions, and looks only at potential and not actual sentence. The admission of evidence of such convictions shall be determined in civil cases by Rule 403 consideration of the balance between prejudicial effect and probative value. The trial judge has discretion to exclude otherwise admissible 609(a)(1) convictions, if the prejudicial effect of the conviction substantially outweighs the probative value of the conviction as it bears on the issue of the credibility of the witness. In making the balance, the trial judge should look to whether it is likely that the jury will utilize the evidence of conviction for some purpose other than the credibility of the witness or whether the conviction evidence will distract the jury from the main issue in the case. For example, in a civil case involving the tort of assault, a conviction of the defendant for an unrelated assault might very well be used by the jury for a substantive purpose, i.e., he committed assault before, so he must have committed an assault in this case. Note that the prejudicial impact of the assault conviction in the previous example may be obviated by limiting cross examination of the defendant to the fact that he was convicted of a crime with a potential penalty in excess of one year, without allowing inquiry into the name of the crime. The problem that remains is that the jury might speculate that the conviction is for a more heinous crime than the crime for which the defendant was convicted.

Rule 609(a)(2) is unequivocal in mandating the admission of prior conviction evidence for impeachment purposes where the conviction is for a crime of dishonesty or false statement, irrespective of whether the crime is a felony or misdemeanor. Dishonesty crimes, also known as crimes in the nature of crimen falsi, will typically include any theft crime and exclude any crime of violence. There is no discretion in the trial judge to exclude evidence of 609(a)(2) convictions.

Rule 609(b) provides that all 609(a) convictions must have occurred within ten years of either the conviction or the release from penalty for the conviction (whichever is later), and the date of impeachment. Note that penalty includes probation or parole time required as the result of conviction. Convictions outside the ten-year rule may only be utilized if written notice is provided to the opposing party *and* the court determines that the probative value of the conviction outweighs the prejudicial effect of the use of conviction. Note that this is a different balance than provided in Rule 403 and the burden of carrying the balance is on the proponent of the conviction evidence.

Rule 609(c) excludes, for impeachment purposes, evidence of a conviction where the conviction has been the subject of a pardon or other equivalent procedure if based on a finding of rehabilitation or innocence *and* there have been no further felony convictions.

Rule 609(d) provides that evidence of juvenile adjudications are not admissible in civil cases.

Rule 609(e) provides that though the pendency of an appeal of the criminal conviction is admissible, the pendency of the appeal does not affect the use of the conviction for impeachment purposes.

Note that an impeaching criminal conviction may be proved in one of two ways: either by cross examination of the witness *or* by way of introduction of a public record of the conviction.

As a matter of practice, because impeachment by prior conviction can have a disproportionately unfavorable impact on the jury, the admissibility of a prior conviction ought to be determined before trial in a motion *in limine.*

Rehabilitation

A witness who has been impeached by a prior conviction can be rehabilitated by showing the circumstances of the conviction if they somehow lessen the blow of the impeachment. If, for example, a witness has been convicted of a crime of theft as a result of attempting to get food for his or her family, that factual basis would lessen the impact of the conviction. Similarly, if the conviction arose out of some other necessitous circumstance such as a crime committed to support a drug addiction, which has now been abandoned for some substantial period of time, that too would tend to rehabilitate the witness. Finally, because impeachment by prior conviction is an attack on the character of a witness for honesty, that witness may be rehabilitated by calling a character witness to testify, by way of reputation or opinion evidence, that the impeached witness has good character for honesty. (See Rule 608(a)(2))

CHAPTER 46
IMPEACHMENT BY PRIOR CONVICTIONS
(Criminal Cases)

Definition

A witness in a criminal case, other than the criminal defendant, may be impeached by a conviction (a) for a crime of dishonesty or false statement, or (b) for any crime which carries a potential penalty of at least one year or death, if the court finds that the prejudicial effect of the impeachment does not substantially outweigh the probative value of the impeachment. Where the witness to be impeached is the criminal defendant, such witness may be impeached by a conviction of a crime of dishonesty or false statement. In addition, the criminal defendant as a witness may be impeached by the conviction of a crime which carries a sentence of at least one year imprisonment or death if the probative value of the conviction on the issue of credibility outweighs the prejudice to the defendant of offering it.

Forms of Objection and Response

Forms of Objection

➤ (Where offered against any witness other than the criminal defendant) *I object. The conviction offered to impeach the witness is neither for a crime of dishonesty or false statement, nor is it for a crime which carries a penalty of at least a year in prison or death. Even if the conviction offered to impeach is for a felony, the prejudicial effect to a party substantially outweighs the probative value of the conviction on the issue of the credibility of the witness.*

➤ *I object because the date of the proffered conviction and the witness' release date from his sentence occurred more than ten years ago, written notice has not been given, and/or the probative value of the conviction on the issue of credibility does not substantially outweigh the prejudice of admitting such conviction.*

➤ (Where offered against the criminal defendant-witness) *I object to the introduction of this conviction because the probative value of the conviction on the issue of credibility does not outweigh the prejudice to the defendant.*

Forms of Response

➤ (Where offered against any witness other than the criminal defendant) *The proffered conviction is for a Rule 609(a)(1) crime, and its prejudicial effect to any party in the case does not substantially outweigh its probative value on the issue of the credibility of the witness.*

➤ (Where offered against the criminal defendant) *The proffered conviction is for a Rule 609(a)(1) crime and its probative value does not outweigh the prejudicial effect to the defendant.*

➤ *The proffered conviction is for activity involving dishonesty or false statement.*

> ➤ *Though the proffered conviction and the witness' release date occurred longer than ten years ago, written notice has been given and the probative value of the conviction on the issue of the witness' credibility substantially outweighs any purported prejudice.*

Federal Rule 609. Impeachment by Evidence of Conviction of Crime

(a) General rule. For the purpose of attacking the credibility of a witness, (1) evidence that a witness other than an accused been convicted of a crime shall be admitted, subject to Rule 403, if the crime was punishable by death or imprisonment in excess of one year under the law under which the witness was convicted, and evidence that an accused has been convicted of such a crime shall be admitted if the court determines that the probative value of admitting this evidence outweighs its prejudicial effect to the accused; and (2) evidence that any witness has been convicted of a crime shall be admitted if it involved dishonesty or false statement, regardless of punishment.

(b) Time limit. Evidence of a conviction under this rule is not admissible if a period of more than ten years has elapsed since the date of the conviction or of the release of the witness from the confinement imposed for that conviction, whichever is the later date, unless the court determines, in the interests of justice, that the probative value of the conviction supported by specific facts and circumstances substantially outweighs its prejudicial effect. However, evidence of a conviction more than 10 years old as calculated herein, is not admissible unless the proponent gives to the adverse party sufficient advance written notice of intent to use such evidence to provide the adverse party with a fair opportunity to contest the use of such evidence.

(c) Effect of pardon, annulment, or certificate of rehabilitation. Evidence of a conviction is not admissible under this rule if (1) the conviction has been the subject of a pardon, annulment, certificate of rehabilitation, or other equivalent procedure based on a finding of the rehabilitation of the person convicted, and that person has not been convicted of a subsequent crime which was punishable by death or imprisonment in excess of one year, or (2) the conviction has been the subject of a pardon, annulment, or other equivalent procedure based on a finding of innocence.

(d) Juvenile adjudications. Evidence of juvenile adjudications is generally not admissible under this rule. The court may, however, in a criminal case allow evidence of a juvenile adjudication of a witness other than the accused if conviction of the offense would be admissible to attack the credibility of an adult and the court is satisfied that admission in evidence is necessary for a fair determination of the issue of guilt or innocence.

(e) Pendency of appeal. The pendency of an appeal therefrom does not render evidence of a conviction inadmissible. Evidence of the pendency of an appeal is admissible.

Commentary

As with the use of convictions for impeachment in civil cases, Rule 609 in criminal cases dispenses with any balancing of probative value against prejudice in the offer of a conviction for a crime of dishonesty or false statement. Thus, such convictions must be admitted against any witness including a criminal defendant. Where, however, a criminal defendant would be impeached with a conviction for a crime that carries a penalty of at least one year in prison that does not involve dishonesty or false statement, Rule 609(a)(1) requires the court to perform a balance which is different from Rule 403 balance and tilts away from admissibility. Such conviction will only be admitted against a criminal defendant where the court finds that the probative value of the conviction on the defendant's credibility outweighs the prejudice to the defendant. The obvious prejudice to a criminal defendant lies in the jury's inclination to find a defendant guilty of the crime charged because of a prior criminal record. Arguably, the similarity between the charged offense and the prior conviction magnifies the prejudicial impact of the prior conviction because of the jury's almost inevitable sense that one who once committed a particular sort of offense is likely to commit a similar offense again. Whatever the common-sense likelihood of such a notion, it is an impermissible inference for a fact-finder to make.

A witness in a criminal case, other than the criminal defendant, is treated like a witness in a civil case for purposes of Rule 609(a).

Rule 609(b) and (c) considerations are identical to those discussed in the preceding chapter entitled, "Impeachment by Prior Conviction (Civil Cases)." Though Rule 609(d) provides for the general inadmissibility of juvenile adjudications for impeachment in civil cases, the court retains discretion in criminal cases to admit juvenile adjudications to impeach a witness, other than the criminal defendant, where (a) the juvenile adjudication is for an offense which would constitute an adult offense which could be used to impeach and (b) admission is necessary for a fair determination of guilt or innocence.

As a matter of practice, the determination of the admissibility of a criminal conviction should always be determined prior to trial so that the defendant can make an informed choice as to whether to testify in his own behalf as well as to avoid the prejudice of being asked about a conviction which is later ruled inadmissible.

Rehabilitation

A witness who has been impeached by a prior conviction can be rehabilitated by showing the circumstances of the conviction if they somehow lessen the blow of the impeachment. If, for example, a witness has been convicted of a crime of theft as a result of attempting to get food for his or her family, that factual basis would lessen the impact of the conviction. Similarly, if the conviction arose out of some other necessitous circumstance such as a crime committed to support a drug habit, which has now been abandoned for some substantial period of time, that too would tend to rehabilitate the witness. Finally, because impeachment by prior conviction is an attack on the character of a witness for honesty, that witness may be rehabilitated by calling a character witness to testify, by way of reputation or opinion evidence, that the impeached witness has good character for honesty. (See Rule 608(a)(2))

CHAPTER 47
IMPEACHMENT BY PRIOR INCONSISTENT STATEMENTS

Definition

A witness may be impeached by showing that the witness has made a statement, prior to trial, which is inconsistent with his testimony on direct examination. The prior inconsistent statement need only be inconsistent with the thrust of the testimony of the witness on direct examination. The inconsistency may appear in the terms of the prior statement or may be inferred by an omission in the prior statement. Unless the prior statement meets the requirements of Rule 801(d)(1)(A), another provision of Rule 801 governing non-hearsay statements, or an exception to the hearsay rule pursuant to Rules 803 or 804, it is not admissible for the truth of its contents but only for the impeaching fact that it was said. This, of course, is a non-hearsay purpose.

Forms of Objection and Response

Forms of Objection

➤ *I object. The proffered statement is not inconsistent with the witness' testimony and is irrelevant.*

➤ (For impeachment by extrinsic evidence of a prior inconsistent statement) *I object. A proper foundation has not been laid for introduction of extrinsic evidence of a prior inconsistent statement in that the witness my adversary is attempting to impeach has not been given an opportunity to explain or deny the alleged inconsistent statement.*

Forms of Response

(For impeachment by prior inconsistent statement on cross examination)

➤ *The witness testified on direct examination that _____ and this statement is inconsistent with the thrust of his direct testimony.*

➤ *The witness testified on direct examination that _____ and this statement is inconsistent in that it omits facts testified to on direct examination.*

(For impeachment by extrinsic evidence of a prior inconsistent statement)

➤ *The witness denied making a prior inconsistent statement during cross examination.*

➤ *This prior inconsistent statement is an admission of a party opponent pursuant to Rule 801(d)(2) and therefore the witness need not be given an opportunity to explain or deny the prior inconsistent statement.*

Federal Rule 613. Prior Statements of Witnesses

(a) Examining witness concerning prior statement. In examining a witness concerning a prior statement made by the witness, whether written or not, the statement need not be shown nor its contents disclosed to the witness at that time, but on request the same shall be shown or disclosed to opposing counsel.

(b) Extrinsic evidence of prior inconsistent statement of witness. Extrinsic evidence of a prior inconsistent statement by a witness is not admissible unless the witness is afforded an opportunity to explain or deny the same and the opposite party is afforded an opportunity to interrogate the witness thereon, or the interests of justice otherwise require. This provision does not apply to admissions of a party-opponent as defined in rule 801(d)(2).

Commentary

Impeachment by prior inconsistent statement is premised on the notion that a witness who makes contrary statements about the facts of a lawsuit has diminished credibility. For this reason, the prior statement must be made or adopted by the witness. An unadopted writing made by someone other than the witness is obviously not a prior inconsistent statement by the witness. The prior statement can be either written or oral. Unless it meets the requirements of Rule 801(d)(1)(A), another provision of Rule 801 governing non-hearsay statements, or an exception to the hearsay rule pursuant to Rules 803 or 804, the prior statement is not admissible for its truth but rather only for that fact that it was made.

The federal rule does not require a formal foundation for impeachment by a prior inconsistent statement. Good tactics dictate, however, that counsel show, by way of foundation, the time, place, and circumstances of the inconsistent statement for maximum impact. This is especially important when the prior statement is inconsistent by omission. The foundation should show that it would have been natural for the witness to include the omitted fact at the time of the making of the prior statement.

If a written statement is utilized, the appearance of fairness requires, although the rule does not, that the written statement be shown to the witness and opposing counsel before questioning proceeds. In most circumstances, counsel can read a prior inconsistent statement with greater impact than can be had if the witness is required to read the prior statement. When the witness is asked to read the prior statement, it is likely that the witness will attempt to explain away the contradictory influence of the prior statement thereby lessening its impact.

In order to utilize extrinsic evidence of prior inconsistent statements through the testimony of a witness who heard the prior statement, or by a writing, the witness to be impeached must be given the opportunity to explain or deny making the prior statement. This opportunity normally occurs during cross examination of the witness to be impeached although the rule may allow the opportunity to occur during the redirect examination of the witness. It should be noted that cross examining counsel need only give the witness the opportunity to deny the statement. Explanation should not occur during cross examination. Extrinsic evidence of a prior inconsistent statement is not precluded by Rule 613(b) if the witness admits making the inconsistent statement, as was true at common law. The judge may exclude the extrinsic evidence in such a circumstance, however, pursuant to Rule 403, which allows exclusion of otherwise admissible evidence on the ground that it is cumulative to other evidence in the case.

If counsel desires to have the prior statement considered for its truth, it must fit within Rule 801(d) or hearsay exceptions pursuant to Rule 803 or 804. Rule 801(d)(2) excludes from hearsay treatment admissions of a party-opponent. Rule 801(d)(1)(A) allows prior inconsistent statements for their truth if they are given under oath at a trial, hearing, or other proceeding or in a deposition. The prior testimony under oath need not be, although it usually is, at an earlier examination concerning the instant cause of action. Therefore, a statement under oath at a preliminary hearing or criminal trial will meet Rule 801(d)(1)(A) requirements when utilized at a later civil proceeding.

Rehabilitation

A witness who has been impeached by a prior inconsistent statement may be rehabilitated in a number of ways.

a) On redirect examination, counsel can show that the circumstances of the making of the statement were such that either the witness was mistaken, the witness was misunderstood, or that the prior statement was taken out of context.

b) If the prior statement is written and contains additional statements concerning the subject matter of the impeachment, the entirety of the writing can be read to the jury pursuant to Rule 106. Counsel should attempt to have the explanatory portions of the writing read to the jury during cross examination. If the judge refuses that request, the remainder of the writing should be elicited during redirect examination.

c) If the prior statement was written by someone other than the witness and adopted by the witness, counsel can show that the recording of the statement was inaccurate and that the witness was not given adequate opportunity to review and correct the recording.

d) If the judge views the impeachment by prior statement as amounting to an expressed or implied charge of recent fabrication or improper motive or influence, then the witness can be rehabilitated by use of prior consistent statements pursuant to Rule 801(d)(1)(B).

CHAPTER 48
IMPEACHMENT BY SPECIFIC INSTANCES OF MISCONDUCT

Definition

A witness may be impeached on cross examination by inquiry into specific instances of conduct that relate directly to honesty or truth telling. The conduct must show a lack of truth-telling ability in and of itself, and normally includes conduct involving lying, misstatement, or dishonesty. Extrinsic evidence of such instances of conduct is not admissible.

Forms of Objection and Response

Forms of Objection

➤ (On cross examination) *I object. The specific instance of conduct does not show lack of honesty or truth-telling ability.*

➤ (To extrinsic evidence, written or oral) *I object. Extrinsic evidence of specific instances of conduct relating to honesty is inadmissible.*

Form of Response

➤ *The specific instance of conduct shows lack of honesty or truth-telling ability in that _____.*

Federal Rule 608. Evidence of Character and Conduct of Witness

(b) Specific instances of conduct. Specific instances of the conduct of a witness, for the purpose of attacking or supporting the witness' credibility, other than conviction of crime as provided in rule 609, may not be proved by extrinsic evidence. They may, however, in the discretion of the court, if probative of truthfulness or untruthfulness, be inquired into on cross-examination of the witness (1) concerning the witness' character for truthfulness or untruthfulness, or (2) concerning the character for truthfulness or untruthfulness of another witness as to which character the witness being cross-examined has testified.

The giving of testimony, whether by an accused or by another witness, does not operate as a waiver of the accused's or the witness' privilege against self-incrimination when examined with respect to matters which relate only to credibility.

Commentary

Rule 608(b) presents a narrow exception to the general rule that specific instances of conduct are not admissible to impeach a witness. The general rule evidences a policy that witnesses must be judged by their testimony and not by whether they are good or bad people. The rule, of course, does not preclude impeachment by prior convictions pursuant to Rule 609. The rule allows impeachment on cross examination by inquiry into prior acts that relate directly to honesty or truth-telling ability. Whether or not a prior act relates to truthfulness or honesty is determined by examining the act for an inference that the witness who commits such act fails to be honest or truthful. Note that the act must connote dishonesty irrespective of the lawsuit involved.

Extrinsic evidence of these instances of conduct is not allowed. Counsel is bound by the answers of the witness to be impeached, as given on cross examination. The strict exclusion of extrinsic evidence precludes the conduct of a trial within a trial concerning whether the instance of conduct occurred, which inquiry would deflect the focus of the jury from the substantive issues involved in the trial. Although extrinsic evidence of these acts is not allowed, if the acts used to impeach pursuant to Rule 608(b) also form the factual predicate for a Rule 609(a)(2) conviction for a crime of dishonesty, both impeachments are permissible.

When conducting cross examination on instances of conduct relating to truthfulness and veracity, counsel should carefully inquire about the time, place, and circumstances of such conduct to obtain maximum impact even if the witness denies the conduct.

Cross examining counsel must, of course, have a good-faith basis for believing that the witness actually committed the act or conduct which shows lack of truthfulness or veracity. The proponent of the witness who may be so impeached should move to exclude such cross examination on Rule 403 grounds.

Rehabilitation

A witness who has been impeached by instances of conduct relating to truthfulness and veracity can be rehabilitated on redirect examination by showing the context and circumstances in which the prior conduct occurred, to lessen its impact. In most circumstances, however, it is wise to avoid any further testimony regarding such conduct and to refocus the jury on the substantive issues of the trial. In addition, because impeachment by use of specific instances or conduct relating to honesty is an attack on the character of the witness for honesty, that witness may be rehabilitated by calling a character witness to testify, by way of reputation or opinion evidence, that the impeached witness has good character for honesty. (See Rule 608(a)(2))

Section VIII. Character Evidence

CHAPTER 49
- CHARACTER EVIDENCE -
GENERALLY

Definition

As a general rule, evidence of a person's character trait is inadmissible as irrelevant when offered on the issue of such person's propensity to act in conformity with such character trait. Where, however, a person's character is in issue *within the meaning of Rule 404(a) or Rule 405(b)*, character evidence is admissible to show actions in conformity with that character. Other exceptions to the general rule are contained in other sections of this volume entitled, "Character Evidence—The Accused or Victim in a Criminal Case," "Character Evidence—Other Acts, Crimes, or Wrongs," "Impeachment by Specific Instances of Misconduct," and "Impeachment by Character Evidence."

Forms of Objection and Response

Form of Objection

> ➤ *I object. The question calls for (or the answer provides) evidence of character offered on propensity.*

Form of Response

> ➤ *This evidence is:*
>
> (a) *offered on propensity pursuant to Rule 404(a)(1) or 404(a)(2), or*
>
> (b) *offered for a relevant, non-propensity purpose under Rule 404(b), or*
>
> (c) *offered to prove propensity where character is an essential element of a claim, charge, or defense under Rule 405(b).*

Federal Rule 404. Character Evidence Not Admissible to Prove Conduct; Exceptions; Other Crimes

(a) Character evidence generally. Evidence of a person's character or a trait of character is not admissible for the purpose of proving action in conformity therewith on a particular occasion, except:

(1) Character of accused. Evidence of a pertinent trait of character offered by an accused, or by the prosecution to rebut the same;

(2) Character of victim. Evidence of a pertinent trait of character of the victim of the crime offered by an accused, or by the prosecution to rebut the same, or evidence of a character trait of peacefulness of the victim offered by the prosecution in a homicide case to rebut evidence that the victim was the first aggressor;

(3) Character of witness. Evidence of the character of a witness, as provided in rules 607, 608, and 609.

(b) Other crimes, wrongs, or acts. Evidence of other crimes, wrongs, or acts is not admissible to prove the character of a person in order to show action in conformity therewith. It may, however, be admissible for other purposes, such as proof of motive, opportunity, intent, preparation, plan, knowledge, identity, or absence of mistake or accident, provided that upon request by the accused, the prosecution in a criminal case shall provide reasonable notice in advance of trial, or during trial if the court excuses pretrial notice on good cause shown, of the general nature of any such evidence it intends to introduce at trial.

Federal Rule 405. Methods of Proving Character

(a) Reputation or opinion. In all cases in which evidence of character or a trait of character of a person is admissible, proof may be made by testimony as to reputation or by testimony in the form of an opinion. On cross-examination, inquiry is allowable into relevant specific instances of conduct.

(b) Specific instances of conduct. In cases in which character or a trait of character of a person is an essential element of a charge, claim, or defense, proof may also be made of specific instances of that person's conduct.

Commentary

Rule 404 states the general rule that evidence of a person's character cannot be offered as proof that such person, whether or not a party, has acted in conformity therewith. In other words, character evidence generally cannot be offered on propensity. For example, in a case where the plaintiff claims the defendant caused him damage by negligent driving, the plaintiff is not permitted to offer evidence that the defendant is generally a negligent driver. Similarly, the defendant cannot offer evidence that he is a careful driver.

Where, however, a character trait is an essential element of a claim, charge, or defense in a lawsuit, character evidence is admissible on propensity. For example, where plaintiff sues defendant for defamation, alleging that defendant called him "a liar," plaintiff's character trait, honesty, is an essential element of the claim or defense, and therefore is an issue. Thus, character evidence regarding plaintiff's honesty is admissible.

Rule 405 provides that such character evidence may be offered, where relevant, by way of reputation or opinion evidence, and in more limited circumstances by specific instances of conduct. Reputation and opinion evidence are offered through some witness other than the person whose character trait is in issue. Such *character witness* will be allowed to testify as to reputation or opinion regarding the pertinent character trait only after an appropriate foundation is laid. With respect to reputation evidence, the character witness must, as a preliminary or foundational matter, establish familiarity with some community's view of the person's character trait by testifying that he has heard talk among members of the community regarding the person's character trait. Having done so, he will be permitted to testify as to the person's reputation in the community for the pertinent trait of character.

Where character evidence is offered by way of opinion, the character witness must offer evidence that he knows the person whose character trait is in issue, and is familiar with that person's particular character trait. Once this foundation is laid, the character witness will be permitted to testify as to his opinion regarding the person's pertinent trait of character.

Finally, where the character of a person is an essential element of a claim, charge, or defense, evidence offered in the form of specific instances of conduct which tend to show the person's pertinent trait of character is admissible. Such evidence may be offered through any witness with knowledge of the pertinent character trait, including the person whose character is in issue. In most cases, however, such testimony will be offered through the testimony of a witness other than the person whose character trait is in issue.

Note that a character witness who testifies by way of reputation or opinion may be cross examined by inquiry into specific instances of conduct on the part of the person about whom character evidence has been given which are inconsistent with the character witness' reputation or opinion testimony. This cross examination as to specific instances is allowable on the theory that either (1) the character witness has incomplete information on which to base the reputation, or (2) the character witness has an inappropriate notion as to what constitutes good character. The form of questions for a reputation witness to elicit specific-act evidence on cross examination is, "Have you heard _____ (insert specific act)?" The form of questions for an opinion witness to elicit specific-act evidence on cross examination is, "Do you know _____ (insert specific act)?" Of course, cross examining counsel must have a good-faith basis for believing that the inquired-of specific act occurred.

CHAPTER 50
- CHARACTER EVIDENCE -
THE ACCUSED OR VICTIM IN A CRIMINAL CASE

Definition

Rule 404(a) contains a number of exceptions to the general rule which would bar character evidence on propensity. Rule 404(a)(1) allows the criminal defendant to offer reputation or opinion evidence, through a character witness, to show his lack of propensity to commit the crime charged. Rule 404(a)(2) allows the criminal defendant to offer evidence of the victim's pertinent character trait or propensity of the victim where it is relevant. In homicide cases, Rule 404(a)(2) permits the prosecution to offer evidence of the victim's trait of *peacefulness* to rebut evidence offered by the accused that the victim was the first aggressor.

Where the accused *opens the door* on his own good character pursuant to 404(a)(1) or on the victim's character pursuant to Rule 404(a)(2), then the government is permitted to offer rebuttal character evidence.

Forms of Objection and Response

Forms of Objection

> ➤ *I object. The prosecution is attempting to offer evidence of the defendant's character where the defendant has not offered any character evidence.*

> ➤ *I object. The prosecution is attempting to offer evidence of the victim's character where none has been offered by the defendant.*

Forms of Response

> ➤ *The defendant has opened the door on his character by offering evidence of his pertinent character trait.*

> ➤ *The defendant has opened the door on the victim's character by:*

> (a) *offering evidence of the victim's character, or*

> (b) *offering evidence that the victim was the first aggressor in a homicide case.*

Federal Rule 404. Character Evidence Not Admissible to Prove Conduct; Exceptions; Other Crimes

(a) Character evidence generally. Evidence of a person's character or a trait of character is not admissible for the purpose of proving action in conformity therewith on a particular occasion, except:

(1) Character of accused. Evidence of a pertinent trait of character offered by an accused, or by the prosecution to rebut the same;

(2) Character of victim. Evidence of a pertinent trait of character of the victim of the crime offered by an accused, or by the prosecution to rebut the same, or evidence of a character trait of peacefulness of the victim offered by the prosecution in a homicide case to rebut evidence that the victim was the first aggressor;

Federal Rule 405. Methods of Proving Character

(a) Reputation or opinion. In all cases in which evidence of character or a trait of character of a person is admissible, proof may be made by testimony as to reputation or by testimony in the form of an opinion. On cross examination, inquiry is allowable into relevant specific instances of conduct.

(b) Specific instances of conduct. In cases in which character or a trait of character of a person is an essential element of a charge, claim, or defense, proof may also be made of specific instances of that person's conduct.

Commentary

Rule 404(a)(1) allows the criminal defendant to offer character evidence, by reputation or opinion witnesses, of a pertinent character trait for the purpose of showing his propensity not to commit the crime charged. For example, if a defendant is charged with a violent crime, he would be permitted to offer the opinion or reputation testimony of a character witness regarding the defendant's peaceful nature or character. Similarly, if charged with a dishonesty crime, the defendant could, through character witnesses, offer evidence of his general honesty. This evidence is admissible for the substantive purpose of showing that the criminal defendant acted consistent with the pertinent character trait.

By offering such evidence, however, the defendant *opens the door* to the prosecution's ability to offer contrary character evidence which tends to show the defendant's propensity to commit the charged offense. For example, if the defendant in a homicide case offers reputation evidence as to his peaceful nature, the prosecution can rebut, by offering reputation evidence which demonstrates the defendant's violent nature. Note the defendant's offer of character evidence is often characterized as the *defendant's putting his character in issue*. This is misleading in that it might lead a litigant to believe that he is entitled to offer character evidence by way of specific instances of conduct under Rule 405(b). This is not permitted.

Rule 404(a)(2) permits the criminal defendant to offer evidence, by way of opinion or reputation, regarding the victim's pertinent character trait. For example, a criminal defendant charged with assault and battery who raises the defense of self-defense could offer evidence that the victim has a violent nature as evidence that the victim acted violently or threatened to act violently toward the defendant. Note that neither the substantive criminal law nor Rule 404(a)(2) requires, though it would be strategically helpful to the defense, that the defendant have knowledge of the victim's trait of violence.

Rule 404(a)(2) also provides that where a defendant in a homicide prosecution offers evidence of any sort that the victim was the first aggressor, the door is opened for the prosecution to offer evidence of the victim's character trait of *peacefulness* to rebut such *first aggressor* evidence.

Note that when the defendant puts in issue the character of the victim, the prosecution may only rebut that evidence with contrary evidence concerning the victim's character and not with evidence of the defendant's character. So, in a homicide case, when the defendant puts in evidence of the victims character for violence to show that the victim was the first aggressor in the case, the prosecution may only rebut with evidence of the victim's character for peacefulness. The prosecution may not offer evidence of the defendant's character for violence to rebut the inference of the victim being the first aggressor raised by character evidence for violence concerning the victim.

CHAPTER 51
- CHARACTER EVIDENCE -
OTHER ACTS, CRIMES, OR WRONGS

Definition

Rule 404(b) permits a party to offer evidence of other acts, crimes, or wrongs committed by a person where those acts, crimes, or wrongs are not the subject of the lawsuit, but where such evidence is relevant for some purpose other than propensity.

Forms of Objection and Response

Form of Objection

➤ *I object that this evidence is inadmissible character evidence offered on propensity.*

Form of Response

➤ *This evidence is not offered on propensity, but rather for the purpose of showing _____, a relevant, non-propensity purpose, pursuant to Rule 404(b).*

Federal Rule 404. Character Evidence Not Admissible to Prove Conduct; Exceptions; Other Crimes

(b) Other crimes, wrongs, or acts. Evidence of other crimes, wrongs, or acts is not admissible to prove the character of a person in order to show action in conformity therewith. It may, however, be admissible for other purposes, such as proof of motive, opportunity, intent, preparation, plan, knowledge, identity, or absence of mistake or accident, provided that upon request by the accused, the prosecution in a criminal case shall provide reasonable notice in advance of trial, or during trial if the court excuses pretrial notice on good cause shown, of the general nature of any such evidence it intends to introduce at trial.

Commentary

Rule 404(b) is not an exception to the general rule forbidding the use of character evidence to show propensity. Rather, Rule 404(b) admits character-type evidence where it involves specific crimes, wrongs, or acts, other than those involved in the case at bar, for any relevant, *non-propensity* purpose, including the common, enumerated purposes illustrated in the rule.

For example, in a criminal case charging armed robbery, the prosecution might offer evidence of the theft of a car which was used in the getaway. The car theft, though not a charged offense, may not be offered to show the defendant's general bad character or propensity to crime but rather may be offered to show either the defendant's opportunity to commit the armed robbery, a general plan or scheme, or intent. Likewise, the use of other uncharged acts which bear a close similarity to the charged act may be offered to show the intent of a person, or if the similarities are close to identical, to show a particular *modus operandi*.

A final example might be the offer of an earlier robbery which is offered to show a motive in a murder case where the murder victim is a witness to the robbery.

Note that all of 404(b) offers have an inescapable tendency to inform the jury, as a side issue, on the person's propensity. As with all other evidence (except for prior convictions under Rule 609 and prior sexual acts of a rape victim under Rule 412), evidence offered under Rule 404(b) is subject to the relevancy-prejudice balancing test of Rules 401 and 403. Therefore, it is appropriate for the court to balance the probative value and necessity of the 404(b)-type evidence against its impermissible-propensity impact in determining admissibility.

The court need not make a preliminary finding that the person committed the act. To admit evidence of an act pursuant to Rule 404(b), the court need only determine that there is sufficient evidence under Rule 104 that the defendant committed the act. In making a determination as to the admissibility of Rule 404(b) evidence, most judges will look to the necessity of the evidence to a fair determination of the case, as balanced by the obvious prejudice to the party against whom it is offered. Rule 404(b) evidence is available in both civil and criminal cases.

The chart on the following page provides a complete scheme of the permitted and precluded uses of character evidence which may appear to bear on a person's character trait. The top line of the chart lists the possible purposes for which the evidence might be offered.

When an offer of evidence is made, one must look to see why it is offered. If offered for a permissible purpose, then look to see if the mode of offering is permitted. In so doing, you will find the appropriate box on the chart.

For example, assume that in a civil case arising from alleged negligent driving, a defendant seeks to offer a witness who will testify to her opinion that the defendant is a *careful person*. Find the box on the *civil* chart dealing with propensity and then read down until you find opinion. You can readily see that such evidence is forbidden by Rule 404(a).

Character Evidence
Rules 404, 405, and 413–415

Civil Case

Method of Proof	Purpose of Offer		
	Propensity	Other Relevant Issues	Impeachment
Opinion	No Unless character is an element of claim or defense	No [404(b)]	Yes Only on character trait of honesty [608(a)]
Reputation	No Unless character is an element of claim or defense	No [404(b)]	Yes Only on character trait of honesty [608(a)]
Specific Acts or Instances	No Unless (1) character is an element of claim or defense, or (2) the act involves sexual assault or child molestation	Yes [404(b)]	Yes Only if the prior act shows dishonesty [608(b)]

Criminal Case

Method of Proof	Purpose of Offer		
	Propensity	Other Relevant Issues	Impeachment
Opinion	Defendant – Yes Prosecutor – Yes, if defendant opens door [404(a)(1) & (2)]	No [404(b)]	Yes Only on character trait of honesty [608]
Reputation	Defendant – Yes Prosecutor – Yes, if defendant opens door [404(a)(1) & (2)]	No [404(b)]	Yes Only on character trait of honesty [608]
Specific Acts or Instances	No Unless (1) character is an element of claim or defense, or (2) the act involves sexual assault or child molestation	Yes [404(b)]	Yes Only if the prior act shows dishonesty [608]

CHAPTER 52
- CHARACTER EVIDENCE -
PRIOR SEXUAL ACTIVITY OF ALLEGED VICTIM
(Criminal Cases)

Definition

In any case in which the defendant is alleged to have committed an act of sexual misconduct, evidence of the past sexual behavior or the sexual predisposition of the alleged victim of the crime is generally not admissible. Reputation **or** opinion evidence concerning the alleged victim's past sexual behavior or sexual predisposition is never admissible. Evidence of specific instances of sexual behavior on the part of the alleged victim is admissible in limited circumstances. Before evidence of specific instances of sexual conduct on the part of the alleged victim may be offered, a motion must be filed detailing the evidence sought to be offered, the motion must be served on all parties including the alleged victim, and an in camera hearing must be held where all parties and the alleged victim have the right to be heard.

Forms of Objection and Response

Forms of Objection

➤ (Opinion of reputation evidence) *I object. The question calls for opinion or reputation evidence concerning the victim's sexual behavior or sexual predisposition.*

➤ (Specific instances of conduct) *I object. The question calls for evidence of specific instances of conduct on the issue of the victim's sexual behavior or sexual predisposition.*

Forms of Response

➤ (Opinion or reputation evidence) *There is no appropriate response.*

➤ (Specific instances of conduct) *The evidence of sexual behavior is admissible:*

    (a) *to prove that someone other than the defendant was the source of semen, injury, or physical condition of the alleged victim;*

    (b) *as it was with the defendant and is offered on the issue of consent;*

    (c) *as it is offered by the prosecution;*

    (d) *as it is offered by the defendant and the failure to admit this evidence of sexual behavior or sexual predisposition would violate the constitutional rights of the defendant;* and

        proper notice has been given the alleged victim and the parties, and the judge has determined, in camera, that the evidence is admissible.

Federal Rule 412. Sex Offense Cases; Relevance of Victim's Past Sexual Behavior or Alleged Sexual Predisposition

(a) Evidence generally inadmissible. The following evidence is not admissible in any civil or criminal proceeding involving alleged sexual misconduct except as provided in subdivisions (b) and (c):

(1) Evidence offered to prove that any alleged victim engaged in other sexual behavior.

(2) Evidence offered to prove any alleged victim's sexual predisposition.

(b) Exceptions.

(1) In a criminal case, the following evidence is admissible, if otherwise admissible under these rules:

(A) evidence of specific instances of sexual behavior by the alleged victim offered to prove that a person other than the accused was the source of semen, injury or other physical evidence;

(B) evidence of specific instances of sexual behavior by the alleged victim with respect to the person accused of the sexual misconduct offered by the accused to prove consent or by the prosecution; and

(C) evidence the exclusion of which would violate the constitutional rights of the defendant.

(2) In a civil case, evidence offered to prove the sexual behavior or sexual predisposition of any alleged victim is admissible if it is otherwise admissible under these rules and its probative value substantially outweighs the danger of harm to any victim and of unfair prejudice to any party. Evidence of an alleged victim's reputation is admissible only if it has been placed in controversy by the alleged victim.

(c) Procedure to determine admissibility.

(1) A party intending to offer evidence under subdivision (b) must

(A) file a written motion at least 14 days before trial specifically describing the evidence and stating the purpose for which it is offered unless the court, for good cause requires a different time for filing or permits filing during trial; and

(B) serve the motion on all parties and notify the alleged victim or, when appropriate, the alleged victim's guardian or representative.

(2) Before admitting evidence under this rule the court must conduct a hearing in camera and afford the victim and parties a right to attend and be heard. The motion, related papers, and the record of the hearing must be sealed and remain under seal unless the court orders otherwise.

Commentary

Rule 412 was amended in 1994. It is a comprehensive statement of the federal "rape shield statute." The Rule supersedes Rules 404 and 405 concerning character evidence when dealing with evidence of the sexual behavior or sexual predisposition of the victim in a criminal case where the defendant is charged with alleged sexual misconduct.

The rule is designed to encourage the reporting of offenses involving sexual misconduct by protecting the victim from inappropriate inquiry concerning sexual behavior or sexual predisposition. It does so by precluding completely any reputation or opinion evidence concerning the sexual behavior or sexual predisposition of the victim. It also severely narrows the circumstances in which specific instances of conduct evidencing sexual conduct or sexual predisposition may be admissible.

There are four situations where specific instances of conduct as evidence of sexual behavior or sexual predisposition of the victim may be admissible. First, the conduct of the victim may be admissible to explain that someone other than the defendant is the source of semen, or the cause of physical injury or physical condition of the victim. Second, if the conduct of the victim was with the defendant, it may be admissible on the issue of the consent of the victim to the charged conduct of the defendant. Third, the sexual conduct of the victim may be admissible if the failure to do so would somehow violate the constitutional rights of the defendant. And fourth, the sexual conduct of the victim is offered by the prosecution.

This third situation, involving the constitutional rights of the defendant, commonly arises when it is the claim of the defendant that the accusation against the defendant is an effort to explain a situation that the victim is trying to hide, that can only have resulted from sexual activity. For example, a defendant may claim that a teenager, in a effort to hide from her parents her voluntary sexual activity that resulted in a pregnancy, accused the defendant of rape. In such a situation, a judge might rule that precluding evidence of the victim's sexual activity with someone other than the defendant might infringe on his confrontation rights pursuant to the 6th Amendment to the U.S. Constitution, as the proffered evidence is relevant to show the victim's motive for falsely accusing the defendant.

Whenever a party seeks to introduce evidence of the sexual behavior or disposition of the victim, it must give notice to all parties and to the victim. The notice must state the conduct of the victim which is sought to be proved and the purpose of the proffer. The judge must then hold an in camera hearing on the admissibility of the proffered evidence, during which the parties and the victim have a right to be heard. All records of this proceeding are sealed.

CHAPTER 53
- CHARACTER EVIDENCE -
PRIOR SEXUAL ACTIVITY OF ALLEGED VICTIM
(Civil Cases)

Definition

In any civil case involving alleged sexual misconduct, evidence of the past sexual behavior **or** the sexual predisposition of the alleged victim of such misconduct is generally not admissible. Evidence offered to prove sexual behavior or sexual predisposition of the alleged victim, to be admissible, must be otherwise admissible pursuant to the Federal Rules of Evidence, and the probative value of the evidence must substantially outweigh the danger of harm to the victim or of unfair prejudice to any party. Even then, the form of the proof of sexual behavior or predisposition is generally limited to specific instances of conduct. Opinion evidence as to the victim's sexual behavior or predisposition is never admissible. Evidence of the victim's reputation as to these matters is admissible only if first placed in controversy by the victim.

Forms of Objection and Response

Forms of Objection

- ➤ (Opinion evidence) *I object. The question calls for opinion evidence concerning sexual behavior or sexual predisposition of a victim of sexual misconduct.*

- ➤ (Reputation evidence) *I object. The question calls for reputation evidence concerning sexual behavior or sexual predisposition of a victim or sexual misconduct, and the victim has not placed that reputation in issue.*

- ➤ (Specific instances of conduct) *I object.*

  (a) *The question calls for evidence concerning the sexual behavior or sexual predisposition of a victim of sexual misconduct and it is irrelevant;* or

  (b) *The question calls for evidence concerning the sexual behavior or sexual predisposition of a victim of sexual misconduct, and the probative value of the evidence does not substantially outweigh the danger or harm to the victim and/or unfair prejudice to my client.*

Forms of Response

- ➤ (Opinion evidence) There is no appropriate response.

- ➤ (Reputation evidence) *The victim of the alleged sexual misconduct put his/her reputation for sexual behavior or sexual predisposition in issue when the following evidence was offered* (insert evidence, as offered by the victim, that put his/her reputation for sexual behavior or sexual predisposition in issue).

- ➤ (Specific instances of conduct) *The evidence of sexual behavior or sexual predisposition is otherwise admissible pursuant to Federal Rules of Evidence 404, 405, or 406, and the probative value of the evidence substantially outweighs the danger of harm to the victim or unfair prejudice to any party.*

Federal Rule 412. Sex Offense Cases; Relevance of Victim's Past Sexual Behavior or Alleged Sexual Predisposition

(a) Evidence generally inadmissible. The following evidence is not admissible in any civil or criminal proceeding involving alleged sexual misconduct except as provided in subdivisions (b) and (c):

(1) Evidence offered to prove that any alleged victim engaged in other sexual behavior.

(2) Evidence offered to prove any alleged victim's sexual predisposition.

(b) Exceptions.

(1) In a criminal case, the following evidence is admissible, if otherwise admissible under these rules:

(A) evidence of specific instances of sexual behavior by the alleged victim offered to prove that a person other than the accused was the source of semen, injury or other physical evidence;

(B) evidence of specific instances of sexual behavior by the alleged victim with respect to the person accused of the sexual misconduct offered by the accused to prove consent or by the prosecution; and

(C) evidence the exclusion of which would violate the constitutional rights of the defendant.

(2) In a civil case, evidence offered to prove the sexual behavior or sexual predisposition of any alleged victim is admissible if it is otherwise admissible under these rules and its probative value substantially outweighs the danger of harm to any victim and of unfair prejudice to any party. Evidence of an alleged victim's reputation is admissible only if it has been placed in controversy by the alleged victim.

(c) Procedure to determine admissibility.

(1) A party intending to offer evidence under subdivision (b) must

(A) file a written motion at least 14 days before trial specifically describing the evidence and stating the purpose for which it is offered unless the court, for good cause requires a different time for filing or permits filing during trial; and

(B) serve the motion on all parties and notify the alleged victim or, when appropriate, the alleged victim's guardian or representative.

(2) Before admitting evidence under this rule the court must conduct a hearing in camera and afford the victim and parties a right to attend and be heard. The motion, related papers, and the record of the hearing must be sealed and remain under seal unless the court orders otherwise.

Commentary

Rule 412 was amended in 1994 to make clear that the rule applies to civil cases, while setting different standards for the admissibility of sexual behavior or predisposition evidence regarding the victim of sexual misconduct in a relevant civil case, than for a case involving the same or similar issues in the criminal setting. The rule is designed to facilitate the making of claims by victims of alleged sexual misconduct concerning that misconduct, by providing them with protection from inappropriate use evidence of the victim's sexual behavior or sexual predisposition, while at the same time allowing parties to utilize such evidence if otherwise relevant in limited circumstances.

In civil cases, as in criminal cases, opinion evidence concerning the sexual behavior or predisposition of the victim of sexual misconduct is never admissible. Reputation evidence concerning these matters may, however, be admissible if first raised by the victim of sexual misconduct.

The most typical proffer concerning the sexual behavior or predisposition of the victim of sexual misconduct will be in the form of specific instances of conduct. Before such evidence is admissible, the court must first determine that the evidence is otherwise admissible under the rules of evidence. In most cases, therefore, the proffered evidence of conduct must be admissible pursuant to:

1. Rule 404(b), as a specific instance of conduct, relevant to something other than the general character of the victim or conformity of conduct;

2. Rule 405, as an essential element of the claim or defense in the case; or

3. Rule 406 as evidence of habitual conduct.

Once that hurdle is cleared, a further determination must be made that the probative value of the evidence substantially outweighs the danger of harm to any victim or of unfair prejudice to any party. Note that the balancing test of Rule 412 is a special one. The Rule 412 balance is weighted against admissibility of the evidence, as the proponent must show that the probative value of the evidence overcomes presumed harm to the victim as well as unfair prejudice to a party, and it must do so in a substantial way.

Just as in criminal cases, the party seeking to introduce evidence of the sexual behavior or disposition of a victim of sexual misconduct must give notice to all parties and the victim. The notice must state the evidence sought to be proved and the purpose for the proffer. The judge must then hold an in camera hearing on the admissibility of the proffered evidence, during which the parties and the victim have a right to be heard. All records of this proceeding are sealed.

CHAPTER 54

- CHARACTER EVIDENCE -
EVIDENCE OF SIMILAR CRIMES OR ACTS IN
CIVIL OR CRIMINAL SEXUAL ASSAULT OR
CHILD MOLESTATION CASES

Definition

Rules 413, 414, and 415 admit evidence of similar crimes against civil and criminal defendants in cases involving sexual assault or child molestation.

Forms of Objection and Response

Form of Objection

> *I object that this evidence is inadmissible character evidence offered on propensity.*

Form of Response

> *This offer involves evidence of a similar crime of sexual assault or child molestation, offered*

>> (a) *in a criminal case charging sexual assault or child molestation,* or

>> (b) *in a civil case concerning sexual assault or child molestation.*

Federal Rule 413. Evidence of Similar Crimes in Sexual Assault Cases

(a) In a criminal case in which the defendant is accused of an offense of sexual assault, evidence of the defendant's commission of another offense or offenses of sexual assault is admissible, and may be considered for its bearing on any matter to which it is relevant.

(b) In a case in which the Government intends to offer evidence under this rule, the attorney for the Government shall disclose the evidence to the defendant, including statements of witnesses or a summary of the substance of any testimony that is expected to be offered, at least fifteen days before the scheduled date of trial or at such later time as the court may allow for good cause.

(c) This rule shall not be construed to limit the admission or consideration of evidence under any other rule.

(d) For purposes of this rule and Rule 415, "offense of sexual assault" means a crime under Federal law or the law of a State (as defined in section 513 of title 18, United States Code) that involved—

(1) any conduct proscribed by chapter 109A of title 18, United States Code;

(2) contact, without consent, between any part of the defendant's body or an object and the genitals or anus of another person;

(3) contact, without consent, between the genitals or anus of the defendant and any part of another person's body;

(4) deriving sexual pleasure or gratification from the infliction of death, bodily injury, or physical pain on another person; or

(5) an attempt or conspiracy to engage in conduct described in paragraph (1)–(4).

Federal Rule 414. Evidence of Similar Crimes in Child Molestation Cases

(a) In a criminal case in which the defendant is accused of an offense of child molestation, evidence of the defendant's commission of another offense or offenses of child molestation is admissible, and may be considered for its bearing on any matter to which it is relevant.

(b) In a case in which the Government intends to offer evidence under this rule, the attorney for the Government shall disclose the evidence to the defendant, including statements of witnesses or a summary of the substance of any testimony that is expected to be offered, at least fifteen days before the scheduled date of trial or at such later time as the court may allow for good cause.

(c) This rule shall not be construed to limit the admission or consideration of evidence under any other rule.

(d) For purposes of this rule and Rule 415, "child" means a person below the age of fourteen, and "offense of child molestation" means a crime under Federal law or the law of a State (as defined in section 513 of title 18, United States Code) that involved—

(1) any conduct proscribed by chapter 109A of title 18, United States Code, that was committed in relation to a child;

(2) any conduct proscribed by chapter 110 of title 18, United States Code;

(3) contact between any part of the defendant's body or an object and the genitals or anus of a child;

(4) contact between the genitals or anus of the defendant and any part of the body of a child;

(5) deriving sexual pleasure or gratification from the infliction of death, bodily injury, or physical pain on a child; or

(6) an attempt or conspiracy to engage in conduct described in paragraphs (1)–(5).

Federal Rule 415. Evidence of Similar Acts in Civil Cases Concerning Sexual Assault or Child Molestation

(a) In a civil case in which a claim for damages or other relief is predicated on a party's alleged commission of conduct constituting an offense of sexual assault or child molestation, evidence of that party's commission of another offense or offenses of sexual assault or child molestation is admissible and may be considered as provided in Rule 413 and Rule 414 of these rules.

(b) A party who intends to offer evidence under this Rule shall disclose the evidence to the party against whom it will be offered, including statements of witnesses or a summary of the substance of any testimony that is expect to be offered, at least fifteen days before the scheduled date of trial or at such later time as the court may allow for good cause.

(c) This rule shall not be construed to limit the admission or consideration of evidence under any other rule.

Commentary

Rules 413, 414, and 415 governing the admissibility of character evidence in civil and criminal cases involving a claim of sexual assault or child molestation became law in July of 1995. Although Rule 404(a) generally excludes evidence of similar acts when offered to prove the propensity of the civil or criminal defendant to commit the act which is charged, Rules 413, 414, and 415 create an exception for such offers in cases involving sexual assault or child molestation.

Of course, the admission of such evidence is subject to exclusion if it is prejudicial or confusing, or involves an undue waste of time pursuant to Rule 403. Relevant factors to be considered in the 403 balance are:

(1) proximity in time to the charged or predicate conduct;

(2) similarity to the charged or predicate conduct;

(3) frequency of the prior acts;

(4) surrounding circumstances;

(5) relevant intervening events; and

(6) other relevant similarities or differences.

However, it is unavailing to argue that the evidence of similar crimes will prejudice the jury by inviting the inference that the defendant committed the crime or act alleged charged in the instant case because he committed a similar crime on an earlier occasion. After all, that inference is the very basis for admitting the similar crime evidence pursuant to Rules 413, 414, and 415.

What is the standard of proof required to obtain admission of similar crimes evidence? As with offers made pursuant to Rule 404(b), the court will admit the similar crimes evidence where the proponent offers evidence sufficient to persuade a reasonable fact-finder by a preponderance of the evidence that the defendant committed the earlier act of sexual assault or child molestation. Note that there is no requirement that the defendant had been convicted of the similar act, nor does the rule require that the similar act be excluded if the defendant was tried and acquitted of the similar act.

Finally, in both civil and criminal cases, the proponent of an offer of similar crimes evidence pursuant to Rules 413, 414, and 415 must disclose such evidence to the party against whom it is offered fifteen days before trial.

Section IX. Hearsay

CHAPTER 55
- HEARSAY -
GENERALLY

Definition

Hearsay is an out-of-court statement offered for truth of the contents of the statement.

Forms of Objection and Response

Forms of Objection

- ➤ *I object. The question calls for a hearsay answer.*
- ➤ *I move to strike the answer as hearsay.*

Form of Response

- ➤ *The statement is not being offered for the truth of the matter asserted, but rather is offered to show the statement was made. The making of the statement is relevant to show:*
  - (a) *the effect on a person who heard the statement, or*
  - (b) *a prior inconsistent statement, or*
  - (c) *the operative facts or a verbal act, or*
  - (d) *the knowledge of the declarant.*

Federal Rule 801. Definitions

(a) Statement. A "statement" is (1) an oral or written assertion or (2) nonverbal conduct of a person, if it is intended by him as an assertion.

(b) Declarant. A "declarant" is a person who makes a statement.

(c) Hearsay. "Hearsay" is a statement, other than one made by the declarant while testifying at the trial or hearing, offered in evidence to prove the truth of the matter asserted.

Commentary

Hearsay is an out-of-court statement, written or oral, which is offered to prove the truth of the matter contained in the statement. An out-of-court statement which is offered for any relevant purpose other than the truth of the matter asserted is non-hearsay. Thus, where the mere fact that an out-of-court statement was made is relevant, independent of whether the statement is true, the statement is non-hearsay.

In determining whether an out-of-court statement is hearsay, there is an essentially foolproof practical test by which one can persuade the trial judge that evidence is, in fact, hearsay. First, ask the question whether or not the only relevant purpose for the offering of the out-of-court statement is its truth. If the answer to that question is "yes," then the out-of-court statement is hearsay. If the answer to that question, however, is not clearly "yes," then ask the next question—(2) whether the content of the out-of-court statement need be believed in order to be relevant. If the answer to that question is "yes," then the evidence is hearsay. If it makes no difference as to a relevant purpose in the lawsuit whether the statement is true, it is not hearsay.

For example, where a statement is offered to show that it was made in the hearing of a person, and such person's being on notice of the words contained in the statement is relevant in the lawsuit, the statement is not hearsay.

Likewise, where a prior inconsistent statement is offered for the purpose of showing that a witness ought not be believed because he has spoken inconsistently, the truth of the statement is not necessary to its relevance. Thus, the statement is non-hearsay.

Furthermore, where the uttering or the writing of the out-of-court statement has legal significance irrespective of truth, it is non-hearsay. For example, the offer and acceptance of a contract are out-of-court statements which create legal duties and obligations when made. Likewise, the statement, "It's a gift," when uttered by a person who hands another money, has legal significance. Such statements which have legal significance independent of their truth, are called *operative words* or *verbal acts* and are non-hearsay because their relevance derives from the mere fact that they were made. That is, they are offered merely to show that they were uttered or written.

Moreover, the proponent may offer an out-of-court statement in order to prove the state of the knowledge of the maker of the statement, the declarant. In other words, the uttering of the statement tells the fact-finder something about what the declarant knows or intends. For example, in a civil commitment hearing, the petitioner may offer the following statement uttered by the person whose commitment to a mental institution is sought, "I am Napoleon." This out-of-court statement is not offered for its truth, but rather for the purpose of showing the mental state of the declarant. The statement is not offered for its truth, but rather to show it was made. Thus, it is non-hearsay.

Finally, note that in a federal court, as well as in most of the state courts, the mere presence of the declarant in court as a witness, without more, fails to obviate the hearsay objection to the declarant's out-of-court statements unless this statement falls within the narrow requirements of Rule 801(d)(1).

CHAPTER 56
HEARSAY WITHIN HEARSAY

Definition

Where an out-of-court statement contains another out-of-court statement, then both statements are admissible only if each statement is either: (a) within a hearsay exception or (b) is defined as non-hearsay.

Forms of Objection and Response

Forms of Objection

➤ *I object. The question calls for hearsay within hearsay.*

➤ *I move to strike the answer because it contains hearsay within hearsay.*

Form of Response

➤ *Both statements are admissible because each either comes within a hearsay exception or is non-hearsay.*

Federal Rule 805. Hearsay Within Hearsay

Hearsay included within hearsay is not excluded under the hearsay rule if each part of the combined statements conforms with an exception to the hearsay rule provided in these rules.

Commentary

This is the multiple or "totem pole" hearsay rule. The rule often applies to writings that contain attributed statements. In order to admit the *second* statement, i.e., the statement within the statement, the proponent must account for both out-of-court statements with either a hearsay exception or an argument that the out-of-court statement is offered for a relevant, non-hearsay purpose.

For example, assume a wrongful death case where a police report contains a statement from a victim who is mortally wounded. The report itself would be admissible as a public record or report pursuant to Rule 803(8) and the statement of the victim, assuming proper foundation could be admissible as a dying declaration pursuant to Rule 804(b)(2). Another typical example is a medical record that contains statements attributed to the patient. The record itself would likely be admissible as a business record pursuant to Rule 803(6) and the statements of the patient if made for the purpose of diagnosis or treatment would be admissible pursuant to Rule 803(4). Unless the proponent of the evidence can account for both levels of hearsay in the document, the part of the statement which is hearsay will not be admissible. It is possible, of course, to redact inadmissible hearsay within hearsay if a document meets an exception to the rule or is non-hearsay and the reported statement within it is inadmissible on hearsay grounds. If, in the above example of the police report, there is no way to account for the victim's statement and it remains as inadmissible hearsay, then after redacting the victim's statement from the report, the remainder of this report, to the extent it is relevant, will be admitted. If neither the report nor the victim's declaration can be accounted for with a hearsay exception or a non-hearsay purpose, then neither statement will be admitted.

The proscription of hearsay within hearsay, although typically raised in the context of documents, also applies to out-of-court oral statements where the out-of-court declarant reports the statement of another. In those cases as well, both levels of hearsay must meet an exception or qualify for non-hearsay treatment.

CHAPTER 57
- HEARSAY -
ATTACKING AND SUPPORTING THE
CREDIBILITY OF A HEARSAY DECLARANT

Definition

When an out-of-court statement is admitted, the declarant's credibility may be impeached, and if impeached, then rehabilitated, in the same manner as if the declarant had testified as a witness. In addition, where a hearsay statement is offered against a party, that party may call the declarant and examine as if on cross examination.

Forms of Objection and Response

Form of Objection

> ➤ *I object. The question seeks to attack the credibility of a person who has not appeared as a witness.*

Form of Response

> ➤ *This impeachment of an out-of-court declarant is permissible to the same extent available for a testifying witness.*

Federal Rule 806. Attacking and Supporting Credibility of Declarant

When a hearsay statement, or a statement defined in Rule 801(d)(2)(C), (D), or (E) has been admitted in evidence, the credibility of the declarant may be attacked, and if attacked may be supported, by any evidence which would be admissible for those purposes if declarant had testified as a witness. Evidence of a statement or conduct by the declarant at any time, inconsistent with the declarant's hearsay statement, is not subject to any requirement that the declarant may have been afforded an opportunity to deny or explain. If the party against whom a hearsay statement has been admitted calls the declarant as a witness, the party is entitled to examine the declarant on the statement as if under cross-examination.

Commentary

Where an out-of-court statement is admitted, the opponent may impeach the credibility of the absent (from court) declarant to the same extent that one could impeach a live witness. In other words, all of the usual impeachment modes are available.

Moreover, impeachment by prior inconsistent statement is permitted despite the inability to confront the declarant with the inconsistency to afford him an opportunity to admit or deny it, as is required in the impeachment of an in-court witness by extrinsic evidence pursuant to Rule 613(b). Similarly, impeachment of the absent declarant as to bias, prejudice, interest, or improper motive may be accomplished without the usual foundational requirement of denial of the same. Perhaps most important, all impeachment of an out-of-court declarant must, of necessity, be performed by the offer of extrinsic evidence.

Therefore, except with regard to prior inconsistent statements, impeachment of the out-of-court declarant is only allowable to the extent that extrinsic evidence of impeachment is allowable. Furthermore, where the declarant is called as a witness, the party against whom the witness' out-of-court statement has been offered, may lead the witness, because such witness is perforce considered hostile pursuant to Rule 611(c).

CHAPTER 58
- HEARSAY -
NON-HEARSAY PRIOR STATEMENTS

Definition

Rule 801(d)(1) excludes from the definition of hearsay, out-of-court statements made by a declarant who is testifying at trial (a) where the declarant is subject to cross examination on the out-of-court statement and where the statement is inconsistent with his/her trial testimony and given under oath at some earlier proceeding or deposition; or (b) where the statement is consistent with his/her trial testimony and is offered for the purpose of rebutting an express or implied charge of recent fabrication or improper influence or motive; or (c) where the statement is one of identification of a person made after perceiving him/her.

Forms of Objection and Response

Forms of Objection

> ➤ *I object. The question calls for a hearsay answer.*

> ➤ *I move to strike the answer as hearsay.*

Form of Response

> ➤ *The statement is not hearsay pursuant to Rule 801(d)(1) because I have shown that:*

>> (a) *it is inconsistent with the witness' trial testimony and was given under oath at an earlier proceeding or deposition, or*

>> (b) *it is consistent with the witness' trial testimony and is offered to rebut an expressed or implied charge of recent fabrication, or improper influence or motive, or*

>> (c) *the statement by the testifying witness is an identification of a person made after perceiving such person.*

Federal Rule 801. Definitions

(d) Statements which are not hearsay. A statement is not hearsay if—

(1) Prior statement by witness. The declarant testifies at the trial or hearing and is subject to cross-examination concerning the statement, and the statement is (A) inconsistent with the declarant's testimony, and was given under oath subject to the penalty of perjury at a trial, hearing, or other proceeding, or in a deposition, or (B) consistent with the declarant's testimony and is offered to rebut an expressed or implied charge against the declarant of recent fabrication or improper influence or motive, or (C) one of identification of a person made after perceiving the person;

Commentary

The federal rules define as non-hearsay the three categories of out-of-court statements contained in Rules 801(d)(1)(A)–(C), despite the fact that they can be offered for the truth of what is asserted in the statements. Note that each category of 801(d)(1) statements requires the declarant to be present and testifying in court and available for cross examination. Unlike the common-law rule in some states, however, the mere presence of the declarant in court without meeting the additional foundational requirements of the 801(d)(1) rules fails to obviate the hearsay objection.

Prior inconsistent statements

A prior inconsistent statement may be offered only to impeach the credibility of a witness-declarant unless it comes within an exception to the hearsay rule or the terms of Rule 801(d)(1)(A). An 801(d)(1)(A) prior inconsistent statement gains its non-hearsay nature from the reliability presumed from its having been made under oath and from the added protection of the out-of-court declarant's presence in court to be cross examined about the prior inconsistent statement.

Prior consistent statements

Although many federal courts had traditionally admitted prior consistent statements made outside of court for the rehabilitation of witnesses who had been impeached, such statements were not offered for their truth but only to show that they had been made. The federal rules, in Rule 801(d)(1)(B), admit a prior consistent statement for its truth, where the consistent statement is offered to rebut attacks on the credibility of a witness which tend to show that the witness' testimony on direct examination has been recently fabricated or is the result of some improper motive or influence. Note that the purpose of the prior consistent statement is to negate the inference that the witness' direct testimony is the first occasion on which the witness has given a particular account of the facts.

Some federal courts have ruled that the admissibility of a prior consistent statement for its truth is triggered by the impeachment of the witness by a prior inconsistent statement. Other courts have taken the position that the mere impeachment by prior inconsistent statement fails to amount to a charge of recent fabrication required by Rule 801(d)(1)(B). The usual example of evidence of improper influence or motive would be impeachment which tends to show that the witness has been bribed or otherwise has exchanged his/her testimony for some consideration.

Additionally, the federal courts are split on whether a *time-line* analysis is crucial to the admissibility of prior consistent statements. Many courts take the position that because the relevance of the prior consistent statement lies in its showing that the witness has not recently fabricated his/her in-court account because the witness gave a similar account at a time prior to the existence of any improper motive or influence to fabricate (or before a prior inconsistent statement), the consistent statement must have been communicated prior to the existence of either the improper influence or motive or the prior inconsistent statement (depending on which triggers the admissibility of a prior consistent statement).

Finally, many federal courts continue to admit prior consistent statements, irrespective of whether they meet the requirements of Rule 801(d)(1)(B), for the limited purpose of rehabilitation, though not for the truth asserted. Most federal courts, however, have adopted the view that only those prior consistent statements which meet the requirements of the rule are admissible for any purpose.

Prior statements of identification

Rule 801(d)(1)(C) admits an out-of-court statement of identification where the declarant testifies at trial and is subject to cross examination on the statement. The identification is admissible only where it is a statement which is made during or shortly after viewing either the person identified or a photograph of such person. This rule recognizes the likelihood that an identification is accurate when made, even if the memory of the identifying witness has faded by the time of trial. This rule permits the out-of-court statement of identification to rehabilitate an impeached identification witness without meeting the requirement of a prior consistent statement set out in Rule 801(d)(1)(B).

Although not required by Rule 801(d)(1)(C), some judges will not admit such prior statements of identification unless the witness is unable to make an in-court identification.

CHAPTER 59
- HEARSAY -
NON-HEARSAY ADMISSIONS

Definition

The federal rules define as non-hearsay any admission by a party opponent. An admission is an out-of-court statement made by a party or attributable to a party offered for its truth by the opponent in the lawsuit.

Forms of Objection and Response

Forms of Objection

> ➤ *I object. The question calls for a hearsay answer.*

> ➤ *I move to strike the answer as hearsay.*

Form of Response

> ➤ *The statement is not hearsay pursuant to Rule 801(d)(2) because I have shown that:*

    (a) *the statement was made by the party opponent,* or

    (b) *the statement was made by a person and was adopted by the party opponent as his/her own, and is, thus, a vicarious admission of the party opponent,* or

    (c) *the statement was made by an agent authorized to speak on behalf of a party opponent, and is, thus, a vicarious admission of the party opponent,* or

    (d) (1) *the statement was made by an agent or servant of the party opponent,*

        (2) *concerning a matter within the scope of the declarant's agency or employment,* and

        (3) *was made during the existence of the declarant's agency or employment, and is, thus, a vicarious admission of the party opponent,* or

    (e) (1) *the statement was made by a co-conspirator of the party opponent,*

        (2) *during the course of the conspiracy,* and

        (3) *in furtherance of the conspiracy, and is thus, a vicarious admission of the party opponent.*

Federal Rule 801. Definitions

(d) Statements which are not hearsay. A statement is not hearsay if–

(2) Admission by party-opponent. The statement is offered against a party and is (A) the party's own statement, in either an individual or a representative capacity or (B) a statement of which the party has manifested an adoption or belief in its truth, or (C) a statement by a person authorized by the party to make a statement concerning the subject, or (D) a statement by the party's agent or servant concerning a matter within the scope of the agency or employment, made during the existence of the relationship, or (E) a statement by a coconspirator of a party during the course and in furtherance of the conspiracy. The contents of the statement shall be considered but are not alone sufficient to establish the declarant's authority under subdivision (C), the agency or employment relationship and scope thereof under subdivision (D), or the existence of the conspiracy and the participation therein of the declarant and the party against whom the statement is offered under subdivision (E).

Commentary

The common law in many jurisdictions treats party admissions as an exception to the hearsay rule. Rule 801(d)(2) simply treats admissions as non-hearsay. The distinction is merely formal, yielding the same result—admissions of a party opponent are admissible for their truth as against a hearsay objection.

Party admissions are statements made by a party in a lawsuit which are offered by the opponent. Though the simplest form of admission is a statement made by the opposing party in either his individual or representative capacity, Rule 801(d)(2) provides for a number of vicarious admissions (statements of a declarant other than the party opponent) which are attributed to the party opponent because of either the party's adoption of the statement or because of some relationship between the party opponent and the declarant.

Rule 801(d)(2)(B) provides that where a statement is made by a person and is adopted by a party opponent, such statement qualifies as an admission of the party opponent. Note that historically, adoption can be construed from the silence of the party opponent in circumstances where it is shown that the party opponent heard the statement, and where the party opponent would have been expected to deny the thrust of the statement. These tacit admissions, however, are carefully scrutinized in light of the inherent ambiguity of silence in response to a statement.

Rule 801(d)(2)(C) provides that a statement by an agent authorized to speak on behalf of the party opponent is a vicarious admission which can be attributed to the party opponent. To meet this rule the declarant must be specifically authorized by the party to speak for the party, e.g., an attorney.

Rule 801(d)(2)(D) provides a liberalized departure from the common law. This rule provides for the attribution of a statement to a party as an admission where the statement is made by an agent or employee of the party, the statement concerns a matter within the scope of the declarant's employment, and the statement is made while the employment relationship between the declarant and the party exists. Note that the agent, employee, or servant need not be a *speaking agent,* i.e., an agent employed for the expressed purpose of speaking on behalf of the party (as is the agent described in Rule 801(d)(2)(C) above). For example, in a lawsuit brought against a corporation that owns a truck involved in a collision which gives rise to the claim, a statement of the truck driver as to the cause of the collision is treated as a vicarious admission of the defendant corporation. In laying the foundation for an admission pursuant Rules 801(d)(2)(C) or (D), the proponent must show the existence of the foundation facts sufficient to enable a reasonable juror to find their existence by a preponderance of the evidence.

Rule 801(d)(2)(E) provides for the vicarious attribution to a party opponent of an out-of-court statement made by a person who is shown to be a co-conspirator of a party opponent. In order to bring a statement within the so-called *co-conspirator exception*, the proponent must demonstrate to the court as a preliminary matter that a conspiracy exists, that the declarant and the party opponent were co-conspirators, and that the declarant's statement was made during the existence of the conspiracy and was made in the furtherance of the conspiracy. In a case where conspiracy is not independently charged, the foundation should be laid outside of the hearing of the jury, with the proponent required to meet the standard of offering evidence sufficient for a reasonable juror to find the existence of the above foundational facts by a preponderance of the evidence.

The United States Supreme Court ruled in 1987 that a trial judge may consider the co-conspirator admission itself in deciding whether the proponent has made the preliminary showing of conspiracy necessary to admit the co-conspirator admission. Though the court left open whether the co-conspirator admission standing alone can form a sufficient foundation for its own admissibility, a 1997 amendment to Rule 801(d)(2)(E) clearly answered that question in the negative. It is important to note that Rule 801(d)(2)(E) admissions are admissible even when conspiracy has not been alleged as a claim or charge in a civil or criminal case, respectively, by either party, so long as the foundational requirements are met. Furthermore, a number of federal courts have ruled that Rule 801(d)(2)(E) applies to statements made during the course and in furtherance of any enterprise, whether legal or illegal, in which the declarant and the defendant jointly participated.

As to all party admissions, the rules precluding opinions in Rule 701 and 702 of the federal rules and the requirement of firsthand knowledge pursuant to Rule 602 do not apply. It is presumed that a party should be made to answer for all relevant statements made concerning the subject matter of any lawsuit.

CHAPTER 60
- HEARSAY EXCEPTION -
PRESENT SENSE IMPRESSION

Definition

A present sense impression is an out-of-court statement which describes or explains an occurrence or condition made at the time the declarant was perceiving the occurrence or condition, or immediately thereafter.

Forms of Objection and Response

Forms of Objection

> ➤ *I object. The question calls for a hearsay answer.*

> ➤ *I move to strike the answer as hearsay.*

Form of Response

> ➤ *This statement is admissible as a present sense impression pursuant to Rule 803(1). I have shown through the testimony of_____ (insert name of witness) that the statement describes or explains an event or condition, and was made:*
>
>   (a) *while the declarant was perceiving the event or condition, or*
>
>   (b) *immediately thereafter.*

Federal Rule 803. Hearsay Exceptions; Availability of Declarant Immaterial

(1) Present sense impression. A statement describing or explaining an event or condition made while the declarant was perceiving the event or condition, or immediately thereafter.

Commentary

Present sense impressions gain their reliability from the virtual contemporaneity of the making of the out-of-court statement and the occurrence of the event described or explained. The substantial contemporaneity of the event and the statement negate the likelihood of deliberation or conscious misrepresentation. Note that the event described in the statement need not be *exciting* or *startling*. Because the only guarantee of reliability for this exception is contemporaneity, the event and the statement must be extremely close in time. Even a brief reflective period may destroy the spontaneity required.

The statement is admissible for the truth of the occurrence which it describes, and the admissibility of the statement is limited to so much of the statement as describes the event or condition perceived by the declarant.

This exception is a codification of the *Houston Oxygen* exception to the hearsay rule. It does not, however, as in *Houston Oxygen*, require that another person must have also seen the event in question and be in a position to correct the declarant at the time the declaration is made.

CHAPTER 61
- HEARSAY EXCEPTION -
EXCITED UTTERANCE

Definition

An excited utterance is a spontaneous out-of-court statement which relates to a startling event and which is made while the declarant is under the stress or excitement caused by the event.

Forms of Objection and Response

Forms of Objection

> ➤ *I object. The question calls for a hearsay answer.*

> ➤ *I move to strike the answer as hearsay.*

Form of Response

> ➤ *This statement is admissible as an excited utterance pursuant to Rule 803(2). I have shown through the testimony of_____* (insert name of witness) *that the statement:*

>> (a) *relates to a startling event or condition,* and

>> (b) *was made while the declarant was under the stress or excitement caused by the event or condition.*

Federal Rule 803. Hearsay Exceptions; Availability of Declarant Immaterial

(2) Excited utterance. A statement relating to a startling event or condition made while the declarant was under the stress of excitement caused by the event or condition.

Commentary

Excited or spontaneous utterances gain their reliability from the connection between the making of the statement and the startling event. In other words, when one is sufficiently startled into making a spontaneous utterance, we assume that there was neither sufficient time nor presence of mind to prevaricate. Thus, to qualify as an excited utterance, the event which gives rise to the statement relating to it must be sufficiently startling so as to remove the likelihood of self-serving reflection in the making of the statement.

In order to demonstrate that a statement falls within Rule 803(2), the proponent of the statement must lay a foundation for the context of the statement which shows the startling event and the statement's connection to it prior to offering the statement itself. Unlike present sense impressions, an excited utterance need not be contemporaneous with the pertinent event as long as it can be fairly said that the declarant was acting under the stress of the exciting or startling event when the statement was made. For example, if the declarant were injured by a startling event and lost consciousness, if upon regaining consciousness, the declarant makes a spontaneous statement regarding that event, it could still be said that the declarant is acting under the stress of that event and the statement could meet the requirements for this exception.

The exception has also been found to be available in a circumstance where a sufficiently startling event occurs and the excitement continues until the declarant has an opportunity to report the event to another person. As a general rule, however, the passage of time between the event and the statement will be given strong consideration because necessarily, over time, excitement wears off and reflection takes its place.

Further, courts, in considering the admissibility of purported excited utterances, will look to whether the offered statement was in response to questions. Although not determinative of admissibility, where a statement is made in response to a question, there may arise an inference that reflection or suggestion prompted the statement, thereby negating the impact of the startling event on the declarant.

CHAPTER 62

- HEARSAY EXCEPTION -
THEN EXISTING MENTAL OR EMOTIONAL CONDITION

Definition

An out-of-court statement which sets forth the declarant's present state of mind or present emotional condition is admissible as an exception to the hearsay rule.

Forms of Objection and Response

Forms of Objection

➤ *I object. The question call for a hearsay answer.*

➤ *I move to strike the answer as hearsay.*

Form of Response

➤ *This statement is admissible as a statement of a then existing mental or emotional condition pursuant to Rule 803(3). I have shown through the testimony of* _____ (insert name of witness) *that the statement:*

    (a)   *is of the declarant's then existing:*

        (1)   *state of mind,* or

        (2)   *emotions,* or

        (3)   *sensation,* and

    (b)   (1)   *it does not include a statement of memory or belief offered to prove the fact remembered or believed,* or

        (2)   *it relates to the execution, revocation, identification, or terms of declarant's will.*

Federal Rule 803. Hearsay Exceptions; Availability of Declarant Immaterial

(3) Then existing mental, emotional, or physical condition. A statement of the declarant's then existing state of mind, emotion, sensation, or physical condition (such as intent, plan, motive, design, mental feeling, pain, and bodily health), but not including a statement of memory or belief to prove the fact remembered or believed unless it relates to the execution, revocation, identification, or terms of declarant's will.

Commentary

Statements of then existing mental or emotional condition gain their reliability from the contemporaneity of the statement and the state of mind, sensation, or condition that is described by the declarant. It is critical to note that only statements regarding a *present* (at the time of the making of the statement) mental or emotional condition fit within the exception. A statement regarding a past emotional or mental condition will not be admissible because there is no substantial guarantee of reliability. In addition, statements of the cause of a current mental or emotional condition are not admissible pursuant to this exception at least where the cause is not contemporaneous with the present condition. This hearsay exception is based on the premise that there can be no better evidence of the existing mental or emotional condition of a declarant than the declarant's own statement.

There is a relevance problem that arises in conjunction with the use of this hearsay exception. Under the well-known, pre-federal rules Supreme Court case of *Hillmon v. Mutual Life Insurance Co.,* the statement of the then existing state of mind which involves an intention to do an act is admissible to show that the declarant actually performed the act intended. The theory behind the *Hillmon* case is that one is more likely to perform an act which one has the intention of performing. Furthermore, *Hillmon* permits the further inference that where the declarant's statement of intention includes the declarant's intention to perform an act with another person, the out-of-court statement of intention may be admitted not only to prove that the declarant acted in conformity with the declarant's intention but for the inference that the *other person* did as well. Though Rule 803(3) is clearly designed, according to the Advisory Committee's Note, to leave intact *Hillmon's* holding to the effect that evidence of the declarant's intention may be offered as evidence that the declarant acted in conformity with that intention, the legislative history leaves unanswered the question as to whether or not the statement of the declarant's intent is admissible as evidence of the action of another.

CHAPTER 63

- HEARSAY EXCEPTION -
THEN EXISTING PHYSICAL CONDITION

Definition

A statement of the declarant's then existing physical condition is an out-of-court statement which sets forth such condition. In other words, in order to qualify for this exception to the hearsay rule, a statement must communicate the physical condition.

Forms of Objection and Response

Forms of Objection

> *I object. The statement is hearsay.*

> *I move to strike the answer as hearsay.*

Form of Response

> *This statement is admissible as a statement of a then existing physical condition pursuant to Rule 803(3). I have shown through the testimony of _____* (insert name of witness) *that the statement:*

    (a) *is of the declarant's then existing physical condition,* and

    (b) *does not include a statement of memory or belief to prove the fact remembered or believed.*

Federal Rule 803. Hearsay Exception; Availability of Declarant Immaterial

(3) Then existing mental, emotional, or physical condition. A statement of the declarant's then existing state of mind, emotion, sensation, or physical condition (such as intent, plan, motive, design, mental feeling, pain, and bodily health), but not including a statement of memory or belief to prove the fact remembered or believed unless it relates to the execution, revocation, identification, or terms of declarant's will.

Commentary

A statement of a then existing physical condition gains its reliability from the contemporaneity of the statement and the existence of the physical condition described by the declarant. It is critical to note that only statements regarding present (at the time of the making of the statement) physical conditions come within the exception. A statement regarding a *past* condition will not be admissible because there is no substantial guarantee of reliability. Statements which qualify for admissibility pursuant to Rule 803(3) need not be made to a physician and need not be made for purposes of obtaining medical diagnosis or treatment.

For example, in a personal injury action, statements of pain, made while the pain is experienced by the declarant, are admissible. Such statements are easily impeachable on grounds of interest of the plaintiff. In addition, the court may exclude cumulative statements of present bodily condition pursuant to Rule 403.

CHAPTER 64

- HEARSAY EXCEPTION -
STATEMENTS FOR PURPOSES OF MEDICAL
DIAGNOSIS OR TREATMENT

Definition

A statement for purposes of medical diagnosis or treatment is an out-of-court declaration which describes past or present symptoms, pain, the patient's medical history, or the onset of the medical problem insofar as such cause or source of the medical condition relates to medical diagnosis or treatment and is made for the purpose of obtaining medical assistance.

Forms of Objection and Response

Forms of Objection

➤ *I object. The question calls for a hearsay answer.*

➤ *I move to strike the answer as hearsay.*

Form of Response

➤ *This statement is admissible as a statement for purposes of medical diagnosis or treatment pursuant to Rule 803(4). I have shown through the testimony of _____ (insert name of witness) that the statement:*

    (a) *was made for purposes of medical diagnosis or treatment,* and

    (b) *was made to describe medical history; or to describe past or present symptoms, pain, or sensations; or to describe the inception or general character of the cause or external source thereof,* and

    (c) *was reasonably pertinent to diagnosis or treatment.*

Federal Rule 803. Hearsay Exceptions; Availability of Declarant Immaterial

(4) Statements for purposes of medical diagnosis or treatment. Statements made for purposes of medical diagnosis or treatment and describing medical history, or past or present symptoms, pain, or sensations, or the inception or general character of the cause or external source thereof insofar as reasonably pertinent to diagnosis or treatment.

Commentary

Statements made for purposes of medical diagnosis or treatment gain their reliability from the notion that one who is seeking medical treatment would not likely lie to a doctor or other person who is in the position to render medical assistance or indeed, in the extreme case, save the life of the declarant. This would include, of course, statements to any medical professional.

The former common-law distinction which permitted such statements to be admissible only so long as they were made to a treating as opposed to an examining (i.e., for purposes of litigation) physician has been obliterated by the Rule 803(4). Therefore, a statement made to a doctor who is examining a litigant only for purposes of testimony and trial will be admissible under this exception to the hearsay rule.

In addition, statements made to persons other than those immediately able to render medical assistance will qualify for this hearsay exception if made for purposes of obtaining medical diagnosis or treatment. For example, a statement made by a child to his mother for the purposes of receiving medical assistance can qualify for the Rule 803(4) exception. Note that in this example, the child's statement might also qualify as a hearsay exception under Rule 803(3) if it is a statement of a physical condition.

Finally, statements of causation or the external source of the physical condition mentioned in the out-of-court statement will only be admissible if pertinent to the medical diagnosis or treatment. For example, a patient's statement to a doctor that the patient was hit with a club would be pertinent to diagnosis of treatment while the name of the person who assaulted the patient would not. The key inquiry then, is whether or not the statement is *pathologically germane* to the diagnosis or treatment of a medical patient. Where and how an injury occurs is usually germane to treatment; who caused the injury usually is not.

CHAPTER 65
- HEARSAY EXCEPTION -
RECORDED RECOLLECTION

Definition

Past recollection recorded is an out-of-court statement contained in a memorandum or writing which describes or contains a matter about which the out-of-court declarant once had knowledge, but now, as a witness, lacks sufficient recollection to enable the witness to testify completely about such matter. Such memorandum must have been created or adopted by the declarant-witness at a time when the matter contained in the writing was fresh in the witness' memory and reflected the witness' knowledge accurately.

Forms of Objection and Response

Forms of Objection

➤ *I object. The question calls for a hearsay answer.*

➤ *I move to strike the answer as hearsay.*

Form of Response

➤ *This statement is admissible as a recorded recollection pursuant to Rule 803(5). I have shown through the testimony of _____ (insert name of witness) that it is:*

    (a) *a memorandum or record concerning a matter,*

    (b) *about which a witness once had knowledge,*

    (c) *but now has insufficient recollection to enable the witness to testify fully and accurately,* and

    (d) *shown to have been made or adopted by the witness when the matter was fresh in the witness' memory and to reflect that knowledge correctly.*

Federal Rule 803. Hearsay Exceptions; Availability of Declarant Immaterial

(5) Recorded recollection. A memorandum or record concerning a matter about which a witness once had knowledge but now has insufficient recollection to enable the witness to testify fully and accurately, shown to have been made or adopted by the witness when the matter was fresh in the witness' memory and to reflect that knowledge correctly. If admitted, the memorandum or record may be read into evidence but may not itself be received as an exhibit unless offered by an adverse party.

Commentary

Past recollection recorded must be distinguished from *present recollection refreshed.* Though both require a failure of memory as a predicate, present recollection refreshed presents no hearsay problem at all. Present recollection refreshed refers to a situation where (a) a witness has a failure of memory, (b) the witness is shown some item which serves to refresh the witness' recollection, (c) the item is then taken away from the witness, and (d) the witness testifies from a refreshed recollection. Past recollection recorded also involves a situation where the witness' memory fails. However, instead of the witness testifying from a refreshed recollection, the witness, after the laying of the appropriate foundation pursuant to Rule 803(5), reads from a memorandum which contains facts to which the witness is not able to testify in whole or in part because of lack of recollection at trial.

Though in some common-law jurisdictions counsel must attempt to refresh the witness' recollection prior to offering a memorandum under the hearsay exception for past recollection recorded, this is not a requirement of Rule 803(5). The foundation for past recollection recorded is the following:

(a) the witness must have a failure of recollection while on the witness stand,

(b) the witness must authenticate a memorandum,

(c) the memorandum must contain facts of which the witness testifies he once had personal knowledge,

(d) the memorandum was created or adopted by the witness at a time when the matter was fresh in the witness' memory, and

(e) the memorandum accurately reflects the witness' knowledge.

Note that the witness need not have actually written the document, but rather may read the contents of the document into evidence so long as the memorandum was adopted by the witness. Adoption includes a situation where another person creates the document but the witness compared the contents of the document with the witness' firsthand knowledge of the facts contained in the document when the document was made. Note as well that the creation of the document or memorandum, though not necessarily made contemporaneously with the facts recorded therein, must at least have been made at a time when the facts were *fresh* in the witness' mind. Therefore, a substantial lapse of time between the observations and the recording thereof would tend to argue against admission of the contents of the document under Rule 803(5). Furthermore, the requirement that the memorandum "reflect that knowledge correctly," must permit the witness to testify that although the witness has no recollection or incomplete recollection of the contents of the document at the time of testifying, the witness always or ordinarily took great care in the preparation of such documents (habit or routine practice testimony pursuant to Rule 406) or at least took great care in the preparation of this document in this particular situation.

Note that the memorandum itself cannot be offered into evidence by the proponent of it. The proponent may publish the exhibit by having the contents of the recorded memorandum read into evidence. This rule is designed to encourage witnesses to testify from memory rather than attempting to gain an advantage by the introduction of a writing that may be referred to by the jury during deliberations. Only an adverse party is permitted to actually offer the memorandum as an exhibit.

The impeachment of a witness whose recorded recollection is introduced into evidence is easily accomplished by obtaining agreement from the witness that the witness has no recollection of the events reported and no current knowledge that the recorded recollection is accurate.

CHAPTER 66

- HEARSAY EXCEPTION -
RECORDS OF REGULARLY CONDUCTED ACTIVITY
(BUSINESS RECORDS)

Definition

A record of regularly conducted activity, known in the common law as a *business record*, is a writing or data compilation which records activities or happenings, including opinions, which are made in the ordinary course of a regularly conducted activity, kept in the course of such activity, and created by or from a person with personal knowledge of the contents of the record, at or near the time of the event recorded.

Forms of Objection and Response

Forms of Objections

> ➤ *I object. The question calls for a hearsay answer.*

> ➤ *I move to strike the answer as hearsay.*

Form of Response

> ➤ *This statement is admissible as a business record pursuant to Rule 803(6). I have shown through the testimony of _____ (insert name of witness) who is a custodian of the record or person who has knowledge of the record keeping system, that the statement is contained in a:*

(a) (for a man-made record)

    (1) *memorandum, report, record, or data compilation,*

    (2) *recording acts, events, conditions, opinions, or diagnoses,*

    (3) *made at or near the time the acts or events took place,*

    (4) *by or from information transmitted by one with personal knowledge of the event or act,*

    (5) *where such record is kept in the course of a regularly conducted business activity,* and

    (6) *it was the regular practice of the business to make such record.*

(b) (for a computer-generated record, repeat foundation steps (a)(1) to (6) above, and add:)

    (7) *the computer and the program used are generally accepted in the field,*

    (8) *the computer was in good working order at the relevant times,* and

    (9) *the computer operator possessed the knowledge and training to correctly operate the computer.*

Federal Rule 803. Hearsay Exceptions; Availability of Declarant Immaterial

(6) Records of regularly conducted activity. A memorandum report, record, or data compilation, in any form, of acts, events, conditions, opinions, or diagnoses, made at or near the time by, or from information transmitted by, a person with knowledge, if kept in the course of regularly conducted business activity, and if it was the regular practice of that business activity to make the memorandum, report, record, or data compilation, all as shown by the testimony of the custodian or other qualified witness, unless the source of information or the method or circumstances of preparation indicate lack of trustworthiness. The term "business" as used in this paragraph includes business, institution, association, profession, occupation, and calling of every kind, whether or not conducted for profit.

Commentary

The business records exception codified in Rule 803(6) is one of the most important and most utilized exceptions to the hearsay rule. A record of regularly conducted activity gains its reliability from the regularity of the record keeping operation and function which is ordinary and necessary for the transaction of regularly conducted activity. The exception is premised on the notion that if the record is good enough to do business on, then it ought to be reliable enough for admissibility in court where issues regarding the business are litigated.

The rule applies to the records of any business, institution, association, profession, or occupation. It is irrelevant whether the entity in question has a profit motive for its existence. The rule includes within its purview opinions and diagnoses that might have run afoul of the common-law operation of the rule.

The most litigated issues regarding Rule 803(6) concern: (a) the regularity of both the activity recorded and the making of records concerning the activity; (b) the source of the information contained in the record; (c) the timing of the making of the record; and (d) as an overriding concern, the reliability and trustworthiness of the record in question. Each of these issues focuses on the need to show the reliability of the document offered as a business record.

The regularity of both the activity recorded and the making of records concerning the activity

For the record to meet the requirements of Rule 803(6), the proponent of the evidence must show that the activity is one that is normally conducted by the entity that makes the record and that the making of the record was germane to the *business* of that entity. For example, a hospital record history is, of course, germane to the business of the hospital, i.e., to treat patients. That history may, however, include a statement by the patient as to how the patient was injured. Only those statements that are germane to diagnosis and treatment are properly included in the record. Thus, a statement that the patient was injured when a car ran into him is within the rule. A statement that the car was driven by a particular person and that the car ran a red light is not and would have to be redacted from the record. It is of no matter that the hospital records include in the recorded medical history the names of other parties involved and what the parties were doing at the time of the incident. Because this information does not aid diagnosis or treatment, which is the business of a hospital, it does not meet the requirement of Rule 803(6).

The source of the information contained in the record

In order to ensure the reliability of Rule 803(6) records, the rule also incorporates the so-called "business duty to report" rule. For a record to meet Rule 803(6) requirements, the person who supplies the information contained in the record must have a business duty to the entity that keeps the record to provide such information. For example, a statement by a bank teller regarding the amount of money stolen during a bank robbery which is recorded in a police report would not qualify pursuant to Rule 803(6). There is no business duty on the part of the teller to report the lost amount to the police. If, however, the teller provides the same information to the bank which records the amount stolen in its ledger, that information contained on the bank's ledger would qualify pursuant to Rule 803(6) as the teller does have a business duty to report such information to the bank. In short, the business duty must be imposed on the employee or agent by the organization which maintains the record.

The source of information is also in issue where a record contains a statement of either diagnosis or opinion. For example, a statement of diagnosis or opinion in a hospital record must be made by a person qualified to render such a diagnosis or opinion. Most courts do not require any particular statement of qualifications, such as would be required for expert testimony, as long as it appears from the record that the diagnosis or opinion was made by a person who is likely to be qualified to render such a diagnosis or opinion (e.g., a medical doctor).

The timing of the making of the record

Again, to ensure reliability, Rule 803(6) requires that the record be made at or near the time of the business event that it reflects. For example, consider the situation where a nurse is required by a hospital to record the medication dispensed to patients. If an emergency occurs during a nurse's shift, the nurse fails to record medication given to a patient on a particular day, leaves the hospital for a weekend off, returns, notices the omission in the patient's records, and fills in the patient's chart as to dispensing medication, this record may not have been made sufficiently contemporaneously with the event in question to qualify pursuant to Rule 803(6).

The reliability and trustworthiness of the record in question

Rule 803(6) contains a saving clause which requires exclusion of the record from evidence if "the source of information or the method or circumstance of preparation indicate lack of trustworthiness." It is pursuant to this clause that *business records* made solely for litigation purposes are generally excluded from evidence. Otherwise, cases could be litigated solely on the basis of a business record of an investigation of an incident that was conducted by one of the parties which in all likelihood would contain self-serving statements. The *saving clause* of Rule 803(6) is a reflection of the rule of the Supreme Court case of *Palmer v. Hoffman,* which excluded exculpatory statements made by a train engineer during an investigation by the railroad into a train collision that was the subject of the litigation. The Supreme Court held that the business of the railroad was operating a railroad and not litigation, and therefore, there was a lack of reliability on the part of the record. With the advent of federal regulations requiring investigation of all accidents by common carriers, *Palmer v. Hoffman* has been limited narrowly to its facts. Most courts allow the admissibility of such records together with impeachment of the records on grounds of interest.

CHAPTER 67
- HEARSAY EXCEPTION -
ABSENCE OF ENTRY IN BUSINESS RECORDS

Definition

If a proponent is able to lay a foundation for a record of regularly conducted activity under Rule 803(6), testimony or the offer of the record for the purpose of demonstrating that a particular entry does not appear in the record is permitted. The lack of entry is admissible to show that an event, which had it occurred would have been recorded, did not, in fact, take place.

Forms of Objection and Response

Forms of Objection

➤ *I object. The question calls for hearsay.*

➤ *I move to strike the answer as hearsay.*

Form of Response

➤ *The absence of an entry in this record is admissible to show the nonoccurrence of an event pursuant to Rule 803(7). I have shown through the testimony of* _____ (insert name of witness) *who is the custodian of the business records, other qualified person that:*

    (a) *a business record exists, pursuant to Rule 803(6),* and

    (b) *the matter which is not recorded in the record is of a kind for which a record would regularly be made and preserved,* and

    (c) *the source of information or other circumstances fail to indicate a lack of trustworthiness.*

Federal Rule 803. Hearsay Exceptions; Availability of Declarant Immaterial

(7) Absence of entry in records kept in accordance with the provisions of paragraph (6). Evidence that a matter is not included in the memoranda, reports, records, or data compilations, in any form, kept in accordance with provisions of paragraph (6), to prove the nonoccurrence or nonexistence of the matter, if the matter was of a kind of which a memorandum, report, record, or data compilation was regularly made and preserved, unless the sources of information or other circumstances indicate lack of trustworthiness.

Commentary

The absence of any entry concerning an event which would ordinarily be recorded in a business record may be offered to show that such event never occurred. The reliability of the absence of such entry lies in the regularity of the keeping of records of events that do occur for the purposes of the careful and conscientious running of a business operation.

Such evidence is normally coupled with direct testimony from a witness with knowledge of the nonoccurrence of the event, but is independently sufficient evidence to support a verdict on the issue of the nonoccurrence of the event.

The foundation for the business record is a predicate showing, which is required before the absence of an entry in such a record may be established for its relevant purpose.

CHAPTER 68

- HEARSAY EXCEPTION -
PUBLIC RECORDS AND REPORTS

Definition

A public record or report is a record prepared by a public officer or agency which does one of the following:

a) sets forth the activities of the office or agency, or

b) describes facts, events, or occurrences observed by a public official or officer in accordance with a duty imposed on that person by law and which it is such person's duty to report.

It is admissible unless the source of information or other circumstances indicate a lack of trustworthiness in the making or keeping of such records or reports.

Forms of Objection and Response

Forms of Objections

> ➤ *I object. The question calls for a hearsay answer.*

> ➤ *I move to strike the answer as hearsay.*

> ➤ (In a criminal case) *I object. The report is not admissible against a criminal defendant.*

Form of Response

> ➤ *The out-of-court statement is admissible under the hearsay exception (Rule 803(8)) for public records and reports. I have shown through the testimony of* _____ (insert name of witness) *that:*

> (a) *the document is a record, report, statement, or data compilation,*

> (b) *of a public office or agency setting forth*

> (1) *the activities of the office or agency, or*

> (2) *matters observed pursuant to duty imposed by law as to which matters there was a duty to report.*

Federal Rule 803. Hearsay Exceptions; Availability of Declarant Immaterial

(8) Public records and reports. Records, reports, statements, or data compilations, in any form, of public offices or agencies, setting forth (A) the activities of the office or agency, or (B) matters observed pursuant to duty imposed by law as to which matters there was a duty to report, excluding, however, in criminal cases matters observed by police officers and other law enforcement personnel, or (C) in civil actions and proceedings and against the Government in criminal cases, factual findings resulting from an investigation made pursuant to authority granted by law, unless the sources of information or other circumstances indicate lack of trustworthiness.

Commentary

Public records or reports gain their reliability from the public duty or the duty imposed by law which accompanies the maker's obligation to observe and record the kinds of events contained in such public records or reports. In addition, the maker of the record or report will have no interest in reporting or recording information favoring one side over another. Note that there are three types of matters which are admissible under the public records exception:

(a) records or reports that disclose the activities of the public agency,

(b) observations made pursuant to legal duty and which the public official has a legal requirement to record,

(c) factual findings (and conclusions and opinions derived therefrom) which are derived from an investigation made pursuant to law. *Beech Aircraft v. Rainey,* 109 S.Ct. 439 (1988).

Note that the rule strictly forbids the use of public records or reports against criminal defendants where such reports are made by law enforcement officers, while permitting the use of public records and reports including the results of official investigations to be used in any civil action or to be offered against the government in a criminal case.

As with the business records exception (Rule 803(6)), the entrant must have personal knowledge of the matters contained in the report or must obtain such information from one with personal knowledge assuming that the person who furnishes such information to the official entrant is under a business duty to do so. Furthermore, as with Rule 803(6), there is a trustworthiness proviso which provides an additional check on admissibility pursuant to rule 803(8). In determining whether the circumstances surrounding the creation of the report or record indicate trustworthiness, the Advisory Committee notes list the following factors as appropriate for consideration:

(1) the timeliness of the investigation,

(2) the special skill or experience of the official performing the investigation,

(3) whether a hearing was held, and the agency level at which it was held, and

(4) any possible bias on the part of the investigator or preparer with a view toward possible litigation.

There is, of course, overlap between the public records and reports exception and the business records exception, and there are many records which would qualify as both. In order to avoid the government's use of the business records exception to offer the results of a police investigation against a criminal defendant under the business records exception, courts have held that the business records exception is as unavailable as is the public records exception for the purpose of offering police reports against criminal defendants. Others have ruled that evidence which does not qualify for admission against a criminal defendant under Rule 803(8) may be admissible under Rule 803(6), the exception for Records of Regularly Conducted Activity. Admission of hearsay against a criminal defendant must, of course, not run afoul of the Confrontation Clause of the Sixth Amendment to the United States Constitution.

CHAPTER 69
- HEARSAY EXCEPTION -
ABSENCE OF PUBLIC RECORD OR ENTRY

Definition

An out-of-court certification which describes a diligent, but unavailing search for a particular record in the records of a public office or agency is admissible as an exception to the hearsay rule as an extension of the theory which would admit official documents or public records or records of vital statistics under Rules 803(8) and 803(9). The relevance of such evidence is that where one would expect to find a public record or entry therein, the absence of such entry tends to show that the purported event which is absent from the record never took place. Testimony of such a search is equally admissible against a hearsay objection.

Forms of Objection and Response

Forms of Objection

> *I object. The question calls for a hearsay answer.*

> *I move to strike the answer as hearsay.*

Forms of Response

> *Evidence of a diligent but unavailing search of the records of the public agency or office is admissible pursuant to the hearsay exception contained in Rule 803(10). I have shown through a certification which complies with Rule 902 or through the testimony of_____* (insert name of witness) *that:*

>> (a) *a public agency or office regularly makes and preserves records of a particular kind of matter,* and

>> (b) *a diligent, but unavailing search of such records failed to disclose a record, report, statement, data compilation or entry regarding a particular alleged happening of such a matter.*

Federal Rule 803. Hearsay Exceptions; Availability of Declarant Immaterial

(10) Absence of public record or entry. To prove the absence of a record, report, statement, or data compilation, in any form, or the nonoccurrence or nonexistence of a matter of which a record, report, statement, or data compilation, in any form, was regularly made and preserved by a public office or agency, evidence in the form of a certification in accordance with rule 902, or testimony, that diligent search failed to disclose the record, report, statement, or data compilation, or entry.

Commentary

As with Rule 803(7), this rule provides a hearsay exception for evidence of the absence of a record or record entry. The proof which the rule contemplates is evidence of a diligent but unavailing search of the records or record keeping system of a public office or agency which regularly maintains such records.

The rule provides two acceptable methods to prove the unavailing search. The proponent may offer testimony from one with personal knowledge which describes the unavailing search. Alternatively, the proponent may offer a certification which complies with the self-authentication provisions of Rule 902 and which states that a diligent search of the records of the public office or agency failed to disclose the record or entry sought.

The reliability factor in this hearsay exception is found in the regularity of the maintenance of the records of the public agency or office. If it is the official practice to keep records of the happening of particular events in such an office, then the absence of a record or entry would be relevant to show the nonoccurrence of an event which is not recorded or entered. Therefore, evidence of the regularity and official nature of the record keeping of the agency or office should be offered as a matter of foundation under Rule 803(10).

It is unclear whether or not testimony regarding a diligent but unavailing search would even be considered hearsay because the search and its lack of success, reported in court, would not seem to amount to an out-of-court statement by a person. However, to the extent such testimony could arguably be considered hearsay, Rule 803(10) provides an exception.

CHAPTER 70
- HEARSAY EXCEPTION -
RECORDS OF VITAL STATISTICS

Definition

Records of a vital statistic are out-of-court statements in the form of records which are reported to a public office or official who is required by law to create and maintain a record of such report.

Forms of Objection and Response

Form of Objection

> ➤ *I object. The record is an out-of-court statement offered for its truth and is hearsay.*

Form of Response

> ➤ *The out-of-court statement is admissible pursuant to Rule 803(9) for records of a vital statistic in that it:*

>   (a) *is a record regarding a vital statistic*

>   (b) *which records a report made to a public official required by law to keep such a record.*

Federal Rule 803. Hearsay Exceptions; Availability of Declarant Immaterial

(9) Records of vital statistics. Records or data compilations, in any form, of births, fetal deaths, deaths, or marriages, if the report thereof was made to a public office pursuant to requirements of law.

Commentary

Records of vital statistics gain their reliability from the circumstances of their making. Ordinarily, the information contained in such records is provided by doctors or other persons who have no interest in the outcome of any future litigation. Furthermore, they are recorded by public officials who have an official duty to receive, record, and maintain such records.

As with all other out-of-court writings which are offered pursuant to a hearsay exception, records of vital statistics must be authenticated either through the testimony of the public officer who creates and maintains the records or, more easily, by the proffer of a certified copy of the public record pursuant to Rule 902(4).

CHAPTER 71
- HEARSAY EXCEPTION -
RECORDS OF RELIGIOUS ORGANIZATIONS

Definition

This rule creates a hearsay exception for records of personal and family history so long as such records are maintained in a regularly kept record of some religious organization.

Forms of Objection and Response

Form of Objection

➤ *I object. The record is an out-of-court statement offered for its truth and is hearsay.*

Form of Response

➤ *This statement is admissible as a record of a religious organization pursuant to Rule 803(11). I have shown through the testimony of* _____ (insert name of witness) *that the statement:*

(a) *is one of personal or family history,* and

(b) *is contained in a regularly kept record of a religious organization.*

Federal Rule 803. Hearsay Exceptions; Availability of Declarant Immaterial

(11) Records of religious organizations. Statements of births, marriages, divorces, deaths, legitimacy, ancestry, relationship by blood or marriage, or other similar facts of personal or family history, contained in a regularly kept record of a religious organization.

Commentary

This exception for regularly kept records of personal or family history gains its reliability from the fact that such events are ordinarily contemporaneously recorded by a religious functionary or clergyman with no motive to falsify in a record on which persons ordinarily rely.

Though bearing some superficial similarity to business records under Rule 803(6), note there is no requirement that: (a) the entry be contemporaneous to the event recorded, or (b) the entrant have personal knowledge or a source with personal knowledge.

CHAPTER 72

- HEARSAY EXCEPTION -
MARRIAGE, BAPTISMAL, AND SIMILAR CERTIFICATES

Definition

A statement of fact which appears in a certificate which memorializes some religious act is admissible for its truth where the certificate is completed by a person authorized to perform such acts and where the statement is entered at or near the time of the act.

Forms of Objection and Response

Form of Objection

> *I object. The document is an out-of-court statement offered for its truth and is hearsay.*

Form of Response

> *This statement is admissible as a marriage, baptismal, or similar certificate pursuant to Rule 803(12). I have shown through the testimony of _____ (insert name of witness) that this is a statement of fact:*

>> (a) *contained in a certificate that shows that the maker performed a marriage or other similar ceremony,*

>> (b) *made by a clergyman, public official, or other person authorized by law or the practices of a religious organization to perform the act certified, and*

>> (c) *which purports to be issued at the time of the act or within a reasonable time thereafter.*

Federal Rule 803. Hearsay Exceptions; Availability of Declarant Immaterial

(12) Marriage, baptismal, and similar certificates. Statements of fact contained in a certificate that the maker performed a marriage or other ceremony or administered a sacrament, made by a clergyman, public official, or other person authorized by the rules or practices of a religious organization or by law to perform the act certified, and purporting to have been issued at the time of the act or within a reasonable time thereafter.

Commentary

This hearsay exception admits the facts relating to religious ceremonies, like marriages or baptisms, so long as the entrant is authorized by law or religious practice to perform such ceremony and records the facts contained in the certificate essentially contemporaneously with the occurrence of the ceremony.

The reliability factor here derives from the solemnity of the occasion, the entrant's legal authorization, and the contemporaneity of the entry with the fact or ceremony entered.

Examples of facts which could be proved by the use of Rule 803(12) would be paternity (in a baptismal certificate) and marriage (in a marriage certificate).

CHAPTER 73
- HEARSAY EXCEPTION -
FAMILY RECORDS

Definition
This rule creates a hearsay exception for facts relating to family or personal history which are found in a variety of writings ranging from Bibles to tombstones.

Forms of Objection and Response
Forms of Objection

> ➤ *I object. The question calls for a hearsay answer.*

> ➤ *I move to strike the answer as hearsay.*

Form of Response

> ➤ *This statement is admissible as a family record pursuant to Rule 803(13). I have shown through the testimony of _____* (insert name of witness) *that this is a statement of fact:*

> (a) *concerning personal or family history,*

> (b) *contained in family Bibles, genealogies, or the like.*

Federal Rule 803. Hearsay Exceptions; Availability of Declarant Immaterial

(13) Family records. Statements of fact concerning personal or family history contained in family Bibles, genealogies, charts, engravings on rings, inscriptions on family portraits, engravings on urns, crypts, or tombstones, or the like.

Commentary
This rule gains its reliability from the simple fact that an entry in such a document or item would not be erroneously made without family or personal protest.

Note the absence of a requirement of contemporaneity of entry. Such writing must, however, like any other, be authenticated. Because the writing or entry is only reliable if generally accepted by the family or person to whom it refers, the proponent's offer of evidence of family acceptance or lack of protest regarding the writing or inscription would support admissibility.

CHAPTER 74
- HEARSAY EXCEPTION -
RECORDS OF DOCUMENTS AFFECTING
AN INTEREST IN PROPERTY

Definition

A record of a document affecting an interest in property is an out-of-court writing which either relates to or establishes an interest in property. Such a record can be offered for the truth of the contents of the original recorded document as well as for the fact of its having been executed and delivered by the parties to the appropriate public office, so long as the record is of a type which is maintained in a public office as authorized by statute which requires the recording of documents of that type.

Forms of Objection and Response

Form of Objection

> ➤ *I object. The document is an out-of-court statement offered for its truth and is therefore hearsay.*

Form of Response

> ➤ *This statement is admissible as a record of a document affecting an interest in property pursuant to Rule 803(14). I have shown through the testimony of _____* (insert name of witness) *that:*
>> (a) *this is a record of a public office,* and
>> (b) *an applicable statute authorizes the recording of documents of that kind in that office.*

Federal Rule 803. Hearsay Exceptions; Availability of Declarant Immaterial

(14) Records of documents affecting an interest in property. The record of a document purporting to establish or affect an interest in property, as proof of the content of the original recorded document in its execution and delivery by each person by whom it purports to have been executed, if the record is a record of a public office and an applicable statute authorizes the recording of documents of that kind in that office.

Commentary

The record of a document of the type described in this rule is admissible for its truth in regard to the contents of the original recorded document, as well as for the fact of its execution by the parties to the document. The reliability factor which supports admissibility here is the fact that the record is of a type kept by a public office, like a registry of deeds, pursuant to recording statutes. Note that this exception is distinguishable from Rule 803(8), the public records exception, in that Rule 803(8) addresses entries in all sorts of public records which record activities of the public office or observations made and recorded pursuant to public duty.

Of course, the proponent could always simply offer the original document, for example, a deed, and then offer testimony that such document was in fact recorded as well as executed by both parties.

CHAPTER 75

- HEARSAY EXCEPTION -
STATEMENTS IN DOCUMENTS AFFECTING
AN INTEREST IN PROPERTY

Definition

A statement in a document affecting an interest in property is admissible against a hearsay objection so long as the matter contained in the document which the proponent offers was indeed relevant to the purpose of the creation of the document.

Forms of Objection and Response

Forms of Objection

> ➤ *I object. The question calls for a hearsay answer.*

> ➤ *I move to strike the answer as hearsay.*

Form of Response

> ➤ *This statement is admissible pursuant to Rule 803(15) as a statement in a document affecting an interest in property. I have shown through the testimony of_____ (insert name of witness) that:*

>> (a) *the statement is contained in a document purporting to establish or affect an interest in property,*

>> (b) *the matter stated was relevant to the purpose of the document,* and

>> (c) *dealings with the property since the document was made have not been inconsistent with the truth of the statement or the purpose of the document.*

Federal Rule 803. Hearsay Exceptions; Availability of Declarant Immaterial

(15) Statements in documents affecting an interest in property. A statement contained in a document purporting to establish or affect an interest in property if the matter stated was relevant to the purpose of the document, unless dealings with the property since the document was made have been inconsistent with the truth of the statement or the purport of the document.

Commentary

While Rule 803(14) is limited to the proof of the content of the officially recorded document, Rule 803(15) is a broader rule permitting the admission of out-of-court statements contained in a document, whether or not recorded, which creates, relates to, or affects an interest in property. Note there are two further requirements which are qualifications for admissibility. First, the factual statement contained in the document must relate or be relevant to the purpose of the document, and second, the document would only be admissible so long as dealings with the property after the time that the document was created have not been inconsistent with the truth of the statement or the purport of the document which was offered.

CHAPTER 76
- HEARSAY EXCEPTION -
STATEMENTS IN ANCIENT DOCUMENTS

Definition

A statement contained in a writing which was created at least twenty years prior to the date of its offer is admissible as against a hearsay objection where the authenticity of the document has been established.

Forms of Objection and Response

Form of Objection

> ➤ *I object. This statement is contained in an out-of-court writing offered for its truth, which is hearsay.*

Form of Response

> ➤ *This statement is admissible as a statement contained in an ancient document pursuant to Rule 803(16). I have shown through the testimony of* _____ (insert name of witness) *that the statement is contained in:*
>
> (a) *a document in existence twenty years or more,*
>
> (b) *the authenticity of which is established.*

Federal Rule 803. Hearsay Exceptions; Availability of Declarant Immaterial

(16) Statements in ancient documents. Statements in a document in existence twenty years or more the authenticity of which is established.

Commentary

Statements contained in ancient documents are admissible as against the hearsay objection and gain their reliability from the notion that a document created twenty or more years prior to its being offered during litigation is unlikely to be created at a time when there was any motive to falsify such document, at least for purposes of the current litigation. Rule 803(16) is unusual in that it states in its terms a requirement of authenticity. Thus, there is a direct tie-in between Rule 803(16) and the authentication argument of Rule 901(b)(8), which provides a foundation for demonstrating the authenticity of an ancient document. That foundation requires the following showing:

(a) the condition of the document creates no suspicion regarding its authenticity,

(b) the document has been kept in a place where it likely would be kept if it were authentic, and

(c) it has indeed been in existence for at least twenty years at the time of its proffer at trial.

Obviously, there are many situations when the creator of the document is not available to testify as to the authenticity of its contents based on personal knowledge of the document's creation. Thus, the authentication provided by Rule 901(b)(8) is an appropriate substitute for authentication by one with personal knowledge.

CHAPTER 77
- HEARSAY EXCEPTION -
MARKET REPORTS AND COMMERCIAL PUBLICATIONS

Definition

Market reports or commercial publications are out-of-court statements which compile facts or data which are used either by the general public or by persons in particular professions or occupations, and are relied on for the purposes of carrying out their daily business.

Forms of Objection and Response

Form of Objection

> *I object. The document is an out-of-court statement and therefore hearsay.*

Form of Response

> *This statement is admissible as a market report or commercial publication pursuant to Rule 803(17). I have shown that the document is:*
>
> (a) *a market quotation, tabulation, list, directory, or other published compilation,*
>
> (b) *which is generally used and relied upon by the public or persons in particular occupations.*

Federal Rule 803. Hearsay Exceptions; Availability of Declarant Immaterial

(17) Market reports, commercial publications. Market quotations, tabulations, lists, directories, or other published compilations generally used or relied upon by the public or by persons in particular occupations.

Commentary

Market reports or quotations and commercial publications including commercial newspapers, actuarial papers, and the like are admissible against a hearsay objection, gaining their reliability from the general reliance placed upon them by the entities that utilize them. As a result, the person or entity that creates such documents for use in a business or profession, in order to be successful, must be reliable and therefore accurate. In addition, any inaccuracies are likely to be corrected.

Note that the exception does not merely permit the admission of documents containing factual matters, but seems to also permit the admission of interpretive or evaluative reports if they are documents upon which entities in a particular setting rely.

CHAPTER 78
- HEARSAY EXCEPTION -
LEARNED TREATISES

Definition

A learned treatise is a book or article established as a reliable authority on a matter, ordinarily the subject of expert opinion, which is called to the attention of an expert witness upon cross examination or which is relied upon by the expert in direct examination.

Forms of Objection and Response

Forms of Objection

> ➤ *I object. The question calls for a hearsay answer.*

> ➤ *I move to strike answer as hearsay.*

Form of Response

> ➤ *This statement is admissible as a statement contained in a learned treatise pursuant to Rule 803(18). I have shown through the testimony of _____ (insert name of witness) that:*

> (a) (on direct examination) *the expert witness has relied on the statement,* or

> (b) (on cross examination)

> (1) *I have called the statement to the attention of the expert,* and

> (2) *the statement is contained in a published treatise, periodical, or pamphlet on a subject of history, medicine, or other science or art,*

> (3) *which has been established as a reliable authority by the testimony or admission of the expert witness or by other expert testimony, or by judicial notice.*

Federal Rule 803. Hearsay Exceptions; Availability of Declarant Immaterial

(18) Learned treatises. To the extent called to the attention of an expert witness upon cross-examination or relied upon by the expert witness in direct examination, statements contained in published treatises, periodicals, or pamphlets on a subject of history, medicine, or other science or art, established as a reliable authority by the testimony or admission of the witness or by other expert testimony or by judicial notice. If admitted, the statements may be read into evidence but may not be received as exhibits.

Commentary

The learned treatise exception to the hearsay rule allows admissibility of passages, excerpts, or on occasion, the entire contents of a book, article, or other writing on a subject ordinarily the subject of expert testimony. The learned treatise, or parts thereof, are only to be admitted where used to cross examine an expert witness or where an expert witness has relied on a learned treatise in his direct examination.

A foundation for the learned treatise may be laid through the expert who is on the stand, some other expert, or the taking of judicial notice by the trial judge of the learned nature of the writing. Note as well, that whether or not a learned treatise or a passage therefrom is offered either during direct or cross, it may be admitted for its substantive truth. Finally, note in order that the jury not be misled in giving the treatise undue weight in its deliberations, the passage or entire learned treatise to the extent it is admissible, may only be read to the jury, rather than its being taken into the jury room where it might be given undue weight by the fact-finder.

Note that Rule 803(18) ties in clearly with the impeachment of an expert. The ordinary way in which to use a learned treatise on impeachment is to lead the adverse expert into admitting that a particular treatise or article is in fact authoritative and then calling to the witness' attention some inconsistency between the expert's testimony and the contents of the *authoritative* treatise. This is not the use of a prior inconsistent statement to impeach, unless the treatise was in fact written by the expert witness. Rather this impeachment mode serves to impeach the expertise of the expert witness on the theory that his views are at variance with an authoritative text.

The foundation for the admissibility of Rule 803(18) writings will typically include a statement of qualifications of the author and reliance on the treatise by experts in the field so that the jury can properly evaluate the weight of the evidence. Care must always be taken to ensure that the treatise does not contain conflicting matter on the same matter for which it is offered to avoid damaging cross examination or admission under the rule of completeness in Rule 106. The proponent should also examine later writings of the author to see if the author's opinion or findings have changed over time.

CHAPTER 79
- HEARSAY EXCEPTION -
REPUTATION CONCERNING PERSONAL OR
FAMILY HISTORY

Definition

A statement of reputation is a collection of hearsay. Reputation concerning personal or family history involves a collection of hearsay concerning personal or family history within a particular group of associates or community regarding such matters as marriages, births, deaths, or other like events of family significance.

Forms of Objection and Response

Forms of Objection

> ➤ *I object. The question calls for a hearsay answer.*

> ➤ *I move to strike the answer as hearsay.*

Form of Response

> ➤ *This statement is admissible as a statement of reputation concerning personal or family history pursuant to Rule 803(19). I have shown through the testimony of* _____ (insert name of witness) *that this is a statement of reputation:*
>
> > (a) *among members of one's family,* or
> >
> > (b) *among one's associates,* or
> >
> > (c) *in the community,*
> >
> > (d) *concerning a person's adoption, birth, marriage, divorce, death, legitimacy, relationship by blood adoption or marriage, ancestry, or other similar fact of personal or family history.*

Federal Rule 803. Hearsay Exceptions; Availability of Declarant Immaterial

(19) Reputation concerning personal or family history. Reputation among members of a person's family by blood, adoption, or marriage, or among a person's associates, or in the community concerning a person's birth, adoption, marriage, divorce, death, legitimacy, relationship by blood, adoption, or marriage, ancestry, or other similar fact of personal or family history.

Commentary

Reputation concerning personal or family history is admissible against the hearsay objection so long as it is generally accepted among the family, associates, or community where the reputation is known. The witness who testifies concerning the reputation clearly must be familiar with that reputation which is shown by (a) his being a member of the family, community, or group of associates which is relevant, and (b) the witness' familiarity with the reputation, having either heard it discussed or taken part in such discussions.

CHAPTER 80
- HEARSAY EXCEPTION -
REPUTATION CONCERNING BOUNDARIES
OR GENERAL HISTORY

Definition

Reputation concerning boundaries or general history involves a collection of hearsay drawn from a community regarding events of general import or of general knowledge in that community, as well as boundaries or customs regarding land located in that community.

Forms of Objection and Response

Forms of Objection

> *I object. The question calls for a hearsay answer.*

> *I move to strike the answer as hearsay.*

Form of Response

> *This statement is admissible as a statement of reputation concerning boundaries or general history pursuant to Rule 803(20). I have shown through the testimony of* _____ (insert name of witness) *that this is a statement of reputation:*

   (a) *in a community,*

   (b) *arising before the controversy,*

   (c) *as to boundaries of, or customs affecting, lands in the community,* or

   (d) *as to events of general history important to the community or state or nation in which located.*

Federal Rule 803. Hearsay Exceptions; Availability of Declarant Immaterial

(20) Reputation concerning boundaries or general history. Reputation in a community, arising before the controversy, as to boundaries of or customs affecting lands in the community, and reputation as to events of general history important to the community or State or nation in which located.

Commentary

Reputation concerning boundaries or general history, though a collection of hearsay statements, is admissible under this exception so long as the reputation had arisen prior to the controversy involved in the trial, and the witness is familiar with the reputation by having heard it discussed in the relevant community.

CHAPTER 81

- HEARSAY EXCEPTION -
REPUTATION AS TO CHARACTER

Definition

Reputation of a person's character which is found among his associates in some community is admissible as a hearsay exception, subject, of course, to the relevance requirements of Rules 404, 405, and 608.

Forms of Objection and Response

Forms of Objection

> ➤ *I object. The question calls for a hearsay answer.*

> ➤ *I move to strike the answer as hearsay.*

Form of Response

> ➤ *This statement is admissible as reputation as to character pursuant to Rule 803(21). I have shown through the testimony of* _____ (insert name of witness) *that this is a statement of:*
>
>   (a) *reputation of a person's character*
>
>   (b) *among associates or in the community.*

Federal Rule 803. Hearsay Exceptions; Availability of Declarant Immaterial

(21) Reputation as to character. Reputation of a person's character among associates or in the community.

Commentary

Reputation is a collection of hearsay. It must be reported by a witness on the stand who has had occasion to overhear discussion of the person's character either among such person's associates or in the community. Reputation is distinguished from opinion on the question of character since opinion raises no hearsay problems but merely refers to a notion formed by the witness from personal experience.

It is, of course, critical to note that reputation as to character, although not hearsay, is admissible only in a limited number of circumstances discussed in Rules 405(a) and 608(a), 404(a)(1), and 404(a)(2). The hearsay exception for character is really an exception that simply enables a witness to testify as to reputation where other rules establish the admissibility, on relevance grounds, of reputation testimony.

CHAPTER 82
- HEARSAY EXCEPTION -
JUDGMENT OF PREVIOUS CONVICTION

Definition

A prior conviction for a crime which carries a sentence of at least one year in prison or death is admissible as against a hearsay objection where it is offered against the person convicted in a later case for the proof of any fact which was *essential* to sustain the judgment of conviction.

Forms of Objection and Response

Forms of Objection

> ➤ *I object. The question calls for a hearsay answer.*

> ➤ *I move to strike the answer as hearsay.*

Form of Response

> ➤ *This statement is admissible as a judgment of previous conviction pursuant to Rule 803(22). I have shown through a certified record or the testimony of* _____ (insert name of witness) *that this statement is evidence of:*
>
> (a) *a final judgment,*
>
> (b) *entered after a trial or upon a plea of guilty,*
>
> (c) *adjudging a person guilty of a crime punishable by either death or imprisonment for more than one year,*
>
> (d) *which is offered to prove any fact essential to sustain the judgment,*
>
> (e) (in a criminal prosecution) *which is not the conviction of someone other than the accused.*

Federal Rule 803. Hearsay Exceptions; Availability of Declarant Immaterial

(22) Judgment of previous conviction. Evidence of a final judgment, entered after a trial or upon a plea of guilty (but not upon a plea of nolo contendere), adjudging a person guilty of a crime punishable by death or imprisonment in excess of one year, to prove any fact essential to sustain the judgment, but not including, when offered by the Government in a criminal prosecution for purposes other than impeachment, judgments against persons other than the accused. The pendency of an appeal may be shown but does not affect admissibility.

Commentary

The exception provides for the admission of prior felony convictions for the truth of facts essential to the judgment of conviction. Such conviction is admissible for its truth in a second case only against the person convicted in a first case.

This hearsay exception actually provides the means to give collateral estoppel effect in a later action to facts found or admitted by guilty pleas in an earlier criminal case. The term "essential" under the rules of collateral estoppel refers to facts which support the judgment of conviction, are consistent with it, and which were tried and necessarily found by the jury or necessarily admitted by the plea of guilty.

Although Rule 803(22) permits the offer of the prior conviction in a civil or criminal case, note that Rule 803(22) precludes the government's use of a prior judgment of conviction of a third person against a criminal defendant for the purpose of proving facts essential to the conviction of a third person against a criminal defendant in a later action.

Of course, a prior conviction can always be offered, where appropriate, for the non-hearsay purpose of impeachment.

Finally, where a judgment of prior conviction is offered, the person against whom it is offered will, within the limits of Rule 403, be permitted to explain the circumstances of the conviction or attempt to rebut the *essential* facts offered against him.

The decision as to whether or not to admit the prior conviction rests with the trial judge who must rule, based on either the fact of the conviction or on the record at an earlier trial, whether or not the underlying facts for which the conviction is offered was tried or admitted and decided in the first case.

CHAPTER 83
- HEARSAY EXCEPTION -
JUDGMENT AS TO PERSONAL, FAMILY, OR
GENERAL HISTORY, OR BOUNDARIES

Definition

This exception admits a prior judgment as to personal, family, or general history, or boundaries which are permitted to be proved otherwise by reputation evidence pursuant to Rule 803(23).

Forms of Objection and Response

Forms of Objection

➤ *I object. The question calls for a hearsay answer.*

➤ *I move to strike the answer as hearsay.*

Form of Response

➤ *This statement is admissible as a judgment as to personal, family, or general history, or boundaries pursuant to Rule 803(23). I have shown through the testimony of _____ (insert name of witness) that this statement is a:*

   (a) *judgment offered as proof of*

   (b) *matters of personal, family, or general history, or boundaries,*

   (c) *essential to the judgment,* and

   (d) *which is provable by evidence of reputation.*

Federal Rule 803. Hearsay Exceptions; Availability of Declarant Immaterial

(23) Judgment as to personal, family or general history, or boundaries. Judgments as proof of matters of personal, family or general history, or boundaries, essential to the judgment, if the same would be provable by evidence of reputation.

Commentary

This exception provides a means to prove a fact essential to an earlier judgment as to personal, family, or general history, or as to boundaries. Note that this rule must be read in conjunction with Rules 803(19) and 803(20), because Rule 803(23) only permits the admissibility where the judgment proves facts which would be provable by reputation evidence.

CHAPTER 84
- HEARSAY EXCEPTION -
REQUIREMENT OF UNAVAILABILITY

Definition

The hearsay exceptions in Rule 804(b)(1)–(5) all require the unavailability of the declarant at trial as a prerequisite to admissibility. The definition of *unavailability* includes (a) exemption by privilege from testifying, (b) persistence in a refusal to testify despite court order, (c) lack of memory, (d) death or sufficient mental or physical illness, or (e) absence where attempts to procure the declarant's presence are unavailing.

Forms of Objection and Response

Forms of Objection

> ➤ *I object. The question calls for a hearsay answer.*

> ➤ *I move to strike the answer as hearsay.*

Form of Response

> ➤ *The out-of-court statements meets* _____ (insert the appropriate Rule 804(b) exception). *The declarant is unavailable because the declarant:*

> (a) *is exempted from testifying concerning the subject of the statement by ruling by the court on the ground of privilege,* or

> (b) *persists in refusing to testify concerning the subject of the statement despite a court order to do so,* or

> (c) *testifies to a lack of memory on the subject of the statement,* or

> (d) *is unable to testify at the hearing because of death or illness,* or

> (e) *is absent from the hearing and I, as the proponent of the declarant's statement, have been unable to procure the declarant's attendance through process or other means,* or

> (f) _____ (insert reason for the witness' absence).

Federal Rule 804. Hearsay Exceptions; Declarant Unavailable

(a) Definition of unavailability. "Unavailability as a witness" includes situations in which the declarant–

(1) is exempted by ruling of the court on the ground of privilege from testifying concerning the subject matter of the declarant's statement; or

(2) persists in refusing to testify concerning the subject matter of the declarant's statement despite an order of the court to do so; or

(3) testifies to a lack of memory of the subject matter of the declarant's statement; or

(4) is unable to be present or to testify at the hearing because of death or then existing physical or mental illness or infirmity; or

(5) is absent from the hearing and the proponent of a statement has been unable to procure the declarant's attendance (or in the case of hearsay exception under subdivision (b)(2), (3), or (4), the declarant's attendance or testimony) by process or other reasonable means.

A declarant is not unavailable as a witness if the declarant's exemption, refusal, claim of lack of memory, inability, or absence is due to the procurement or wrongdoing of the proponent of a statement for the purpose of preventing the witness from attending or testifying.

Commentary

The Rule 804(b) exceptions require the declarant's unavailability. Note that the types of unavailability listed in Rule 804(a) are not the exclusive circumstances of unavailability. Rather, Rule 804(a) lists circumstance which *per se* amount to unavailability, but fails to exclude any other legitimate showing of unavailability which the trial judge determines acceptable pursuant to Rule 804.

Unavailability pursuant to Rule 804(a) is merely a necessary foundation for Rule 804(b) exceptions to the hearsay rule. Unavailability of the declarant alone does not meet a hearsay objection.

CHAPTER 85
- HEARSAY EXCEPTION -
FORMER TESTIMONY

Definition

Former testimony is any testimony given under oath in an earlier proceeding. It is admissible at a later hearing if the declarant is unavailable, and the party against whom it is now offered had the opportunity and a similar motive to *develop*, by the questioning of the declarant, the earlier testimony when it was given.

Forms of Objection and Response

Forms of Objection

➤ *I object. The question calls for a hearsay answer.*

➤ *I move to strike the answer as hearsay.*

Form of Response

➤ *This statement is admissible as former testimony pursuant to Rule 804(b)(1). I have shown through the testimony of _____ (insert name of witness) that:*

   (a) *the declarant is unavailable pursuant to Rule 804(a),*

   (b) *the statement is testimony given*

   (c) *at another hearing of the same of a different proceeding, or in a deposition in the course of the same or a different proceeding, and*

   (d) *the party against whom it is offered had an opportunity and similar motive to develop the testimony by direct, cross, or redirect examination.*

Federal Rule 804. Hearsay Exceptions; Declarant Unavailable

(b) Hearsay exceptions. The following are not excluded by the hearsay rule if the declarant is unavailable as a witness:

(1) Former testimony. Testimony given as a witness at another hearing of the same or a different proceeding, or in a deposition taken in compliance with law in the course of the same or another proceeding, if the party against whom the testimony is now offered, or, in a civil action or proceeding, a predecessor in interest, had an opportunity and similar motive to develop the testimony by direct, cross, or redirect examination.

Commentary

This exception draws its reliability from the general lack of the hearsay dangers at the time the statement was made. The now out-of-court statement was made under oath and the person against whom it is now offered had the opportunity to examine and confront the witness with a similar motive as he would have when the statement is now offered.

Opposing counsel need not be the same counsel at the time the former testimony was originally taken, so long as the opponent possessed the opportunity to develop testimony at the earlier hearing. Furthermore, the party against whom the former testimony is offered in the present case must have also had a motive at the time the former testimony was taken similar to its motive to develop or impeach the statement when the former testimony is offered at the present trial. If the issues were different at the first hearing as opposed to the present hearing or if the posture of the parties or the case was sufficiently different so that the motive to cross examine, for example, was not the same, then the former testimony may not be offered.

Motive, however, is viewed generally. For example, in a criminal case, testimony from the preliminary hearing assuming proper foundation will often be admissible pursuant to Rule 804(b)(1) (and despite Confrontation Clause objections) at the later trial of the case. This is so even though the tactics of counsel at the preliminary hearing may have been different from the tactics at trial. Typically, at the preliminary hearing, the prosecution will only present such evidence as necessary to support a finding of probable cause while defense counsel will utilize the hearing as a discovery device. At trial, a prosecutor would expand the testimony of the witness and the defense would seek to impeach and limit. Defense counsel might also choose to save some known impeachment until trial. Most courts, however, will view the *motive* to be conviction for the prosecution and acquittal by the defense, and assuming other foundation, admit the testimony pursuant to Rule 804(b)(1).

A similar analysis as to motive applies in civil cases when dealing with depositions where the tactics of the proponent and opponent of witnesses often differ at the time of deposition and at the time of trial.

CHAPTER 86
- HEARSAY EXCEPTION -
STATEMENT UNDER BELIEF OF IMPENDING DEATH

Definition

This out-of-court statement, referred to at common law as a *dying declaration,* is available only in limited situations, i.e., a prosecution for homicide or a civil action. This statement is one made by a presently unavailable, out-of-court declarant who had sufficient reason to believe that the declarant's death was imminent. The statement must relate to the cause or circumstances of what the declarant believed to be the declarant's impending death.

Forms of Objection and Response

Forms of Objection

> ➤ *I object. The question calls for a hearsay answer.*
> ➤ *I move to strike the statement as hearsay.*

Form of Response

> ➤ *This statement is admissible as a statement under belief of impending death pursuant to Rule 804(b)(2). I have shown through the testimony of _____ (insert name of witness) that the statement:*
>
>   (a) *was made by a declarant who is now unavailable pursuant to Rule 804(a),*
>   (b) *is offered in a prosecution for homicide or a civil action or proceeding,*
>   (c) *was made by the declarant while believing that death was imminent,* and
>   (d) *concerns the causes or circumstances of what the declarant believed to be impending death.*

Federal Rule 804. Hearsay Exceptions; Declarant Unavailable

(b) Hearsay exceptions. The following are not excluded by the hearsay rule if the declarant is unavailable as a witness:

(2) Statement under the belief of impending death. In a prosecution for homicide or in a civil action or proceeding, a statement made by a declarant while believing that the declarant's death was imminent, concerning the cause or circumstances of what the declarant believed to be impending death.

Commentary

A statement made under belief of impending death gains its reliability from the notion that a declarant who in good faith believes that (s)he is about to die would not fabricate either the cause of death or the name of the person who has caused the declarant's condition. Unlike the common law, the federal rule does not require a declarant to die as a foundation or requirement to the offering of a statement under belief of impending death. The guarantee of reliability is found in the reasonable *belief* on the part of the declarant that (s)he is about to die.

This belief can be established in a number of ways. First of all, the type of wounds suffered may be so serious as to lead the declarant to believe that, in fact, death is imminent. Second, some other person on the scene may inform the witness that it is unlikely that the witness will survive and will die in a very short time, which, if reasonably believed, would appropriately lay the foundation for a belief of impending death. (Note that the out-of-court statement informing the declarant that death is imminent is not hearsay because it is offered on the issue of the state of mind of the listener—the maker of the dying declaration). Third, the declarant may have other reasons for believing that death is imminent.

Note that once the predicate foundation of a reasonable belief in impending death is shown, then the types of statements that are admissible under the Rule 804(b)(2) are limited to those which relate to the cause or circumstances of what the declarant believes to be impending death. This would certainly include the identification of the person or persons who so injured the declarant as to make the declarant believe that death is imminent as well as the manner in which the declarant was injured.

The dying declaration may be, and often is, elicited from a mortally injured person in the form of leading questions by an observer (typically a police officer at the scene of a homicide or an automobile accident). The leading form of the questions put to the declarant does not *per se* render the declaration inadmissible, but would bear on the weight to be given the admissible dying declaration.

Finally, note that the only type of criminal case in which statements under the belief of impending death are admissible is a prosecution for homicide while such a statement is admissible in a civil action of any type.

CHAPTER 87
- HEARSAY EXCEPTIONS -
STATEMENT AGAINST INTEREST

Definition

A declaration against interest is an out-of-court statement made by an unavailable declarant which is so far against the pecuniary or proprietary interest of the maker of the statement or would so likely tend to subject the declarant to civil or criminal liability that a reasonable person would not make such a statement unless (s)he believed it to be true at the time of the making of the statement.

Forms of Objection and Response

Forms of Objection

> *I object. The question calls for a hearsay answer.*

> *I move to strike the answer as hearsay.*

Form of Response

> *This statement is admissible as a statement against interest pursuant to Rule 804(b)(3). I have shown through the testimony of* _____ (insert name of witness) *that the statement:*

>> (a) *was made by a declarant who is now unavailable pursuant to Rule 804(a),* and

>> (b) (1) *was, at the time of its making, so far contrary to the declarant's pecuniary or proprietary interest,* or

>>> (2) *so far tended to subject him to criminal or civil liability,* or

>>> (3) *to render invalid a claim by him against another,*

>> (c) *that a reasonable person in his position would not have made the statement unless he believed it to be true,* and

>> (d) (If the statement tends to expose the declarant to criminal liability, and is offered to exculpate the accused) *corroborating circumstances clearly indicate the trustworthiness of the statement.*

Federal Rule 804. Hearsay Exceptions; Declarant Unavailable

(b) Hearsay exceptions. The following are not excluded by the hearsay rule if the declarant is unavailable as a witness:

(3) Statement against interest. A statement which was at the time of its making so far contrary to the declarant's pecuniary or proprietary interest, or so far tended to subject the declarant to civil or criminal liability, or to render invalid a claim by the declarant against another, that a reasonable person in the declarant's position would not have made the statement unless believing it to be true. A statement tending to expose the declarant to criminal liability and offered to exculpate the accused is not admissible unless corroborating circumstances clearly indicate the trustworthiness of the statement.

Commentary

A statement against interest is an out-of-court declaration which at the time of its making is so far against a particular enumerated interest of the declarant that the declarant would have believed its truth when he made the statement. This guarantee of reliability is what justifies this hearsay exception.

The key to this exception is proof that the declarant knew, at the time of the making of the statement, that it was against his interest. This proof is usually had by the circumstances surrounding the making of the statement. In situations where a witness may have both a self-serving and a disserving purpose in making a statement (e.g., a hope to have an immediate gain while risking a longer term loss), the court must determine whether, in the mind of the declarant, the statement was primarily in the interest or against the interest of the declarant.

It is irrelevant whether or not the statement turns out to be contrary to the position of the declarant, as is often the case in party admissions. The witness must realize the adverse nature of the statement when it was made. Also, unlike in the case of party admissions, the rules requiring firsthand knowledge and the rules precluding opinions do apply.

Note that there is special treatment for a statement against criminal or penal interest, where offered to exculpate an accused, which requires that there be corroborating circumstances which indicate the truthfulness or the reliability of the statement against criminal liability or criminal interest. The reason for this special requirement lies in the reality that there are people who will confess to all sorts of crimes because of mental problems, or situations where people already serving long terms in correctional institutions will take the blame for a variety of crimes which will not effectively add sufficiently to their sentences but would exculpate associates who are in fact guilty. There is less inherent reliability in such statements against criminal or penal interest and thus the requirement for corroborating circumstances.

CHAPTER 88

- HEARSAY EXCEPTION -
STATEMENT OF PERSONAL OR FAMILY HISTORY

Definition

A statement of personal or family history is an out-of-court declaration by an unavailable declarant which relates to the declarant's own personal history or the personal history of a family member or someone with whom (s)he is so intimately associated that (s)he would likely have accurate knowledge concerning the matter declared.

Forms of Objection and Response

Forms of Objection

➤ *I object. The question calls for a hearsay answer.*

➤ *I move to strike the answer as hearsay.*

Form of Response

➤ *This statement is admissible as a statement of personal or family history pursuant to Rule 804(b)(4). I have shown through the testimony of _____* (insert name of witness) *that:*

    (a) (1)   *the declarant is now unavailable pursuant to Rule 804(a),* and

         (2)   *the statement concerns the declarant's own birth, adoption, marriage, divorce, legitimacy, relationship by blood, adoption, or marriage, ancestry, or other similar fact of personal or family history,*

         (3)   *even though the declarant had no means of acquiring personal knowledge of the matter stated,* or

    (b) *the statement concerns the foregoing matters, as well as the death of another person, where the declarant was related to the other person by blood, adoption, or marriage, or was so intimately associated with the other's family as to be likely to give accurate information concerning the matter declared.*

Federal Rule 804. Hearsay Exceptions; Declarant Unavailable

(b) Hearsay exceptions. The following are not excluded by the hearsay rule if the declarant is unavailable as witness:

(4) Statement of personal or family history. (A) A statement concerning the declarant's own birth, adoption, marriage, divorce, legitimacy, relationship by blood, adoption, or marriage, ancestry, or other similar fact of personal or family history, even though declarant had no means of acquiring personal knowledge of the matter stated; or (B) a statement concerning the foregoing matters, and death also, of another person, if the declarant was related to the other by blood, adoption, or marriage or was so intimately associated with the other's family as to be likely to have accurate information concerning the matter declared.

Commentary

This exception gains its reliability from the fact of the declarant's likely reliance on such information throughout the course of the declarant's life. Note that the requirement of the declarant's personal knowledge which ordinarily must be apparent from the circumstances of the making of a declarant's admissible hearsay statement is explicitly dispensed with pursuant to Rule 804(b)(4).

CHAPTER 89

- HEARSAY EXCEPTION -
FORFEITURE BY WRONGDOING

Definition

A party forfeits the right to object on hearsay grounds to any statement made by a person whose unavailability has been procured by the wrongdoing of the party. Forfeiture also applies if the wrongful conduct that procured the unavailability of the hearsay declarant was acquiesced in by the party.

Forms of Objection and Response

Forms of Objection

➤ *I object. The question calls for hearsay.*

➤ *I move to strike the answer as hearsay.*

Form of Response

➤ *This statement is admissible pursuant to Rule 804(b)(6). I have shown through the testimony of* _____ (insert the name of the witness(es)) that:

    (a) (1) *the declarant is now unavailable pursuant to Rule 804(a),* and

          (2) *objecting counsel's client engaged in wrongdoing that was intended to, and did, procure the unavailability of the declarant,* or

          (3) *objecting counsel's client acquiesced in wrongdoing that was intended to, and did, procure the unavailability of the declarant.*

Federal Rule 804. Hearsay Exceptions; Declarant Unavailable

(b) Hearsay Exceptions. The following are not excluded by the hearsay rule if the declarant is unavailable as a witness:

(6) Forfeiture by wrongdoing. A statement offered against a party that has engaged or acquiesced in wrongdoing that was intended to, and did, procure the unavailability of the declarant as a witness.

Commentary

This exception became effective on December 1, 1997. It gains its reliability from the notion that a party should not be allowed to benefit from wrongful conduct that would otherwise preclude relevant evidence. It codifies the law in every circuit that has considered the matter, and provides that a party forfeits the right to object to a hearsay statement if the declarant's unavailability was procured by the wrongdoing of the party, or wrongdoing acquiesced in by the party, that was intended to and, in fact did, procure the unavailability of the declarant.

The rule applies to any statement by a declarant that meets the rules requirements. The statement need not be given under oath. The rule also applies to all parties in civil or criminal cases, including both individuals and institutions.

"Wrongdoing" is undefined, but need not amount to criminal activity. Presumably any conduct intended to prevent a witness from giving testimony by making the witness unavailable would meet the definition of "wrongdoing." Such conduct thwarts the legitimate goals of both the civil and criminal justice system and would properly implicate the rule.

In order to present a statement pursuant to this exception, the wrongdoing that procured the declarant's unavailability must be proved by the Rule 104(a) quantum of proof of sufficient evidence that a jury could find the necessary foundational facts by a preponderance of the evidence.

CHAPTER 90
- HEARSAY EXCEPTION -
RESIDUAL EXCEPTION

Definition

The residual exception to the hearsay rule, formerly contained in Rules 803(24) and 804(b)(5), is recodified after 1997, as Rule 807. It provides a catch-all provision which permits the admission of hearsay where, although not fitting within one of the enumerated exceptions, the proffered hearsay possesses guarantees of trustworthiness equivalent to that of the enumerated exceptions, and is more probative of the fact for which it is offered than any other available evidence.

Forms of Objection and Response

Forms of Objection

> *I object. The question calls for a hearsay answer.*

> *I move to strike the answer as hearsay.*

Form of Response

> *This statement is admissible pursuant to the residual exception to the hearsay rule contained in Rule 807. I have shown through the testimony of _____ (insert name of witness) that:*

> (a) *the statement is not specifically covered by any of the other enumerated hearsay exceptions, and*

> (b) *the statement has circumstantial guarantees of trustworthiness equivalent to that of the enumerated exceptions, and*

> (c) *the statement is offered as evidence of a material fact, and*

> (d) *the statement is more probative on the point for which it is offered than any other which I can procure through reasonable efforts, and*

> (e) *the general purposes of these rules and the interests of justice will best be served by the admission of this statement into evidence, and*

> (f) *I have given the adverse parties notice sufficiently in advance of trial of my intention to offer the statement so as to afford them a fair opportunity to prepare to meet it.*

Federal Rule 807. Residual Exception

A statement not specifically covered by Rule 803 or 804 but having equivalent circumstantial guarantees of trustworthiness, is not excluded by the hearsay rule, if the court determines that (A) the statement is offered as evidence of a material fact; (B) the statement is more probative on the point for which it is offered than any other evidence which the proponent can procure through reasonable efforts; and (C) the general purposes of these rules and the interests of justice will best be served by admission of the statement into evidence. However, a statement may not be admitted under this exception unless the proponent of it makes known to the adverse party sufficiently in advance of the trial or hearing to provide the adverse party with a fair opportunity to prepare to meet it, the proponent's intention to offer the statement and the particulars of it, including the name and address of the declarant.

Commentary

The residual exception to the hearsay rule was designed by Congress to deal with evidentiary offers of hearsay statements not anticipated nor covered by the foregoing enumerated exceptions. The foundational requirements for a proffer pursuant to the residual exception are the following: (a) the offer must relate to a material fact, (b) admission must serve the interests of justice and general purposes of the Federal Rules, (c) the proffered hearsay must bear circumstantial guarantees of trustworthiness equivalent to the reliability of any of the enumerated exceptions, (d) the proffer must be the most probative evidence available on point, and (e) the proponent of the evidence must provide the opponent sufficient pretrial notice of intent to offer evidence pursuant to the residual exception.

The last three components require further explanation. First, the trustworthiness requirement has been treated in two ways by the federal courts. Some courts look solely to the circumstances surrounding the making of the out-of-court statement to see if such circumstances provide sufficient trustworthiness guarantees. Other courts look to extrinsic factors like corroboration to verify the reliability of the proffered hearsay. Note, however, that the 1990 Supreme Court opinion in *Idaho v. Wright* calls into serious question the use of corroborating evidence as the reliability foundation for residual hearsay. In *Wright,* the Court, dealing with a Confrontation Clause challenge to the Idaho residual exception, forbade the use of corroboration to lay the reliability foundation required to overcome the Confrontation Clause objection. The language used to define "reliability" for both Confrontation Clause and residual hearsay purposes is essentially the same.

Second, with respect to the *probativeness* requirement, the clear import of the rule is that the hearsay offer under the residual exception must be rejected where it is cumulative of other equally or more probative evidence available in the case.

A determination of what is meant by *most probative* may be subjective and be decided on a case-by-case basis. Some courts, however, have ruled that direct evidence is more probative than either circumstantial evidence or expert opinion.

Third, courts have split in their dealings with the so-called *near-miss* situation—the case of the hearsay offer which is similar to one of the enumerated exceptions, but is lacking one or more of the enumerated foundational requirements. Some courts *per se* bar the admission of near-miss evidence. Others consider a near-miss as the substantial equivalent of an enumerated exception and admit it. A third, middle view would admit the near-miss if there is some other reliability factor in the making of the statement which substitutes for the missing element.

Finally, though the provision requiring pretrial notice by the proponent of intent to offer an out-of-court statement under the residual exception appears to be unqualified, most courts have dispensed with pretrial notice where the proponent is surprised by the unavailability or lack of memory of a witness and then seeks to offer the residual hearsay instead. These courts offer the opponent a continuance to prepare to meet the offer under Rule 807.

APPENDIX
FEDERAL RULES OF EVIDENCE

As amended to December 1, 1998

ARTICLE I. GENERAL PROVISIONS

Rule 101 — Scope

These rules govern proceedings in the courts of the United States and before United States bankruptcy judges and United States magistrate judges, to the extent and with the exceptions stated in rule 1101.

Rule 102 — Purpose and Construction

These rules shall be construed to secure fairness in administration, elimination of unjustifiable expense and delay, and promotion of growth and development of the law of evidence to the end that the truth may be ascertained and proceedings justly determined.

Rule 103 — Rulings on Evidence

(a) Effect of erroneous ruling. Error may not be predicated upon a ruling which admits or excludes evidence unless a substantial right of the party is affected, and

(1) Objection. In case the ruling is one admitting evidence, a timely objection or motion to strike appears of record, stating the specific ground of objection, if the specific ground was not apparent from the context; or

(2) Offer of proof. In case the ruling is one excluding evidence, the substance of the evidence was made known to the court by offer or was apparent from the context within which questions were asked.

(b) Record of offer and ruling. The court may add any other or further statement which shows the character of the evidence, the form in which it was offered, the objection made, and the ruling thereon. It may direct the making of an offer in question and answer form.

(c) Hearing of jury. In jury cases, proceedings shall be conducted, to the extent practicable, so as to prevent inadmissible evidence from being suggested to the jury by any means, such as making statements or offers of proof or asking questions in the hearing of the jury.

(d) Plain error. Nothing in this rule precludes taking notice of plain errors affecting substantial rights although they were not brought to the attention of the court.

Rule 104 — Preliminary Questions

(a) Questions of admissibility generally. Preliminary questions concerning the qualification of a person to be a witness, the existence of a privilege, or the admissibility of evidence shall be determined by the court, subject to the provisions of subdivision (b). In making its determination it is not bound by the rules of evidence except those with respect to privileges.

(b) Relevancy conditioned on fact. When the relevancy of evidence depends upon the fulfillment of a condition of fact, the court shall admit it upon, or subject to, the introduction of evidence sufficient to support a finding of the fulfillment of the condition.

(c) Hearing of jury. Hearings on the admissibility of confessions shall in all cases be conducted out of the hearing of the jury. Hearings on other preliminary matters shall be so conducted when the interests of justice require, or when an accused is a witness and so requests.

(d) Testimony by accused. The accused does not, by testifying upon a preliminary matter, become subject to cross-examination as to other issues in the case.

(e) Weight and credibility. This rule does not limit the right of a party to introduce before the jury evidence relevant to weight or credibility.

Rule 105 — Limited Admissibility

When evidence which is admissible as to one party or for one purpose but not admissible as to another party or for another purpose is admitted, the court, upon request, shall restrict the evidence to its proper scope and instruct the jury accordingly.

Rule 106 — Remainder of or Related Writings or Recorded Statements

When a writing or recorded statement or part thereof is introduced by a party, an adverse party may require the introduction at that time of any other part or any other writing or recorded statement which ought in fairness to be considered contemporaneously with it.

ARTICLE II. JUDICIAL NOTICE

Rule 201 — Judicial Notice of Adjudicative Facts

(a) Scope of rule. This rule governs only judicial notice of adjudicative facts.

(b) Kinds of facts. A judicially noticed fact must be one not subject to reasonable dispute in that it is either (1) generally known within the territorial jurisdiction of the trial court or (2) capable of accurate and ready determination by resort to sources whose accuracy cannot reasonably be questioned.

(c) When discretionary. A court may take judicial notice, whether requested or not.

(d) When mandatory. A court shall take judicial notice if requested by a party and supplied with the necessary information.

(e) Opportunity to be heard. A party is entitled upon timely request to an opportunity to be heard as to the propriety of taking judicial notice and the tenor of the matter noticed. In the absence of prior notification, the request may be made after judicial notice has been taken.

(f) Time of taking notice. Judicial notice may be taken at any stage of the proceeding.

(g) Instructing jury. In a civil action or proceeding, the court shall instruct the jury to accept as conclusive any fact judicially noticed. In a criminal case, the court shall instruct the jury that it may, but is not required to, accept as conclusive any fact judicially noticed.

ARTICLE III. PRESUMPTIONS IN CIVIL ACTIONS AND PROCEEDINGS

Rule 301 — Presumptions in General in Civil Actions and Proceedings

In all civil actions and proceedings not otherwise provided for by Act of Congress or by these rules, a presumption imposes on the party against whom it is directed the burden of going forward with evidence to rebut or meet the presumption, but does not shift to such party the burden of proof in the sense of the risk of non-persuasion, which remains throughout the trial upon the party on whom it was originally cast.

Rule 302 — Applicability of State Law in Civil Actions and Proceedings

In civil actions and proceedings, the effect of a presumption respecting a fact which is an element of a claim or defense as to which State law supplies the rule of decision is determined in accordance with State law.

ARTICLE IV. RELEVANCY AND ITS LIMITS

Rule 401 — Definition of "Relevant Evidence"

"Relevant evidence" means evidence having any tendency to make the existence of any fact that is of consequence to the determination of the action more probable or less probable than it would be without the evidence.

Rule 402 — Relevant Evidence Generally Admissible; Irrelevant Evidence Inadmissible

All relevant evidence is admissible, except as otherwise provided by the Constitution of the United States, by Act of Congress, by these rules, or by other rules prescribed by the Supreme Court pursuant to statutory authority. Evidence which is not relevant is not admissible.

Rule 403 — Exclusion of Relevant Evidence on Grounds of Prejudice, Confusion, or Waste of Time

Although relevant, evidence may be excluded if its probative value is substantially outweighed by the danger of unfair prejudice, confusion of the issues, or misleading the jury, or by considerations of undue delay, waste of time, or needless presentation of cumulative evidence.

Rule 404 — Character Evidence Not Admissible to Prove Conduct; Exceptions; Other Crimes

(a) **Character evidence generally.** Evidence of a person's character or a trait of character is not admissible for the purpose of proving action in conformity therewith on a particular occasion, except:

(1) **Character of accused.** Evidence of a pertinent trait of character offered by an accused, or by the prosecution to rebut the same;

(2) **Character of victim.** Evidence of a pertinent trait of character of the victim of the crime offered by an accused, or by the prosecution to rebut the same, or evidence of a character trait of peacefulness of the victim offered by the prosecution in a homicide case to rebut evidence that the victim was the first aggressor;

(3) **Character of witness.** Evidence of the character of a witness, as provided in rules 607, 608, and 609.

(b) **Other crimes, wrongs, or acts.** Evidence of other crimes, wrongs, or acts is not admissible to prove the character of a person in order to show action in conformity therewith. It may, however, be admissible for other purposes, such as proof of motive, opportunity, intent, preparation, plan, knowledge, identity, or absence of mistake or accident, provided that upon request by the accused, the prosecution in a criminal case shall provide reasonable notice in advance of trial, or during trial if the court excuses pretrial notice on good cause shown, of the general nature of any such evidence it intends to introduce at trial.

Rule 405 — Methods of Proving Character

(a) Reputation or opinion. In all cases in which evidence of character or a trait of character of a person is admissible, proof may be made by testimony as to reputation or by testimony in the form of an opinion. On cross-examination, inquiry is allowable into relevant specific instances of conduct.

(b) Specific instances of conduct. In cases in which character or a trait of character of a person is an essential element of a charge, claim, or defense, proof may also be made of specific instances of that person's conduct.

Rule 406 — Habit; Routine Practice

Evidence of the habit of a person or of the routine practice of an organization, whether corroborated or not and regardless of the presence of eyewitnesses, is relevant to prove that the conduct of the person or organization on a particular occasion was in conformity with the habit or routine practice.

Rule 407 — Subsequent Remedial Measures

When, after an injury or harm allegedly caused by an event, measures are taken that, if taken previously, would have made the injury or harm less likely to occur, evidence of the subsequent measures is not admissible to prove negligence, culpable conduct, a defect in a product, a defect in a product's design, or a need for a warning or instruction. This rule does not require the exclusion of evidence of subsequent measures when offered for another purpose, such as proving ownership, control, or feasibility of precautionary measures, if controverted, or impeachment.

Rule 408 — Compromise and Offers to Compromise

Evidence of (1) furnishing or offering or promising to furnish, or (2) accepting or offering or promising to accept, a valuable consideration in compromising or attempting to compromise a claim which was disputed as to either validity or amount, is not admissible to prove liability for or invalidity of the claim or its amount. Evidence of conduct or statements made in compromise negotiations is likewise not admissible. This rule does not require the exclusion of any evidence otherwise discoverable merely because it is presented in the course of compromise negotiations. This rule also does not require exclusion when the evidence is offered for another purpose, such as proving bias or prejudice of a witness, negativing a contention of undue delay, or proving an effort to obstruct a criminal investigation or prosecution.

Rule 409 — Payment of Medical and Similar Expenses

Evidence of furnishing or offering or promising to pay medical, hospital, or similar expenses occasioned by an injury is not admissible to prove liability for the injury.

Rule 410 — Inadmissibility of Pleas, Plea Discussions, and Related Statements

Except as otherwise provided in this rule, evidence of the following is not, in any civil or criminal proceeding, admissible against the defendant who made the plea or was a participant in the plea discussions:

(1) a plea of guilty which was later withdrawn;

(2) a plea of nolo contendere;

(3) any statement made in the course of any proceedings under Rule 11 of the Federal Rules of Criminal Procedure or comparable state procedure regarding either of the foregoing pleas; or

(4) any statement made in the course of plea discussions with an attorney for the prosecuting authority which do not result in a plea of guilty or which result in a plea of guilty later withdrawn.

However, such a statement is admissible (i) in any proceeding wherein another statement made in the course of the same plea or plea discussions has been introduced and the statement ought in fairness be considered contemporaneously with it, or (ii) in a criminal proceeding for perjury or false statement if the statement was made by the defendant under oath, on the record and in the presence of counsel.

Rule 411 — Liability Insurance

Evidence that a person was or was not insured against liability is not admissible upon the issue whether the person acted negligently or otherwise wrongfully. This rule does not require the exclusion of evidence of insurance against liability when offered for another purpose, such as proof of agency, ownership, or control, or bias or prejudice of a witness.

Rule 412 — Sex Offense Cases; Relevance of Victim's Past Sexual Behavior or Alleged Sexual Predisposition

(a) Evidence generally inadmissible. The following evidence is not admissible in any civil or criminal proceeding involving alleged sexual misconduct except as provided in subdivisions (b) and (c):

(1) Evidence offered to prove that any alleged victim engaged in other sexual behavior.

(2) Evidence offered to prove any alleged victim's sexual predisposition.

(b) Exceptions.

(1) In a criminal case, the following evidence is admissible, if otherwise admissible under these rules:

(A) evidence of specific instances of sexual behavior by the alleged victim offered to prove that a person other than the accused was the source of semen, injury or other physical evidence;

(B) evidence of specific instances of sexual behavior by the alleged victim with respect to the person accused of the sexual misconduct offered by the accused to prove consent or by the prosecution; and

(C) evidence the exclusion of which would violate the constitutional rights of the defendant.

(2) In a civil case, evidence offered to prove the sexual behavior or sexual predisposition of any alleged victim is admissible if it is otherwise admissible under these rules and its probative value substantially outweighs the danger of harm to any victim and of unfair prejudice to any party. Evidence of an alleged victim's reputation is admissible only if it has been placed in controversy by the alleged victim.

(c) Procedure to determine admissibility.

(1) A party intending to offer evidence under subdivision (b) must

(A) file a written motion at least 14 days before trial specifically describing the evidence and stating the purpose for which it is offered unless the court, for good cause requires a different time for filing or permits filing during trial; and

(B) serve the motion on all parties and notify the alleged victim or, when appropriate, the alleged victim's guardian or representative.

(2) Before admitting evidence under this rule the court must conduct a hearing in camera and afford the victim and parties a right to attend and be heard. The motion, related papers, and the record of the hearing must be sealed and remain under seal unless the court orders otherwise.

Rule 413 — Evidence of Similar Crimes in Sexual Assault Cases

(a) In a criminal case in which the defendant is accused of an offense of sexual assault, evidence of the defendant's commission of another offense or offenses of sexual assault is admissible, and may be considered for its bearing on any matter to which it is relevant.

(b) In a case in which the Government intends to offer evidence under this rule, the attorney for the Government shall disclose the evidence to the defendant, including statements of witnesses or a summary of the substance of any testimony that is expected to be offered, at least fifteen days before the scheduled date of trial or at such later time as the court may allow for good cause.

(c) This rule shall not be construed to limit the admission or consideration of evidence under any other rule.

(d) For purposes of this rule and Rule 415, "offense of sexual assault" means a crime under Federal law or the law of a State (as defined in section 513 of title 18, United States Code) that involved—

(1) any conduct proscribed by chapter 109A of title 18, United States Code;

(2) contact, without consent, between any part of the defendant's body or an object and the genitals or anus of another person;

(3) contact, without consent, between the genitals or anus of the defendant and any part of another person's body;

(4) deriving sexual pleasure or gratification from the infliction of death, bodily injury, or physical pain on another person; or

(5) an attempt or conspiracy to engage in conduct described in paragraphs (1)–(4).

Rule 414 — Evidence of Similar Crimes in Child Molestation Cases

(a) In a criminal case in which the defendant is accused of an offense of child molestation, evidence of the defendant's commission of another offense or offenses of child molestation is admissible, and may be considered for its bearing on any matter to which it is relevant.

(b) In a case in which the Government intends to offer evidence under this rule, the attorney for the Government shall disclose the evidence to the defendant, including statements of witnesses or a summary of the substance of any testimony that is expected to be offered, at least fifteen days before the scheduled date of trial or at such later time as the court may allow for good cause.

(c) This rule shall not be construed to limit the admission or consideration of evidence under any other rule.

(d) For purposes of this rule and Rule 415, "child" means a person below the age of fourteen, and "offense of child molestation" means a crime under Federal law or the law of a State (as defined in section 513 of title 18, United States Code) that involved—

    (1) any conduct proscribed by chapter 109A of title 18, United States Code, that was committed in relation to a child;

    (2) any conduct proscribed by chapter 110 of title 18, United States Code;

    (3) contact between any part of the defendant's body or an object and the genitals or anus of a child;

    (4) contact between the genitals or anus of the defendant and any part of the body of a child;

    (5) deriving sexual pleasure or gratification from the infliction of death, bodily injury, or physical pain on a child; or

    (6) an attempt or conspiracy to engage in conduct described in paragraphs (1)–(5).

Rule 415 — Evidence of Similar Acts in Civil Cases Concerning Sexual Assault or Child Molestation

(a) In a civil case in which a claim for damages or other relief is predicated on a party's alleged commission of conduct constituting an offense of sexual assault or child molestation, evidence of that party's commission of another offense or offenses of sexual assault or child molestation is admissible and may be considered as provided in Rule 413 and Rule 414 of these rules.

(b) A party who intends to offer evidence under this Rule shall disclose the evidence to the party against whom it will be offered, including statements of witnesses or a summary of the substance of any testimony that is expect to be offered, at least fifteen days before the scheduled date of trial or at such later time as the court may allow for good cause.

(c) This rule shall not be construed to limit the admission or consideration of evidence under any other rule.

ARTICLE V. PRIVILEGES

Rule 501 — General Rule

Except as otherwise required by the Constitution of the United States or provided by Act of Congress or in rules prescribed by the Supreme Court pursuant to statutory authority, the privilege of a witness, person, government, State, or political subdivision thereof shall be governed by the principles of the common law as they may be interpreted by the courts of the United States in the light of reason and experience. However, in civil actions and proceedings, with respect to an element of a claim or defense as to which State law supplies the rule of decision, the privilege of a witness, person, government, State, or political subdivision thereof shall be determined in accordance with State law.

ARTICLE VI. WITNESSES

Rule 601 — General Rule of Competency

Every person is competent to be a witness except as otherwise provided in these rules. However, in civil actions and proceedings, with respect to an element of a claim or defense as to which State law supplies the rule of decision, the competency of a witness shall be determined in accordance with State law.

Rule 602 — Lack of Personal Knowledge

A witness may not testify to a matter unless evidence is introduced sufficient to support a finding that the witness has personal knowledge of the matter. Evidence to prove personal knowledge may, but need not, consist of the witness' own testimony. This rule is subject to the provisions of rule 703, relating to opinion testimony by expert witnesses.

Rule 603 — Oath or Affirmation

Before testifying, every witness shall be required to declare that the witness will testify truthfully, by oath or affirmation administered in a form calculated to awaken the witness' conscience and impress the witness' mind with the duty to do so.

Rule 604 — Interpreters

An interpreter is subject to the provisions of these rules relating to qualification as an expert and the administration of an oath or affirmation to make a true translation.

Rule 605 — Competency of Judge as Witness

The judge presiding at the trial may not testify in that trial as a witness. No objection need be made in order to preserve the point.

Rule 606 — Competency of Juror as Witness

(a) At the trial. A member of the jury may not testify as a witness before that jury in the trial of the case in which the juror is sitting. If the juror is called so to testify, the opposing party shall be afforded an opportunity to object out of the presence of the jury.

(b) Inquiry into validity of verdict or indictment. Upon an inquiry into the validity of a verdict or indictment, a juror may not testify as to any matter or statement occurring during the course of the jury's deliberations or to the effect of anything upon that or any other juror's mind or emotions as influencing the juror to assent to or dissent from the verdict or indictment or concerning the juror's mental processes in connection therewith, except that a juror may testify on the question whether extraneous prejudicial information was improperly brought to the jury's attention or whether any outside influence was improperly brought to bear upon any juror. Nor may a juror's affidavit or evidence of any statement by the juror concerning a matter about which the juror would be precluded from testifying be received for these purposes.

Rule 607 — Who May Impeach

The credibility of a witness may be attacked by any party, including the party calling the witness.

Rule 608 — Evidence of Character and Conduct of Witness

(a) Opinion and reputation evidence of character. The credibility of a witness may be attacked or supported by evidence in the form of opinion or reputation, but subject to these limitations: (1) the evidence may refer only to character for truthfulness or untruthfulness, and (2) evidence of truthful character is admissible only after the character of the witness for truthfulness has been attacked by opinion or reputation evidence or otherwise.

(b) Specific instances of conduct. Specific instances of the conduct of a witness, for the purpose of attacking or supporting the witness' credibility, other than conviction of crime as provided in rule 609, may not be proved by extrinsic evidence. They may, however, in the discretion of the court, if probative of truthfulness or untruthfulness, be inquired into on cross-examination of the witness (1) concerning the witness' character for truthfulness or untruthfulness, or (2) concerning the character for truthfulness or untruthfulness of another witness as to which character the witness being cross-examined has testified.

The giving of testimony, whether by an accused or by any other witness, does not operate as a waiver of the accused's or the witness' privilege against self-incrimination when examined with respect to matters which relate only to credibility.

Rule 609 — Impeachment by Evidence of Conviction of Crime

(a) General rule. For the purpose of attacking the credibility of a witness,

(1) evidence that a witness other than an accused has been convicted of a crime shall be admitted subject to Rule 403, if the crime was punishable by death or imprisonment in excess of one year under the law under which the witness was convicted, and evidence that an accused has been convicted of such a crime shall be admitted if the court determines that the probative value of admitting this evidence outweighs its prejudicial effect to the accused; and

(2) evidence that any witness has been convicted of a crime shall be admitted if it involved dishonesty or false statement, regardless of the punishment.

(b) Time limit. Evidence of a conviction under this rule is not admissible if a period of more than ten years has elapsed since the date of the conviction or of the release of the witness from the confinement imposed for that conviction, whichever is the later date, unless the court determines, in the interests of justice, that the probative value of the conviction supported by specific facts and circumstances substantially outweighs its prejudicial effect. However, evidence of a conviction more than 10 years old as calculated herein, is not admissible unless the proponent gives to the adverse party sufficient advance written notice of intent to use such evidence to provide the adverse party with a fair opportunity to contest the use of such evidence.

(c) Effect of pardon, annulment, or certificate of rehabilitation. Evidence of a conviction is not admissible under this rule if (1) the conviction has been the subject of a pardon, annulment, certificate of rehabilitation, or other equivalent procedure based on a finding of the rehabilitation of the person convicted, and that person has not been convicted of a subsequent crime which was punishable by death or imprisonment in excess of one year, or (2) the conviction has been the subject of a pardon, annulment, or other equivalent procedure based on a finding of innocence.

(d) Juvenile adjudications. Evidence of juvenile adjudications is generally not admissible under this rule. The court may, however, in a criminal case allow evidence of a juvenile adjudication of a witness other than the accused if conviction of the offense would be admissible to attack the credibility of an adult and the court is satisfied that admission in evidence is necessary for a fair determination of the issue of guilt or innocence.

(e) Pendency of appeal. The pendency of an appeal therefrom does not render evidence of a conviction inadmissible. Evidence of the pendency of an appeal is admissible.

Rule 610 — Religious Beliefs or Opinions

Evidence of the beliefs or opinions of a witness on matters of religion is not admissible for the purpose of showing that by reason of their nature the witness' credibility is impaired or enhanced.

Rule 611 — Mode and Order of Interrogation and Presentation

(a) Control by court. The court shall exercise reasonable control over the mode and order of interrogating witnesses and presenting evidence so as to (1) make the interrogation and presentation effective for the ascertainment of the truth, (2) avoid needless consumption of time, and (3) protect witnesses from harassment or undue embarrassment.

(b) Scope of cross-examination. Cross-examination should be limited to the subject matter of the direct examination and matters affecting the credibility of the witness. The court may, in the exercise of discretion, permit inquiry into additional matters as if on direct examination.

(c) Leading questions. Leading questions should not be used on the direct examination of a witness except as may be necessary to develop the witness' testimony. Ordinarily leading questions should be permitted on cross-examination. When a party calls a hostile witness, an adverse party, or a witness identified with an adverse party, interrogation may be by leading questions.

Rule 612 — Writing Used to Refresh Memory

Except as otherwise provided in criminal proceedings by section 3500 of title 18, United States Code, if a witness uses a writing to refresh memory for the purpose of testifying, either

(1) while testifying, or

(2) before testifying, if the court in its discretion determines it is necessary in the interests of justice, an adverse party is entitled to have the writing produced at the hearing, to inspect it, to cross-examine the witness thereon, and to introduce in evidence

those portions which relate to the testimony of the witness. If it is claimed that the writing contains matters not related to the subject matter of the testimony the court shall examine the writing in camera, excise any portions not so related, and order delivery of the remainder to the party entitled thereto. Any portion withheld over objections shall be preserved and made available to the appellate court in the event of an appeal. If a writing is not produced or delivered pursuant to order under this rule, the court shall make any order justice requires, except that in criminal cases when the prosecution elects not to comply, the order shall be one striking the testimony or, if the court in its discretion determines that the interests of justice so require, declaring a mistrial.

Rule 613 — Prior Statements of Witnesses

(a) Examining witness concerning prior statement. In examining a witness concerning a prior statement made by the witness, whether written or not, the statement need not be shown nor its contents disclosed to the witness at that time, but on request the same shall be shown or disclosed to opposing counsel.

(b) Extrinsic evidence of prior inconsistent statement of witness. Extrinsic evidence of a prior inconsistent statement by a witness is not admissible unless the witness is afforded an opportunity to explain or deny the same and the opposite party is afforded an opportunity to interrogate the witness thereon, or the interests of justice otherwise require. This provision does not apply to admissions of a party-opponent as defined in rule 801(d)(2).

Rule 614 — Calling and Interrogation of Witnesses by Court

(a) Calling by court. The court may, on its own motion or at the suggestion of a party, call witnesses, and all parties are entitled to cross-examine witnesses thus called.

(b) Interrogation by court. The court may interrogate witnesses, whether called by itself or by a party.

(c) Objections. Objections to the calling of witnesses by the court or to interrogation by it may be made at the time or at the next available opportunity when the jury is not present.

Rule 615 — Exclusion of Witnesses

At the request of a party the court shall order witnesses excluded so that they cannot hear the testimony of other witnesses, and it may make the order of its own motion. This rule does not authorize exclusion of (1) a party who is a natural person, or (2) an officer or employee of a party which is not a natural person designated as its representative by its attorney, or (3) a person whose presence is shown by a party to be essential to the presentation of the party's cause, or (4) a person authorized by statute to be present.

ARTICLE VII. OPINIONS AND EXPERT TESTIMONY

Rule 701 — Opinion Testimony by Lay Witnesses

If the witness is not testifying as an expert, the witness' testimony in the form of opinions or inferences is limited to those opinions or inferences which are (a) rationally based on the perception of the witness and (b) helpful to a clear understanding of the witness' testimony or the determination of a fact in issue.

Rule 702 — Testimony by Experts

If scientific, technical, or other specialized knowledge will assist the trier of fact to understand the evidence or to determine a fact in issue, a witness qualified as an expert by knowledge, skill, experience, training, or education, may testify thereto in the form of an opinion or otherwise.

Rule 703 — Bases of Opinion Testimony by Experts

The facts or data in the particular case upon which an expert bases an opinion or inference may be those perceived by or made known to the expert at or before the hearing. If of a type reasonably relied upon by experts in the particular field in forming opinions or inferences upon the subject, the facts or data need not be admissible in evidence.

Rule 704 — Opinion on Ultimate Issue

(a) Except as provided in subdivision (b), testimony in the form of an opinion or inference otherwise admissible is not objectionable because it embraces an ultimate issue to be decided by the trier of fact.

(b) No expert witness testifying with respect to the mental state or condition of a defendant in a criminal case may state an opinion or inference as to whether the defendant did or did not have the mental state or condition constituting an element of the crime charged or of a defense thereto. Such ultimate issues are matters for the trier of fact alone.

Rule 705 — Disclosure of Facts or Data Underlying Expert Opinion

The expert may testify in terms of opinion or inference and give reasons therefor without first testifying to the underlying facts or data, unless the court requires otherwise. The expert may in any event be required to disclose the underlying facts or data on cross-examination.

Rule 706 — Court Appointed Experts

(a) Appointment. The court may on its own motion or on the motion of any party enter an order to show cause why expert witnesses should not be appointed, and may request the parties to submit nominations. The court may appoint any expert witnesses agreed upon by the parties, and may appoint expert witnesses of its own selection. An expert witness shall not be appointed by the court unless the witness consents to act. A witness so appointed shall be informed of the witness' duties by the court in writing, a copy of which shall be filed with the clerk, or at a conference in which the parties shall have opportunity to participate. A witness so appointed shall advise the parties of the witness' findings, if any; the witness' deposition may be taken by any party; and the witness may be called to testify by the court or any party. The witness shall be subject to cross-examination by each party, including a party calling the witness.

(b) Compensation. Expert witnesses so appointed are entitled to reasonable compensation in whatever sum the court may allow. The compensation thus fixed is payable from funds which may be provided by law in criminal cases and civil actions and proceedings involving just compensation under the fifth amendment. In other civil actions and proceedings the compensation shall be paid by the parties in such proportion and at such time as the court directs, and thereafter charged in like manner as other costs.

(c) Disclosure of appointment. In the exercise of its discretion, the court may authorize disclosure to the jury of the fact that the court appointed the expert witness.

(d) Parties' experts of own selection. Nothing in this rule limits the parties in calling expert witnesses of their own selection.

ARTICLE VIII. HEARSAY

Rule 801 — Definitions

The following definitions apply under this article:

(a) Statement. A "statement" is (1) an oral or written assertion or (2) nonverbal conduct of a person, if it is intended by the person as an assertion.

(b) Declarant. A "declarant" is a person who makes a statement.

(c) Hearsay. "Hearsay" is a statement, other than one made by the declarant while testifying at the trial or hearing, offered in evidence to prove the truth of the matter asserted.

(d) Statements which are not hearsay. A statement is not hearsay if —

(1) Prior statement by witness. The declarant testifies at the trial or hearing and is subject to cross-examination concerning the statement, and the statement is (A) inconsistent with the declarant's testimony, and was given under oath subject to the penalty of perjury at a trial, hearing, or other proceeding, or in a deposition, or (B) consistent with the declarant's testimony and is offered to rebut an express or implied charge against the declarant of recent fabrication or improper influence or motive, or (C) one of identification of a person made after perceiving the person; or

(2) Admission by party-opponent. The statement is offered against a party and is (A) the party's own statement, in either an individual or a representative capacity or (B) a statement of which the party has manifested an adoption or belief in its truth, or (C) a statement by a person authorized by the party to make a statement concerning the subject, or (D) a statement by the party's agent or servant concerning a matter within the scope of the agency or employment, made during the existence of the relationship, or (E) a statement by a coconspirator of a party during the course and in furtherance of the conspiracy. The contents of the statement shall be considered but are not alone sufficient to establish the declarant's authority under subdivision (C), the agency or employment relationship and scope thereof under subdivision (D), or the existence of the conspiracy and the participation therein of the declarant and the party against whom the statement is offered under subdivision (E).

Rule 802 — Hearsay Rule

Hearsay is not admissible except as provided by these rules or by other rules prescribed by the Supreme Court pursuant to statutory authority or by Act of Congress.

Rule 803 — Hearsay Exceptions; Availability of Declarant Immaterial

The following are not excluded by the hearsay rule, even though the declarant is available as a witness:

(1) Present sense impression. A statement describing or explaining an event or condition made while the declarant was perceiving the event or condition, or immediately thereafter.

(2) Excited utterance. A statement relating to a startling event or condition made while the declarant was under the stress of excitement caused by the event or condition.

(3) Then existing mental, emotional, or physical condition. A statement of the declarant's then existing state of mind, emotion, sensation, or physical condition (such as intent, plan, motive, design, mental feeling, pain, and bodily health), but not including a statement of memory or belief to prove the fact remembered or believed unless it relates to the execution, revocation, identification, or terms of declarant's will.

(4) Statements for purposes of medical diagnosis or treatment. Statements made for purposes of medical diagnosis or treatment and describing medical history, or past or present symptoms, pain, or sensations, or the inception or general character of the cause or external source thereof insofar as reasonably pertinent to diagnosis or treatment.

(docs prepared for litigation) **(5) Recorded recollection.** A memorandum or record concerning a matter about which a witness once had knowledge but now has insufficient recollection to enable the witness to testify fully and accurately, shown to have been made or adopted by the witness when the matter was fresh in the witness' memory and to reflect that knowledge correctly. If admitted, the memorandum or record may be read into evidence but may not itself be received as an exhibit unless offered by an adverse party.

(not prepared for litigation) **(6) Records of regularly conducted activity.** A memorandum, report, record, or data compilation, in any form, of acts, events, conditions, opinions, or diagnoses, made at or near the time by, or from information transmitted by, a person with knowledge, if kept in the course of a regularly conducted business activity, and if it was the regular practice of that business activity to make the memorandum, report, record, or data compilation, all as shown by the testimony of the custodian or other qualified witness, unless the source of information or the method or circumstances of preparation indicate lack of trustworthiness. The term "business" as used in this paragraph includes business, institution, association, profession, occupation, and calling of every kind, whether or not conducted for profit.

(7) Absence of entry in records kept in accordance with the provisions of paragraph (6). Evidence that a matter is not included in the memoranda reports, records, or data compilations, in any form, kept in accordance with the provisions of paragraph (6), to prove the nonoccurrence or nonexistence of the matter, if the matter was of a kind of which a memorandum, report, record, or data compilation was regularly made and preserved, unless the sources of information or other circumstances indicate lack of trustworthiness.

(8) Public records and reports. Records, reports, statements, or data compilations, in any form, of public offices or agencies, setting forth (A) the activities of the office or agency, or (B) matters observed pursuant to duty imposed by law as to which matters there was a duty to report, excluding, however, in criminal cases matters observed by police officers and other law enforcement personnel, or (C) in civil actions and proceedings and against the Government in criminal cases, factual findings resulting from an investigation made pursuant to authority granted by law, unless the sources of information or other circumstances indicate lack of trustworthiness.

(9) Records of vital statistics. Records or data compilations, in any form, of births, fetal deaths, deaths, or marriages, if the report thereof was made to a public office pursuant to requirements of law.

(10) Absence of public record or entry. To prove the absence of a record, report, statement, or data compilation, in any form, or the nonoccurrence or nonexistence of a matter of which a record, report, statement, or data compilation, in any form, was regularly made and preserved by a public office or agency, evidence in the form of a certification in accordance with rule 902, or testimony, that diligent search failed to disclose the record, report, statement, or data compilation, or entry.

(11) Records of religious organizations. Statements of births, marriages, divorces, deaths, legitimacy, ancestry, relationship by blood or marriage, or other similar facts of personal or family history, contained in a regularly kept record of a religious organization.

(12) Marriage, baptismal, and similar certificates. Statements of fact contained in a certificate that the maker performed a marriage or other ceremony or administered a sacrament, made by a clergyman, public official, or other person authorized by the rules or practices of a religious organization or by law to perform the act certified, and purporting to have been issued at the time of the act or within a reasonable time thereafter.

(13) Family records. Statements of fact concerning personal or family history contained in family Bibles, genealogies, charts, engravings on rings, inscriptions on family portraits, engravings on urns, crypts, or tombstones, or the like.

(14) Records of documents affecting an interest in property. The record of a document purporting to establish or affect an interest in property, as proof of the content of the original recorded document and its execution and delivery by each person by whom it purports to have been executed, if the record is a record of a public office and an applicable statute authorizes the recording of documents of that kind in that office.

(15) Statements in documents affecting an interest in property. A statement contained in a document purporting to establish or affect an interest in property if the matter stated was relevant to the purpose of the document, unless dealings with the property since the document was made have been inconsistent with the truth of the statement or the purport of the document.

(16) Statements in ancient documents. Statements in a document in existence twenty years or more the authenticity of which is established.

(17) Market reports, commercial publications. Market quotations, tabulations, lists, directories, or other published compilations, generally used and relied upon by the public or by persons in particular occupations.

(18) Learned treatises. To the extent called to the attention of an expert witness upon cross-examination or relied upon by the expert witness in direct examination, statements contained in published treatises, periodicals, or pamphlets on a subject of history, medicine, or other science or art, established as a reliable authority by the testimony or admission of the witness or by other expert testimony or by judicial notice. If admitted, the statements may be read into evidence but may not be received as exhibits.

(19) Reputation concerning personal or family history. Reputation among members of a person's family by blood, adoption, or marriage, or among a person's associates, or in the community, concerning a person's birth, adoption, marriage, divorce, death, legitimacy, relationship by blood, adoption, or marriage, ancestry, or other similar fact of personal or family history.

(20) Reputation concerning boundaries or general history. Reputation in a community, arising before the controversy, as to boundaries of or customs affecting lands in the community, and reputation as to events of general history important to the community or State or nation in which located.

(21) Reputation as to character. Reputation of a person's character among associates or in the community.

(22) Judgment of previous conviction. Evidence of a final judgment, entered after a trial or upon a plea of guilty (but not upon a plea of nolo contendere), adjudging a person guilty of a crime punishable by death or imprisonment in excess of one year, to prove any fact essential to sustain the judgment, but not including, when offered by the Government in a criminal prosecution for purposes other than impeachment, judgments against persons other than the accused. The pendency of an appeal may be shown but does not affect admissibility.

(23) Judgment as to personal, family or general history, or boundaries. Judgments as proof of matters of personal, family or general history, or boundaries, essential to the judgment, if the same would be provable by evidence of reputation.

(24) [Transferred to Rule 807]

Rule 804 — Hearsay Exceptions; Declarant Unavailable

(a) Definition of unavailability. "Unavailability as a witness" includes situations in which the declarant–

(1) is exempted by ruling of the court on the ground of privilege from testifying concerning the subject matter of the declarant's statement; or

(2) persists in refusing to testify concerning the subject matter of the declarant's statement despite an order of the court to do so; or

(3) testifies to a lack of memory of the subject matter of the declarant's statement; or

(4) is unable to be present or to testify at the hearing because of death or then existing physical or mental illness or infirmity; or

(5) is absent from the hearing and the proponent of a statement has been unable to procure the declarant's attendance (or in the case of a hearsay exception under subdivisions (b)(2), (3), or (4), the declarant's attendance or testimony) by process or other reasonable means.

A declarant is not unavailable as a witness if exemption, refusal, claim of lack of memory, inability, or absence is due to the procurement or wrongdoing of the proponent of a statement for the purpose of preventing the witness from attending or testifying.

(b) Hearsay exceptions. The following are not excluded by the hearsay rule if the declarant is unavailable as a witness:

(1) Former testimony. Testimony given as a witness at another hearing of the same or a different proceeding, or in a deposition taken in compliance with law in the course of the same or another proceeding, if the party against whom the testimony is now offered, or, in a civil action or proceeding, a predecessor in interest, had an opportunity and similar motive to develop the testimony by direct, cross, or redirect examination. *[handwritten: similar importance]*

[handwritten margin: Dying Declarations] **(2) Statement under belief of impending death.** In a prosecution for homicide or in a civil action or proceeding, a statement made by a declarant while believing that the declarant's death was imminent, concerning the cause or circumstances of what the declarant believed to be impending death. *[handwritten: (only admissible for this purpose)]*

(3) Statement against interest. A statement which was at the time of its making so far contrary to the declarant's pecuniary or proprietary interest, or so far tended to subject the declarant to civil or criminal liability, or to render invalid a claim by the declarant against another, that a reasonable person in the declarant's position would not have made the statement unless believing it to be true. A statement tending to expose the declarant to criminal liability and offered to exculpate the accused is not admissible unless corroborating circumstances clearly indicate the trustworthiness of the statement. *[handwritten: (concerning monetary/property rights & freedom from crim liab)]*

(4) Statement of personal or family history. (A) A statement concerning the declarant's own birth, adoption, marriage, divorce, legitimacy, relationship by blood, adoption, or marriage, ancestry, or other similar fact of personal or family history, even though declarant had no means of acquiring personal knowledge of the matter stated; or (B) a statement concerning the foregoing matters, and death also, of another person, if the declarant was related to the other by blood, adoption, or marriage or was so intimately associated with the other's family as to be likely to have accurate information concerning the matter declared.

(5) [Transferred to Rule 807]

(6) Forfeiture by wrongdoing. A statement offered against a party that has engaged or acquiesced in wrongdoing that was intended to, and did, procure the unavailability of the declarant as a witness. *[handwritten: — to deter witness tampering / intimidation.]*

Rule 805 — Hearsay Within Hearsay

Hearsay included within hearsay is not excluded under the hearsay rule if each part of the combined statements conforms with an exception to the hearsay rule provided in these rules.

Rule 806 — Attacking and Supporting Credibility of Declarant

When a hearsay statement, or a statement defined in Rule 801(d)(2)(C), (D), or (E), has been admitted in evidence, the credibility of the declarant may be attacked, and if attacked may be supported, by any evidence which would be admissible for those purposes if declarant had testified as a witness. Evidence of a statement or conduct by the declarant at any time, inconsistent with the declarant's hearsay statement, is not subject to any requirement that the declarant may have been afforded an opportunity to deny or explain. If the party against whom a hearsay statement has been admitted calls the declarant as a witness, the party is entitled to examine the declarant on the statement as if under cross-examination.

Rule 807 — Residual Exception

A statement not specifically covered by Rule 803 or 804 but having equivalent circumstantial guarantees of trustworthiness, is not excluded by the hearsay rule, if the court determines that (A) the statement is offered as evidence of a material fact; (B) the statement is more probative on the point for which it is offered than any other evidence which the proponent can procure through reasonable efforts; and (C) the general purposes of these rules and the interests of justice will best be served by admission of the statement into evidence. However, a statement may not be admitted under this exception unless the proponent of it makes known to the adverse party sufficiently in advance of the trial or hearing to provide the adverse party with a fair opportunity to prepare to meet it, the proponent's intention to offer the statement and the particulars of it, including the name and address of the declarant.

ARTICLE IX. AUTHENTICATION AND IDENTIFICATION

Rule 901 — Requirement of Authentication or Identification

(a) **General provision.** The requirement of authentication or identification as a condition precedent to admissibility is satisfied by evidence sufficient to support a finding that the matter in question is what its proponent claims.

(b) **Illustrations.** By way of illustration only, and not by way of limitation, the following are examples of authentication or identification conforming with the requirements of this rule:

(1) **Testimony of witness with knowledge.** Testimony that a matter is what it is claimed to be.

(2) **Nonexpert opinion on handwriting.** Nonexpert opinion as to the genuineness of handwriting, based upon familiarity not acquired for purposes of litigation.

(3) **Comparison by trier or expert witness.** Comparison by the trier of fact or by expert witnesses with specimens which have been authenticated.

(4) **Distinctive characteristics and the like.** Appearance, contents, substance, internal patterns, or other distinctive characteristics, taken in conjunction with circumstances.

(5) **Voice identification.** Identification of a voice, whether heard firsthand or through mechanical or electronic transmission or recording, by opinion based upon hearing the voice at any time under circumstances connecting it with the alleged speaker.

(6) **Telephone conversations.** Telephone conversations, by evidence that a call was made to the number assigned at the time by the telephone company to a particular person or business, if (A) in the case of a person, circumstances, including self-identification, show the person answering to be the one called, or (B) in the case of a business, the call was made to a place of business and the conversation related to business reasonably transacted over the telephone.

(7) **Public records or reports.** Evidence that a writing authorized by law to be recorded or filed and in fact recorded or filed in a public office, or a purported public record, report, statement, or data compilation, in any form, is from the public office where items of this nature are kept.

(8) **Ancient documents or data compilation.** Evidence that a document or data compilation, in any form, (A) is in such condition as to create no suspicion concerning

its authenticity, (B) was in a place where it, if authentic, would likely be, and (C) has been in existence 20 years or more at the time it is offered.

(9) Process or system. Evidence describing a process or system used to produce a result and showing that the process or system produces an accurate result.

(10) Methods provided by statute or rule. Any method of authentication or identification provided by Act of Congress or by other rules prescribed by the Supreme Court pursuant to statutory authority.

Rule 902 — Self-Authentication

Extrinsic evidence of authenticity as a condition precedent to admissibility is not required with respect to the following:

(1) Domestic public documents under seal. A document bearing a seal purporting to be that of the United States, or of any State, district, Commonwealth, territory, or insular possession thereof, or the Panama Canal Zone, or the Trust Territory of the Pacific Islands, or of a political subdivision, department, officer, or agency thereof, and a signature purporting to be an attestation or execution.

(2) Domestic public documents not under seal. A document purporting to bear the signature in the official capacity of an officer or employee of any entity included in paragraph (1) hereof, having no seal, if a public officer having a seal and having official duties in the district or political subdivision of the officer or employee certifies under seal that the signer has the official capacity and that the signature is genuine.

(3) Foreign public documents. A document purporting to be executed or attested in an official capacity by a person authorized by the laws of a foreign country to make the execution or attestation, and accompanied by a final certification as to the genuineness of the signature and official position (A) of the executing or attesting person, or (B) of any foreign official whose certificate of genuineness of signature and official position relates to the execution or attestation or is in a chain of certificates of genuineness of signature and official position relating to the execution or attestation. A final certification may be made by a secretary of embassy or legation, consul general, consul, vice consul, or consular agent of the United States, or a diplomatic or consular official of the foreign country assigned or accredited to the United States. If reasonable opportunity has been given to all parties to investigate the authenticity and accuracy of official documents, the court may, for good cause shown, order that they be treated as presumptively authentic without final certification or permit them to be evidenced by an attested summary with or without final certification.

(4) Certified copies of public records. A copy of an official record or report or entry therein, or of a document authorized by law to be recorded or filed and actually recorded or filed in a public office, including data compilations in any form, certified as correct by the custodian or other person authorized to make the certification, by certificate complying with paragraph (1), (2), or (3) of this rule or complying with any Act of Congress or rule prescribed by the Supreme Court pursuant to statutory authority.

(5) Official publications. Books, pamphlets, or other publications purporting to be issued by public authority.

(6) Newspapers and periodicals. Printed materials purporting to be newspapers or periodicals.

(7) Trade inscriptions and the like. Inscriptions, signs, tags, or labels purporting to have been affixed in the course of business and indicating ownership, control, or origin.

(8) Acknowledged documents. Documents accompanied by a certificate of acknowledgment executed in the manner provided by law by a notary public or other officer authorized by law to take acknowledgments.

(9) Commercial paper and related documents. Commercial paper, signatures thereon, and documents relating thereto to the extent provided by general commercial law.

(10) Presumptions under Acts of Congress. Any signature, document or other matter declared by Act of Congress to be presumptively or prima facie genuine or authentic.

Rule 903 — Subscribing Witness' Testimony Unnecessary

The testimony of a subscribing witness is not necessary to authenticate a writing unless required by the laws of the jurisdiction whose laws govern the validity of the writing.

ARTICLE X. CONTENTS OF WRITINGS, RECORDINGS, AND PHOTOGRAPHS

Rule 1001 — Definitions

For purposes of this article the following definitions are applicable:

(1) Writings and recordings. "Writings" and "recordings" consist of letters, words, or numbers, or their equivalent, set down by handwriting, typewriting, printing, photostating, photographing, magnetic impulse, mechanical or electronic recording, or other form of data compilation.

(2) Photographs. "Photographs" include still photographs, X-ray films, video tapes, and motion pictures.

(3) Original. An "original" of a writing or recording is the writing or recording itself or any counterpart intended to have the same effect by a person executing or issuing it. An "original" of a photograph includes the negative or any print therefrom. If data are stored in a computer or similar device, any printout or other output readable by sight, shown to reflect the data accurately, is an original.

(4) Duplicate. A "duplicate" is a counterpart produced by the same impression as the original, or from the same matrix, or by means of photography, including enlargements and miniatures, or by mechanical or electronic re-recording, or by chemical reproduction, or by other equivalent techniques which accurately reproduces the original.

Rule 1002 — Requirement of Original

To prove the content of a writing, recording, or photograph, the original writing, recording, or photograph is required, except as otherwise provided in these rules or by Act of Congress.

Rule 1003 — Admissibility of Duplicates

A duplicate is admissible to the same extent as an original unless (1) a genuine question is raised as to the authenticity of the original or (2) in the circumstances it would be unfair to admit the duplicate in lieu of the original.

Rule 1004 — Admissibility of Other Evidence of Contents

The original is not required, and other evidence of the contents of a writing, recording, or photograph is admissible if –

(1) Originals lost or destroyed. All originals are lost or have been destroyed, unless the proponent lost or destroyed them in bad faith; or

(2) Original not obtainable. No original can be obtained by any available judicial process or procedure; or

(3) Original in possession of opponent. At a time when an original was under the control of the party against whom offered, that party was put on notice, by the pleadings or otherwise, that the contents would be a subject of proof at the hearing, and that party does not produce the original at the hearing; or

(4) Collateral matters. The writing, recording, or photograph is not closely related to a controlling issue.

Rule 1005 — Public Records

The contents of an official record, or of a document authorized to be recorded or filed and actually recorded or filed, including data compilations in any form, if otherwise admissible, may be proved by copy, certified as correct in accordance with rule 902 or testified to be correct by a witness who has compared it with the original. If a copy which complies with the foregoing cannot be obtained by the exercise of reasonable diligence, then other evidence of the contents may be given.

Rule 1006 — Summaries

The contents of voluminous writings, recordings, or photographs which cannot conveniently be examined in court may be presented in the form of a chart, summary, or calculation. The originals, or duplicates, shall be made available for examination or copying, or both, by other parties at reasonable time and place. The court may order that they be produced in court.

Rule 1007 — Testimony or Written Admission of Party

Contents of writings, recordings, or photographs may be proved by the testimony or deposition of the party against whom offered or by that party's written admission, without accounting for the nonproduction of the original.

Rule 1008 — Functions of Court and Jury

When the admissibility of other evidence of contents of writings, recordings, or photographs under these rules depends upon the fulfillment of a condition of fact, the question whether the condition has been fulfilled is ordinarily for the court to determine in accordance with the provisions of rule 104. However, when an issue is raised (a) whether the asserted writing ever existed, or (b) whether another writing, recording, or photograph produced at the trial is the original, or (c) whether other evidence of contents correctly reflects the contents, the issue is for the trier of fact to determine as in the case of other issues of fact.

ARTICLE XI. MISCELLANEOUS RULES

Rule 1101 — Applicability of Rules

(a) **Courts and judges.** These Rules apply to the United States district courts, the District Court of Guam, the District Court of the Virgin Islands, the District Court for the Northern Mariana Islands, the United States Courts of Appeals, the United States Claims Court, and to United States bankruptcy judges and United States magistrate judges, in the actions, cases, and proceedings and to the extent hereinafter set forth. The terms "judge" and "court" in these rules include United States bankruptcy judges and United States magistrate judges.

(b) **Proceedings generally.** These rules apply generally to civil actions and proceedings, including admiralty and maritime cases, to criminal cases and proceedings, to contempt proceedings except those in which the court may act summarily, and to proceedings and cases under title 11, United States Code.

(c) **Rule of privilege.** The rule with respect to privileges applies at all stages of all actions, cases, and proceedings.

(d) **Rules inapplicable.** The rules (other than with respect to privileges) do not apply in the following situations:

(1) **Preliminary questions of fact.** The determination of questions of fact preliminary to admissibility of evidence when the issue is to be determined by the court under rule 104.

(2) **Grand jury.** Proceedings before grand juries.

(3) **Miscellaneous proceedings.** Proceedings for extradition or rendition; preliminary examinations in criminal cases; sentencing, or granting or revoking probation; issuance of warrants for arrest, criminal summonses, and search warrants; and proceedings with respect to release on bail or otherwise.

(e) **Rules applicable in part.** In the following proceedings these rules apply to the extent that matters of evidence are not provided for in the statutes which govern procedure therein or in other rules prescribed by the Supreme Court pursuant to statutory authority: the trial of misdemeanors and other petty offenses before United States magistrate judges; review of agency actions when the facts are subject to trial de novo under section 706(2)(F) of title 5, United States Code; review of orders of the Secretary of Agriculture under section 2 of the Act entitled "An Act to authorize association of producers of agricultural products" approved February 18, 1922 (7 U.S.C. 292), and under sections 6 and 7(c) of the Perishable Agricultural Commodities Act, 1930 (7 U.S.C. 499f, 499g(c)); naturalization and revocation of naturalization under sections 310–318 of the Immigration and Nationality Act (8 U.S.C. 1421–1429); prize proceedings in admiralty under sections 7651–7681 of title 10, United States Code; review of orders of the Secretary of the Interior under section 2 of the Act entitled "An Act authorizing associations of producers of aquatic products" approved June 25, 1934 (15 U.S.C. 522); review of orders of petroleum control boards under section 5 of the Act entitled "An Act to regulate interstate and foreign commerce in petroleum and its products by prohibiting the shipment in such commerce of petroleum and its products produced in violation of State law, and for other purposes," approved February 22, 1935 (15 U.S.C. 715d); actions for fines, penalties, or forfeitures under part V of title IV of the Tariff Act of 1930 (19 U.S.C. 1581–1624), or under the Anti-Smuggling Act (19 U.S.C. 1701–1711); criminal libel for condemnation, exclusion of imports, or other proceedings under the Federal Food, Drug, and Cosmetic Act (21 U.S.C. 301–392); disputes between seamen under sections 4079, 4080, and 4081 of the Revised Statutes (22 U.S.C. 256–258); habeas corpus under sections 2241–2254 of title 28, United States Code; motions to vacate, set aside or correct sentence under section 2255 of title 28, United States Code; actions for penalties for refusal to transport destitute seamen under section 4578 of the Revised Statutes (46 U.S.C. 679); actions against the United States under the Act entitled "An Act authorizing suits against the United States in admiralty for damage caused by and salvage service rendered to public vessels belonging to the United States, and for other purposes," approved March 3, 1925 (46 U.S.C. 781–790), as implemented by section 7730 of title 10, United States Code.

Rule 1102 — Amendments

Amendments to the Federal Rules of Evidence may be made as provided in section 2072 of title 28 of the United States Code.

28 U.S.C. §2072

The Supreme Court of the United States shall have the power to prescribe amendments to the Federal Rules of Evidence. Such amendments shall not take effect until they have been reported to Congress by the Chief Justice at or after the beginning of a regular session of Congress but not later than the first day of May, and until the expiration of one hundred and eighty days after they have been so reported; but if either House of Congress within that time shall by resolution disapprove any amendment so reported it shall not take effect. The effective date of any amendment so reported may be deferred by either House of Congress to a later date or until approved by Act of Congress. Any rule whether proposed or in force may be amended by Act of Congress. Any provision of law in force at the expiration of such time and in conflict with any such amendment not disapproved shall be of no further force or effect after such amendment has taken effect. Any such amendment creating, abolishing, or modifying a privilege shall have no force or effect unless it shall be approved by Act of Congress.

Rule 1103 — Title

These rules may be known and cited as the Federal Rules of Evidence.

INDEX

This is an index of the "Definition," "Commentary," and "Rehabilitation" sections of each chapter. References in the text to rule number are indexed under "Rules."

E

Emotional condition, hearsay exception, 136
Exceptions to hearsay rule
    See specific topics
Excited utterances, hearsay exception, 134
Exhibits
    demonstrative, 67
    generally, 62
    illustrative, 64
    impeachment, 82
    models, 69
    photographs, 68
    tangible objects, 70
    writings, 62
Expert opinion
    firsthand knowledge requirement, 8
    generally, 74
Expert witnesses
    bases for opinion, 74
    court-appointed, 75
    demonstrative exhibits, 69
    hypothetical questions, 8, 77
    illustrative exhibits, 65
    leading questions, 24
    learned treatises, 77, 161
    limited admissibility for basis, 76
    qualifications, 76
    scientific theories, 76
    ultimate issue, 74
    voice authentication, 56
Extrinsic evidence, 99
    See also Impeachment
    bias, prejudice, interest, or improper
      motive, 85
    credibility attacked, 84, 88
    hearsay, impeachment of, 125
    prior inconsistent statement, 125
    specific instances of misconduct, 101

F

Family history
    hearsay exception
    hearsay exception, judgment, 168

    hearsay exception, reputation, 163
Family records, hearsay exception, 155
Felony convictions
    hearsay exception, 166
    impeachment by, 92
Firsthand knowledge
    admissions, 132
    business records, required in, hearsay
      exceptions, 143
    defined, 8
    demonstrative exhibits, 68
    expert witnesses, 5, 8
    generally, 8
    habit, 41
    public records, required in, hearsay
      exception, 148, 151
Form of questions
    See also Cross examination
    ambiguous, 15
    argumentative, 16
    asked and answered, 18
    assuming facts not in evidence, 20
    compound, 22
    cross examination, exceeding scope of
      direct, 80
    hypothetical, 8, 77
    leading, 23
    leading, dying declarations, 174
    reputation, 89

G

General history, reputation as to, hearsay
    exception, 164
Guilty pleas, admissibility, 48

H

Habit and routine practice, 41
Handwriting, authentication, 53, 55
Hearsay
    See also Limited admissibility
    See also Non-hearsay
    See also Out-of-court statements
    See also Records
    ancient documents, 159

baptismal certificates, 154

belief of impending death, statement under, 173

bias, prejudice, interest or improper motive, 84

boundaries, reputation as to, 164, 168

business records, 144

character, reputation as to, 165

commercial publications, 160

confessions, criminal, 176

contemporaneous statements, 133, 136

convictions, prior, 166

credibility of declarant, 125

data compilations, 143, 160

death, belief of impending, statement under, 173

declarations against interest, 175

defined, 121

diagnosis or treatment, statements for, 139

dying declarations, 123, 173

emotional condition statements, 136

excited utterances, 134

extrinsic evidence, impeachment by, 125

family history, 153, 168, 177

family records, 155

forfeiture by wrongdoing, 179

former testimony, 171

general history, 164, 168

generally, 121

impeachment of declarant, 125

interest in property, document affecting, hearsay exception, 156

judgments, 166

learned treatises, 161

market reports, 160

marriage certificates, 154

medical diagnosis or treatment, statements for, 139

mental condition statements, 136

multiple hearsay, 123

other exceptions, 181

out-of-court statement, 121

out-of-court statement, presence of declarant, 122

past recollection recorded, 141

patient's statements, 123

personal history, 163, 168, 177

physical condition statements, 138

present recollection refreshed, 141

present sense impression, 133

pretrial notice, use of residual exception, 182

prior convictions, 166

prior inconsistent statements, 99, 125

prior testimony, 171

property interest, documents affecting, 156

public records and reports, 148

recorded recollection, 141

records of regularly conducted activity, 143

redaction, 123

relevance, generally, 122

religious organizations, records, 153

reputation concerning boundaries or general history, 164

reputation concerning personal or family history, 163

residual exceptions, 181

spontaneous statements, 133

startled utterances, 134

statements against interest, 158, 175

testimony in earlier proceedings, 171

then existing mental or emotional condition, statements, 136

then existing physical condition, 138

totem pole rules, 123

treatises, 161

unavailability, requirement, 169

vital statistics, 152

within hearsay, 123

Hearsay exception

    public records and reports, 148

Hearsay exceptions

    See specific topics

Hillmon v. Mutual Life Insurance Co., 137

History, hearsay exception, 163

Honesty, character trait
    See Rehabilitation
Hostile witness
    cross examination, 80
    defined, 24
    leading questions, 24
Houston Oxygen, 133
Hypothetical questions
    See Expert witnesses

I

Identification, out-of-court, 127, 129
Illustrative exhibits, 64
    See also Writings
Impeachment
    See also Extrinsic evidence
    See also Rehabilitation
    appeal, convictions under, 93, 94
    by bias, prejudice, interest, or improper motive, 84, 85, 125
    by character evidence, 88
    by subsequent remedial measures, 43
    chart, 83
    civil, prior conviction, 92
    defined, 82
    discretion of court, admissibility of convictions, 93, 95, 97
    dishonesty, specific instances, 101
    faulty memory, 90
    generally, 82
    hearsay declarant, 125
    juvenile adjudications, 93, 96
    limited admissibility, 39, 50
    memory, 90
    misconduct, specific instances, 101
    pardoned convictions, 94
    perception, 91
    pretrial determination of admissibility, convictions, 93, 95, 97
    prior conviction, 94
    prior convictions (criminal), 95
    prior inconsistent statement, 98, 125
    sensory impairment, 91

Impending death, statement under belief of, hearsay exception, 173
Improper motive or influence, impeachment for, 86
Inferences
    drawn on direct, 16
    expert witnesses, 74
    intention to act, 137
    lay opinions, 72
    prior consistent statements, 128
    prior inconsistent statements, 128
    specific instances of misconduct, 101
Instances of misconduct
    character evidence, 103
    impeachment by, 102
Instrument, authentication, 52
Insurance, limited admissibility, 50
Intention to act, admissibility, 137
Interest in outcome, impeachment for, 84, 86
Interpreters, 6

J

Judges, competence to testify, 6
Judgments, hearsay exception, 166
Judicial notice
    defined, 9
    generally, 9
    of law, 9
Jurors, competence to testify, 6
Jury presence
    offers of proof, 3
    relevance obligations, 32
Juvenile adjudications, as impeachment, 93

L

Leading questions
    See Form of questions
    adverse party, 24
    children, 23
    cross examination, 23
    defined, 23
    direct examination, 23
    expert witnesses, 24
    hostile witnesses, 24

P

Palmer v. Hoffman, 145

Pardoned convictions, as impeachment, 94

Past recollection recorded, hearsay exception, 141

Payment of medical expenses, 47

Personal history, hearsay exception, 163, 168, 177

Personal knowledge
    See Firsthand knowledge

Photocopy, as original, 59, 60

Photographs, 67
    See also Writings

Physical condition, statements, hearsay exceptions, 138

Plain error, 2

Pleas and plea agreements
    admissibility, 48
    disclosure for impeachment, 86

Police reports
    See Records

Prejudice
    exclusion of relevant evidence for, 18, 33
    impeachment for, 85

Preliminary matters, leading questions, 23

Present bodily condition, hearsay exception, 138

Present recollection refreshed, not hearsay, 141

Present sense impressions
    hearsay exception, 133

Presumptions
    burden of presumption, 11
    burden of proof shifts, 11
    civil cases, 11
    competence to testify, 6
    defined, 11
    generally, 11
    mailbox rule defined, 12

Pretrial motions
    convictions as impeachment, 93, 95, 97
    hearsay exceptions, residual clause, 181
    relevance issues, 32
    writings, 63

Prior act of misconduct, impeachment by, 101

Prior consistent statements
    identification, 129
    impeachment of hearsay, 128
    limited admissibility, 128
    rehabilitation, 128
    rehabilitation from bias, 87
    relevance, 128

Prior convictions
    hearsay exception, 166
    impeachment by, 92

Prior inconsistent statements
    adoption required, 99
    hearsay, impeachment, 125
    impeachment, generally, 98
    limited admissibility, 17, 39, 99, 100, 128
    non-hearsay, impeachment, 128
    oath, given under, 99

Prior sexual activity, admissibility, 112

Privileges, 13, 14
    attorney-client, 13
    defined, 13
    existing privileges, 13
    generally, 13
    spousal, 14

Profit motive, required for business records, hearsay exception, 144

Propensity
    See Character evidence

Public records
    See Records

R

Rape Shield, 114

Recorded recollection, hearsay exception, 141

Recordings
    See Writings

Records
    See also Hearsay
    See also Limited admissibility
    See also Writings
    absence of entry, records, hearsay exception, 146, 150

S

T

Tape recording
    See Writings
Telephone conversations, authentication, 53, 56
Testimony in earlier proceedings, hearsay exception, 171
Then existing mental or emotional condition, 136
Then existing physical condition, 136, 138
Timing
    business records creation, hearsay exception, 144
    challenge to witness' competence, 6
    excited utterance, 134
    judicial notice, 10
    objections, 2
    offers of proof, 1, 4
    remainder of writings, 37
Treatises, admissibility, 161

U

Ultimate issue, opinion, 72
Unavailability, requirement for hearsay exception, 169
Unfair prejudice, defined, 34

V

Victim, character traits, 103
Vital statistics, hearsay exception, 152
Voices, authentication, 56
Voir dire
    competence of witness, 6
    writing admissibility, 63

W

Waiver, appellate review, 1
Waste of time, exclusion of relevant evidence for, 18, 33
Weight of testimony vs. competence to testify, 6
Writings
    See also Impeachment
    See also Prior inconsistent statements
    See also Records
    authentication, 53, 55, 62

completeness rule, 37
exhibits, 62
original document rule, 58
recorded recollection, hearsay exception, 141
redaction, 63
refreshing present recollection, 29

QUICK REFERENCE GUIDE

This quick reference guide is intended to be used in moot or trial court. It provides the minimum language required to make or respond to an objection. The chapter titles have been reworded to facilitate access. Refer to the chapters listed for the full text of the objection or response.

AMBIGUOUS QUESTIONS

611

Objection

> ➤ *The question is (ambiguous—vague—unintelligible).*

Response

> ➤ In most circumstances, rephrase the question.

ARGUMENTATIVE QUESTIONS

611

Objections

> ➤ *The question is argumentative.*
> ➤ *Counsel is arguing to the jury.*

Response

> ➤ *I am trying to elicit evidence from the witness.*

ASKED AND ANSWERED

611

Objections

> ➤ *That question has been asked and answered.*
> ➤ *The witness has already answered that question.*

Responses

> ➤ *The witness has not yet answered the question.*
> ➤ *The question has not been answered during my examination.*

ASSUMING FACTS NOT IN EVIDENCE

611, 602

Objection

> ➤ *The question assumes a fact not in evidence. There has been no testimony that _____.*

Responses

> ➤ *I will elicit that fact from the witness in a separate question.*
> ➤ *That fact has been proved during the earlier testimony of this witness.*
> ➤ *That fact has been proved by* (insert name of a witness who has already testified).
> ➤ *This fact will be testified to by* (insert name of a witness who will testify later).

AUTHENTICATION OF INSTRUMENTS

901–3

Objection

> ➤ *This exhibit has not been authenticated.*

Responses

➤ *The instrument has been authenticated by stipulation of counsel.*

➤ *The instrument has been authenticated by* (insert name of witness) *who has testified that:*

    (a) *(s)he created the writing,* or

    (b) *(s)he was present at the creation of the writing and testified that it is in substantially the same condition as at the time of its creation,* or

    (c) *(s)he knows the handwriting because (s)he saw the author write or sign the instrument,* or

    (d) *(s)he knows the handwriting from having seen the author sign his name at another time,* or

    (e) *(s)he knows the handwriting by circumstantial evidence that shows* (state circumstances), or

    (f) (where proved by an expert witness) *(s)he has compared the handwriting with an authentic handwriting exemplar and his/her opinion is that the handwriting is that of* (insert name of purported author), or

    (g) *(s)he was present at the time the tape recording was made,* or

    (h) *(s)he saw the scene or items portrayed in the photograph at a relevant time and that the photograph is a fair and accurate representation of what (s)he saw.*

➤ *I request that your honor compare the handwriting in question with an admittedly authentic handwriting exemplar and find that it is the handwriting of* (insert name of purported author).

AUTHENTICATION OF TELEPHONE CONVERSATIONS AND VOICES   901

Objections

➤ *The phone conversation has not been authenticated.*

➤ *The participants in the phone conversation have not been properly identified.*

Response

➤ *The identity of the participants in the phone conversation has been established through the testimony of* (insert name of witness) *who has testified that:*

    (a) *(s)he is familiar with and recognized the voice,* or

    (b) *(s)he called the number listed to* (insert name of participant) *and the other party identified himself as* (insert name of participant), or

    (c) *(s)he called the number listed to* (insert name of participant) *and the content of the conversation showed* (insert name of person) *to be the person who answered the call,* or

(d) *(s)he called the number listed to* (insert name of business) *and the conversation related to business conducted by* (insert name of business) *over the telephone,* or

(e) (where proved by a qualified expert witness) *(s)he has compared the voice with an authentic voice exemplar and his/her opinion is that the voice is that of* (insert name of purported speaker).

BEST EVIDENCE RULE – ORIGINAL DOCUMENT RULE 1001–8
Objection
➤ *The proponent offers to show the contents of a writing by the use of secondary evidence.*

Responses
➤ *The terms of the writing are not in issue and thus the original is not required. The writing is offered to prove _____.*

➤ *The original's absence has been sufficiently accounted for and thus secondary evidence is admissible because the original:*

(a) *has been lost or destroyed,* or

(b) *cannot be obtained by judicial process or procedure,* or

(c) *is in the possession of an opposing party against whom the contents are offered, that the party has failed to produce it, and that party has been put on notice that the contents would be subject of proof at trial.*

CHARACTER EVIDENCE – ACCUSED OR VICTIM (Criminal Cases) 404–5
Objection
➤ *The prosecution is attempting to offer evidence of the defendant's (or victim's) character where the defendant has not offered any character evidence.*

Responses
➤ *The defendant has opened the door on his character by offering evidence of his pertinent character trait.*

➤ *The defendant has opened the door on the victim's character by:*

(a) *offering evidence of the victim's character,* or

(b) *offering evidence that the victim was the first aggressor in a homicide case.*

CHARACTER EVIDENCE GENERALLY 404–5
Objection
➤ *The question calls for (or the answer provides) evidence of character offered on propensity.*

Response

> *This evidence is:*
>
>   (a) *offered on propensity pursuant to Rule 404(a)(1) or 404(a)(2), or*
>
>   (b) *offered for a relevant, non-propensity purpose under Rule 404(b), or*
>
>   (c) *offered to prove propensity where character is an essential element of a claim, charge, or defense under Rule 405(b).*

CHARACTER EVIDENCE – OTHER ACTS, CRIMES, OR WRONGS   404

Objection

> *This is inadmissible character evidence offered on propensity.*

Response

> *This is not offered on propensity, but rather for the purpose of showing _____, a relevant, non-propensity purpose, pursuant to Rule 404(b).*

CHARACTER EVIDENCE – PRIOR SEXUAL ACTIVITY OF   412
ALLEGED VICTIM (Criminal Cases)

Objections

> (Opinion of reputation evidence) *The question calls for opinion or reputation evidence concerning the victim's sexual behavior or sexual predisposition.*
>
> (Specific instances of conduct) *The question calls for evidence of specific instances of conduct on the issue of the victim's sexual behavior or sexual predisposition.*

Responses

> (Opinion or reputation evidence) *There is no appropriate response.*
>
> (Specific instances of conduct) *The evidence of sexual behavior is admissible:*
>
>   (a) *to prove that someone other than the defendant was the source of semen, injury, or physical condition of the alleged victim;*
>
>   (b) *as it was with the defendant and is offered on the issue of consent;*
>
>   (c) *as it is offered by the prosecution;*
>
>   (d) *as it is offered by the defendant and the failure to admit this evidence of sexual behavior or sexual predisposition would violate the constitutional rights of the defendant; and*
>
>   *proper notice has been given the alleged victim and the parties, and the judge has determined, in camera, that the evidence is admissible.*

CHARACTER EVIDENCE – PRIOR SEXUAL ACTIVITY OF   412
ALLEGED VICTIM (Civil Cases)

Objections

> (Opinion evidence) *The question calls for opinion evidence concerning sexual behavior or sexual predisposition of a victim of sexual misconduct.*

- (Reputation evidence) *The question calls for reputation evidence concerning sexual behavior or sexual predisposition of a victim of sexual misconduct, and the victim has not placed that reputation in issue.*
- (Specific instances of conduct)
    - (a) *The question calls for evidence concerning the sexual behavior or sexual predisposition of a victim of sexual misconduct and it is irrelevant;* or
    - (b) *The question calls for evidence concerning the sexual behavior or sexual predisposition of a victim of sexual misconduct and the probative value of the evidence does not substantially outweighs the danger or harm to the victim, and/or unfair prejudice to my client.*

Responses

- (Opinion evidence) *There is no appropriate response.*
- (Reputation evidence) *The victim of the alleged sexual misconduct put his/her reputation for sexual behavior or sexual predisposition in issue when the following evidence was offered* (insert evidence, as offered by the victim, that put his/her reputation for sexual behavior or sexual predisposition in issue).
- (Specific instances of conduct) *The evidence of sexual behavior or sexual predisposition is otherwise admissible pursuant to Federal Rules of Evidence 404, 405, or 406 and the probative value of the evidence substantially outweighs the danger of harm to the victim or unfair prejudice to any party.*

CHARACTER EVIDENCE — EVIDENCE OF SIMILAR ACTS   413–15
OR CRIMES IN CIVIL OR CRIMINAL CASES INVOLVING
SEXUAL ASSAULT OR CHILD MOLESTATION

Objection

- *I object that this evidence is inadmissible character evidence offered on propensity.*

Response

- *This offer involves evidence of a similar crime of sexual assault or child molestation, offered*
    - (a) *in a criminal case charging sexual assault or child molestation,* or
    - (b) *in a civil case concerning sexual assault or child molestation.*

COMPETENCE TO TESTIFY   601–6

Objections

- *This witness is incompetent to testify because he lacks the ability to _____, which has been shown on the voir dire of the witness.*
- *The witness is incompetent in that his testimony shows he lacks the ability to _____.*

Responses

> ➤ *The witness is presumed competent and there has been no showing of any inability on the part of the witness to perceive, remember, communicate, or appreciate the oath.*

> ➤ *The witness is competent to testify and any questions regarding the witness' testimonial capacities go to the weight of the evidence rather than to the competency of the witness.*

COMPOUND QUESTIONS 611

Objection

> ➤ *The question is compound.*

Response

> ➤ *I withdraw the question and will ask separate questions.*

COMPROMISE AND OFFERS OF COMPROMISE 408

Objection

> ➤ *This is evidence of compromise negotiations offered on liability and/or damages.*

Response

> ➤ *This is admissible because:*
>
> (a) *the claim was not in dispute at the time of the compromise discussions, and/or*
>
> (b) *the evidence is not offered on liability or damages issues but to show:*
>
> (1) *bias, or*
>
> (2) *no undue delay, or*
>
> (3) *an effort to subvert a criminal investigation.*

CROSS EXAMINATION GENERALLY 611

Objection

> ➤ *I have not had the opportunity to conduct a full and fair cross examination of the witness. I move to strike the direct testimony of the witness and ask that the jury be instructed to disregard the testimony of the witness.*

Responses

> ➤ *The purposes of cross examination have been substantially completed.*

> ➤ *Counsel has waived the right to a full and complete cross examination by _____.*

CROSS EXAMINATION – SCOPE 611
Objection

> ➤ *The question on cross examination exceeds the scope of direct examination.*

Responses

> ➤ *The subject matter was raised when the witness testified on direct examination that* _____.

> ➤ *The question seeks to elicit information that is relevant to the credibility of the witness.*

> ➤ *I request that the court allow inquiry outside the scope of the direct examination. I will inquire of the witness as if on direct examination.*

EXHIBITS – DEMONSTRATIVE 901, 611
Objections

> ➤ *The proffered exhibit has not been properly authenticated.*

> ➤ *The proffered exhibit has not been shown to be a fair and accurate representation of a relevant scene or an object in issue.*

Responses

> ➤ *The exhibit has been authenticated by* (insert name of witness) *who has testified that the exhibit is a fair and accurate representation of the scene or object in issue.*

> ➤ (Photographs) *The witness has testified that the photograph shows a relevant scene as it appeared at a relevant time and the exhibit is a fair and accurate depiction of that scene.*

> ➤ (To-scale models) *The witness has testified that the exhibit is a to-scale model and is a fair and accurate representation of an object that is in issue.*

EXHIBITS – ILLUSTRATIVE 901, 611
Objections

> ➤ *The proffered exhibit has not been properly authenticated.*

> ➤ *The proffered exhibit is confusing and/or misleading.*

> ➤ *The proffered exhibit contains markings that will lead the witness in the giving of testimony.*

Responses

> ➤ *The exhibit has been authenticated by* (insert name of witness) *who has testified that:*
>> (a) *(s)he recognizes what the exhibit portrays,* and
>>
>> (b) *that the exhibit will aid in explaining the witness' testimony.*

> ➤ *The exhibit is not offered as a to-scale diagram but merely to explain testimony. Any problems with the exhibit can be demonstrated during cross examination.*

> (Insert name of witness) *has already testified as to what the markings contained on the exhibit portray. The exhibit is offered merely to illustrate that testimony.*

EXHIBITS – TANGIBLE OBJECTS   901
Objection
> *The proffered exhibit is incompetent for lack of proper foundation.*

Response
> *I have shown through the testimony of* (insert name of witness) *that:*
>   (a) *he perceived the exhibit at a relevant time,* and
>   (b) *the exhibit is the one perceived,* and
>   (c) *the exhibit is in substantially the same condition as it was at the relevant time.*

EXHIBITS – WRITINGS
Objection
> *I object to the introduction of the exhibit in that there is an improper foundation because:*
>   (a) *it is not relevant,* or
>   (b) *authenticity has not been shown,* or
>   (c) *the original document rule has not been met,* or
>   (d) *the writing is hearsay.*

Response
> *The foundational requirements regarding relevance, authentication, the original document rule, and hearsay have been met through the testimony of* (insert names of witnesses) *who have testified that* _____ .

EXPERT OPINION   702–6
Objections
> *I object to the qualification of the witness as an expert.*
> *The discipline in which the witness purports to qualify as an expert is not generally recognized in the field.*
> *The witness' opinion is beyond the area of expertise in which he has been qualified.*

Responses
> *I have shown that the witness is qualified as an expert in* (insert field) *through his knowledge, skill, experience, training, or education.*
> *I have shown that the area of expertise in which the witness is qualified is generally accepted in the branch of the discipline to which it belongs.*
> *The court has qualified the expert in the area of* (insert field) *and his opinion is within that area.*

FIRSTHAND KNOWLEDGE
Objection
> There has been no foundation to show that the witness has personal knowledge of that matter.

Response
> The witness has shown that he had firsthand knowledge of the subject of his testimony.

GUILTY PLEAS, OFFERS OF PLEAS, AND RELATED STATEMENTS
Objection
> This is inadmissible as a withdrawn guilty plea, as a nolo plea, or as an offer to so plead.

Response
> This is admissible against the criminal defendant because he is charged with perjury and the statement was made under oath, in the presence of counsel, and on the record.

HABIT AND ROUTINE PRACTICE
Objection
> This is such an isolated occurrence as to be insufficient to constitute a habit or routine practice.

Response
> This is relevant because it shows a consistent habit or routine practice which raises a permissible inference that the party or organization likely acted according to the habit or routine practice.

HEARSAY DECLARANT – CREDIBILITY
Objection
> The question attacks the credibility of a person who has not appeared as a witness.

Response
> This impeachment of an out-of-court declarant is permissible to the same extent available for a testifying witness.

HEARSAY – NON-HEARSAY ADMISSIONS
Objections
> The question calls for a hearsay answer.
> I move to strike the answer as hearsay.

Response

> The statement is not hearsay pursuant to Rule 801(d)(2) because I have shown that the statement was made:
>
> (a) *by the party opponent,* or
>
> (b) *by a person and was adopted by the party opponent as his/her own, and is thus a vicarious admission,* or
>
> (c) *by an agent authorized to speak on behalf of a party opponent, and is thus a vicarious admission,* or
>
> (d) (1) *by an agent or servant of the party opponent,*
>
> (2) *concerning a matter within the scope of the declarant's agency or employment,* and
>
> (3) *was made during the existence of the declarant's agency or employment, and is thus a vicarious admission,* or
>
> (e) (1) *by a co-conspirator of the party opponent,*
>
> (2) *during the course of the conspiracy,* and
>
> (3) *in furtherance of the conspiracy, and is thus a vicarious admission.*

HEARSAY – NON-HEARSAY PRIOR STATEMENTS   801

Objections

> *The question calls for a hearsay answer.*

> *I move to strike the answer as hearsay.*

Response

> The statement is not hearsay pursuant to Rule 801(d)(1) because I have shown that:
>
> (a) *it is inconsistent with the witness' trial testimony and was given under oath at an earlier proceeding or at a deposition,* or
>
> (b) *it is consistent with the witness' trial testimony, and is offered to rebut an express or implied charge of recent fabrication, or improper influence or motive,* or
>
> (c) *the statement by the testifying witness is an identification of a person made after perceiving such person.*

HEARSAY EXCEPTION – ABSENCE OF ENTRY IN BUSINESS RECORDS   803

Objections

> *I object. The question calls for hearsay.*

> *I move to strike the answer as hearsay.*

Response

> *The absence of an entry in this record is admissible to show the nonoccurrence of an event pursuant to Rule 803(7). I have shown through the testimony*

of (insert name of witness) *who is the custodian of the business records, or other qualified person that:*

(a) *a business record exists, pursuant to Rule 803(6),* and

(b) *the matter which is not recorded in the record is of a kind for which a record would regularly be made and preserved,* and

(c) *the source of information or other circumstances fail to indicate a lack of trustworthiness.*

HEARSAY EXCEPTION – ABSENCE OF PUBLIC RECORD OR ENTRY 803

Objections

> ➤ *The question calls for hearsay.*

> ➤ *I move to strike the answer as hearsay.*

Response

> ➤ *Evidence of a diligent but unavailing search of the records of the public agency or office is admissible pursuant to the hearsay exception in Rule 803(10). I have shown through a certification which complies with Rule 902 or through the testimony of* (insert name of witness) *that:*

(a) *a public agency or office regularly makes and preserves records of a particular kind,* and

(b) *a diligent, but unavailing search of such records failed to disclose a record or entry regarding a particular alleged happening.*

HEARSAY EXCEPTION – ANCIENT DOCUMENTS 803

Objection

> ➤ *This statement is contained in an out-of-court writing offered for its truth, which is hearsay.*

Response

> ➤ *This is admissible pursuant to Rule 803(16). I have shown through* (insert name of witness) *that the statement is contained in a document in existence twenty years or more, the authenticity of which is established.*

HEARSAY EXCEPTION – BELIEF OF IMPENDING DEATH 804

Objections

> ➤ *The question calls for a hearsay answer.*

> ➤ *I move to strike the statement as hearsay.*

Response

> ➤ *This is admissible pursuant to Rule 804(b)(2). I have shown through* (insert name of witness) *that the statement:*

(a) *was made by a declarant who is now unavailable pursuant to Rule 804(a),*

(b) *is offered in a prosecution for homicide or a civil action,*

(c) *was made by the declarant while believing that his death was imminent,* and

(d) *concerns the cause or circumstances of what the declarant believed to be impending death.*

HEARSAY EXCEPTION – BUSINESS RECORDS – RECORDS OF REGULARLY CONDUCTED ACTIVITY

Objections

➤ *The question calls for a hearsay answer.*

➤ *I move to strike the answer as hearsay.*

Response

➤ *This is admissible pursuant to Rule 803(6). I have shown through* (insert name of witness) *who is a custodian of the record or who is a person with knowledge of the record keeping system, that the statement is contained in a:*

(a) (for a man-made record)

(1) *memorandum, report, record, or data compilation,*

(2) *recording acts, events, conditions, opinions, or diagnoses,*

(3) *made at or near the time the acts or events took place,*

(4) *by or from information transmitted by one with personal knowledge of the event or act,*

(5) *where such record is kept in the course of a regularly conducted business activity,* and

(6) *it was the regular practice of the business to make such record.*

(b) (for a computer-generated record, repeat foundation steps (a)(1–6) above and add:)

(7) *the computer and the program used are generally accepted in the field,*

(8) *the computer was in good working order at the relevant times,* and

(9) *the computer operator possessed the knowledge and training to correctly operate the computer.*

HEARSAY EXCEPTION – DOCUMENTS AFFECTING AN INTEREST IN PROPERTY

Objections

➤ *The question calls for a hearsay answer.*

➤ *I move to strike the answer as hearsay.*

Response

➤ *This is admissible pursuant to Rule 803(15). I have shown through* (insert name of witness) *that:*

(a) *the statement is contained in a document purporting to establish or affect an interest in property,*

(b) *the matter stated was relevant to the purposes of the document,* and

(c) *dealings with the property since the document was made have not been inconsistent with the truth of the statement or the purpose of the document.*

HEARSAY EXCEPTION – EXCITED UTTERANCE 803

Objections

> *The question calls for a hearsay answer.*

> *I move to strike the answer as hearsay.*

Response

> *This is admissible pursuant to Rule 803(2). I have shown through* (insert name of witness) *that the statement:*

(a) *relates to a startling event or condition,* and

(b) *was made while the declarant was under the stress or excitement caused by the event or condition.*

HEARSAY EXCEPTION – FAMILY RECORDS 803

Objections

> *The question calls for a hearsay answer.*

> *I move to strike the answer as hearsay.*

Response

> *This is admissible pursuant to Rule 803(13). I have shown through* (insert name of witness) *that this is a statement of fact concerning personal or family history, and is contained in family Bibles, genealogies, or the like.*

HEARSAY EXCEPTION – FORFEITURE BY WRONGDOING 804

Objections

> *The question calls for hearsay.*

> *I move to strike the answer as hearsay.*

Response

> *This statement is admissible pursuant to Rule 804(b)(6). I have shown through the testimony of* (insert name of the witness(es)) *that:*

(a) (1) *the declarant is now unavailable pursuant to Rule 804(a),* and

(2) *objecting counsel's client engaged in wrongdoing that was intended to, and did, procure the unavailability of the declarant,* or

(3) *objecting counsel's client acquiesced in wrongdoing that was intended to, and did, procure the unavailability of the declarant.*

HEARSAY EXCEPTION – FORMER TESTIMONY

804

Objections

> ➤ *The question calls for a hearsay answer.*
> ➤ *I move to strike the answer as hearsay.*

Response

> ➤ *This is admissible pursuant to Rule 804(b)(1). I have shown through* (insert name of witness) *that:*
>   (a) *the declarant is unavailable pursuant to Rule 804(a), and*
>   (b) *the statement is testimony given*
>   (c) *at another hearing of the same or a different proceeding, or in a deposition in the course of the same or a different proceeding, and*
>   (d) *the party against whom it is offered had an opportunity and similar motive to develop the testimony.*

HEARSAY EXCEPTION – JUDGMENT AS TO PERSONAL, FAMILY, OR GENERAL HISTORY, OR BOUNDARIES

803

Objections

> ➤ *The question calls for a hearsay answer.*
> ➤ *I move to strike the answer as hearsay.*

Response

> ➤ *This statement is admissible pursuant to Rule 803(23). I have shown through* (insert name of witness) *that this statement is a:*
>   (a) *judgment offered as proof of*
>   (b) *matters of personal, family, or general history, or boundaries,*
>   (c) *essential to the judgment, and*
>   (d) *which is provable by evidence of reputation.*

HEARSAY EXCEPTION – JUDGMENT OF PREVIOUS CONVICTION

803

Objections

> ➤ *The question calls for a hearsay answer.*
> ➤ *I move to strike the answer as hearsay.*

Response

> ➤ *This is admissible pursuant to Rule 803(22). I have shown through a certified record or the testimony of* (insert name of witness) *that this statement is evidence of:*
>   (a) *a final judgment,*
>   (b) *entered after a trial or upon a plea of guilty,*
>   (c) *adjudging a person guilty of a felony,*
>   (d) *which is offered to prove any fact essential to sustain the judgment,*

(e) (in a criminal prosecution) *which is not the conviction of someone other than the accused.*

HEARSAY EXCEPTION – LEARNED TREATISES 803
Objections
> ➤ *The question calls for a hearsay answer.*
> ➤ *I move to strike the answer as hearsay.*

Response
> ➤ *This is admissible pursuant to Rule 803(18). I have shown through* (insert name of witness) *that:*
>> (a) (on direct examination) *the expert witness has relied on the statement in the learned treatise,* or
>> (b) (on cross examination)
>>> (1) *I have called the statement to the attention of the expert,* and
>>> (2) *the statement is contained in a published treatise, periodical, or pamphlet on a subject of history, medicine, or other science or art,*
>>> (3) *which has been established as a reliable authority by expert testimony or judicial notice.*

HEARSAY EXCEPTION – MARKET REPORTS AND COMMERCIAL PUBLICATIONS 803
Objection
> ➤ *The document is an out-of-court statement and is therefore hearsay.*

Response
> ➤ *This is admissible pursuant to Rule 803(17). I have shown that the document is:*
>> (a) *a market quotation, directory, or other published compilation,*
>> (b) *which is generally relied upon by the public or persons in particular occupations.*

HEARSAY EXCEPTION – MARRIAGE, BAPTISMAL, AND SIMILAR CERTIFICATES 803
Objection
> ➤ *The document is an out-of-court statement offered for its truth and is hearsay.*

Response
> ➤ *This is admissible pursuant to Rule 803(12). I have shown through* (insert name of witness) *that this is a statement of fact:*
>> (a) *contained in a certificate that shows that the maker performed a marriage or other similar ceremony,*

(b) *made by a clergyman, public official, or other person authorized by law or a religious organization to perform the act certified,* and

(c) *which purports to be issued at the time of the act or within a reasonable time thereafter.*

HEARSAY EXCEPTION – MEDICAL DIAGNOSIS OR TREATMENT 803

Objections

> ➤ *The question calls for a hearsay answer.*
> ➤ *I move to strike the answer as hearsay.*

Response

> ➤ *This is admissible pursuant to Rule 803(4). I have shown through* (insert name of witness) *that the statement:*
>> (a) *was made for purposes of medical diagnosis or treatment,*
>> (b) *was made for describing medical history, past or present symptoms, or the inception or general character of the cause thereof,* and
>> (c) *was reasonably pertinent to diagnosis or treatment.*

HEARSAY EXCEPTION – PERSONAL OR FAMILY HISTORY 804

Objections

> ➤ *The question calls for a hearsay answer.*
> ➤ *I move to strike the answer as hearsay.*

Response

> ➤ *This is admissible pursuant to Rule 804(b)(4). I have shown through* (insert name of witness) *that:*
>> (a) (1) *the declarant is now unavailable pursuant to Rule 804(a),* and
>>> (2) *the statement concerns the declarant's own birth, adoption, marriage, divorce, or other similar fact of personal or family history,*
>>> (3) *even though the declarant had no means of acquiring personal knowledge of the matter stated,* or
>> (b) *the statement concerns the foregoing matters, as well as the death of another person, where the declarant was related to the other person by blood, adoption, or marriage, or was so intimately associated with the other's family as to be likely to give accurate information.*

HEARSAY EXCEPTION – PRESENT SENSE IMPRESSION 803

Objections

> ➤ *The question calls for a hearsay answer.*
> ➤ *I move to strike the answer as hearsay.*

Response

> ➤ *This is admissible pursuant to Rule 803(1). I have shown through* (insert name of witness) *that the statement describes or explains an event or condition, and was made:*
>
>> (a) *while the declarant was perceiving the event or condition,* or
>>
>> (b) *immediately thereafter.*

HEARSAY EXCEPTION – PUBLIC RECORDS AND REPORTS 803
Objections

> ➤ *The question calls for a hearsay answer.*
> ➤ *I move to strike the answer as hearsay.*
> ➤ (In a criminal case) *The report is not admissible against a criminal defendant.*

Response

> ➤ *This is admissible pursuant to Rule 803(8). I have shown through* (insert name of witness) *that:*
>
>> (a) *the document is a record, report, statement, or data compilation,*
>>
>> (b) *of a public office or agency setting forth*
>>
>>> (1) *the activities of the office or agency,* or
>>>
>>> (2) *matters observed pursuant to duty imposed by law as to which matters there was a duty to report.*

HEARSAY EXCEPTION – RECORDED RECOLLECTION 803
Objections

> ➤ *The question calls for a hearsay answer.*
> ➤ *I move to strike the answer as hearsay.*

Response

> ➤ *This is admissible as a recorded recollection pursuant to Rule 803(5). I have shown through* (insert name of witness) *that it is:*
>
>> (a) *a memorandum or record concerning a matter,*
>>
>> (b) *about which a witness once had knowledge,*
>>
>> (c) *but now has insufficient recollection to enable him to testify fully and accurately,* and
>>
>> (d) *shown to have been made or adopted by the witness when the matter was fresh in his memory and to reflect that knowledge correctly.*

HEARSAY EXCEPTION – RECORDS OF DOCUMENTS 803
AFFECTING AN INTEREST IN PROPERTY
Objection

> ➤ *The document is an out-of-court statement offered for its truth and is therefore hearsay.*

Response

> ➤ *This is admissible pursuant to Rule 803(14). I have shown through* (insert name of witness) *that:*
>> (a) *this is a record of a public office,* and
>> (b) *an applicable statute authorizes the recording of documents of that kind in that office.*

HEARSAY EXCEPTION – RECORDS OF RELIGIOUS ORGANIZATIONS   803

Objection

> ➤ *The record is an out-of-court statement offered for its truth and is hearsay.*

Response

> ➤ *This statement is admissible as a record of a religious organization pursuant to Rule 803(11). I have shown through the testimony of* (insert name of witness) *that the statement:*
>> (a) *is one of personal or family history,* and
>> (b) *is contained in a regularly kept record of a religious organization.*

HEARSAY EXCEPTION – RECORDS OF VITAL STATISTICS   803

Objection

> ➤ *The record is an out-of-court statement offered for its truth and is hearsay.*

Response

> ➤ *The out-of-court statement is admissible pursuant to Rule 803(9) in that it:*
>> (a) *is a record regarding a vital statistic*
>> (b) *which records a report made to a public official required by law to keep such a record.*

HEARSAY EXCEPTION – REPUTATION AS TO CHARACTER   803

Objections

> ➤ *The question calls for a hearsay answer.*
> ➤ *I move to strike the answer as hearsay.*

Response

> ➤ *This is admissible pursuant to Rule 803(21). I have shown through the testimony of* (insert name of witness) *that this is a statement of reputation of a person's character among his associates or in the community.*

HEARSAY EXCEPTION – REPUTATION CONCERNING BOUNDARIES OR GENERAL HISTORY

803

Objections

> ➤ *The question calls for a hearsay answer.*
>
> ➤ *I move to strike the answer as hearsay.*

Response

> ➤ *This is admissible pursuant to Rule 803(2). I have shown through the testimony of* (insert name of witness) *that this is a statement of reputation:*
>   - (a) *in a community,*
>   - (b) *arising before the controversy,*
>   - (c) *as to boundaries of, or customs affecting, lands in the community,* or
>   - (d) *as to events of general history important to the community, state, or nation in which located.*

HEARSAY EXCEPTION – REPUTATION CONCERNING PERSONAL OR FAMILY HISTORY

803

Objections

> ➤ *The question calls for a hearsay answer.*
>
> ➤ *I move to strike the answer as hearsay.*

Response

> ➤ *This is admissible pursuant to Rule 803(19). I have shown through the testimony of* (insert name of witness) *that this is a statement of reputation:*
>   - (a) *among members of one's family,* or
>   - (b) *among one's associate,* or
>   - (c) *in the community,*
>   - (d) *concerning a person's adoption, birth, marriage, or other similar fact of personal or family history.*

HEARSAY EXCEPTION – RESIDUAL EXCEPTION

807

Objections

> ➤ *The question calls for a hearsay answer.*
>
> ➤ *I move to strike the answer as hearsay.*

Response

> ➤ *This is admissible pursuant to the residual exception to the hearsay rule contained in Rule 807. I have shown through* (insert name of witness) *that:*
>   - (a) *the statement is not specifically covered by any of the enumerated hearsay exceptions,*
>   - (b) *the statement has circumstantial guarantees of trustworthiness equivalent to that of the enumerated exceptions,*

(c) *the statement is offered as evidence of a material fact,*

(d) *the statement is more probative on the point for which it is offered than any other which I can procure,*

(e) *the general purposes of these rules and the interests of justice will best be served by the admission of this statement,* and

(f) *I have given the adverse parties sufficient notice of my intention to offer the statement.*

HEARSAY EXCEPTION – STATEMENT AGAINST INTEREST 804

Objections

> *The question calls for a hearsay answer.*

> *I move to strike the answer as hearsay.*

Response

> *This is admissible pursuant to Rule 804(b)(3). I have shown through* (insert name of witness) *that the statement:*

(a) *was made by a declarant who is now unavailable pursuant to Rule 804(a),* and

(b) (1) *was, at the time of its making, so far contrary to the declarant's pecuniary or proprietary interest,* or

(2) *so far tended to subject him to criminal or civil liability,* or

(3) *to render invalid a claim by him against another,*

(c) *that a reasonable person would not have made the statement unless he believed it to be true,* and

(d) (if the statement tends to expose the declarant to criminal liability, and is offered to exculpate the accused) *corroborating circumstances clearly indicate the trustworthiness of the statement.*

HEARSAY EXCEPTION – THEN EXISTING MENTAL OR EMOTIONAL CONDITION 803

Objections

> *The question calls for a hearsay answer.*

> *I move to strike the answer as hearsay.*

Response

> *This is admissible pursuant to Rule 803(3). I have shown through* (insert name of witness) *that the statement:*

(a) *is of the declarant's then existing state of mind, emotions, or sensation,* and

(b) (1) *does not include a statement of memory or belief offered to prove the fact remembered or believed,* or

(2) *relates to the execution, revocation, identification, or terms of declarant's will.*

HEARSAY EXCEPTION – THEN EXISTING PHYSICAL CONDITION 803

Objections

> ➤ *The question calls for a hearsay answer.*
> ➤ *I move to strike the answer as hearsay.*

Response

> ➤ *This is admissible pursuant to Rule 803(3). I have shown through* (insert name of witness) *that the statement:*
>> (a) *is of the declarant's then existing physical condition, and*
>> (b) *does not include a statement of memory or belief to prove the fact remembered or believed.*

HEARSAY EXCEPTION – UNAVAILABILITY REQUIREMENT 804

Objections

> ➤ *The question calls for a hearsay answer.*
> ➤ *I move to strike the answer as hearsay.*

Response

> ➤ *The out-of-court statement meets* (insert the appropriate Rule 804(b) exception). *The declarant is unavailable because he:*
>> (a) *is exempted from testifying concerning the subject of the statement by ruling by the court on the ground of privilege, or*
>> (b) *persists in refusing to testify concerning the subject of the statement despite a court order to do so, or*
>> (c) *testifies to a lack of memory on the subject of the statement, or*
>> (d) *is unable to testify at the hearing because of death or illness, or*
>> (e) *is absent from the hearing and I have been unable to procure his attendance, or*
>> (f) (insert other reason for the witness' absence).

HEARSAY GENERALLY 801

Objections

> ➤ *The question calls for a hearsay answer.*
> ➤ *I move to strike the answer as hearsay.*

Response

> ➤ *The statement is not being offered for the truth of the matter asserted, but rather to show the statement was made. This is relevant to show:*
>> (a) *the effect on a person who heard the statement, or*
>> (b) *a prior inconsistent statement, or*
>> (c) *the operative facts or a verbal act, or*
>> (d) *the knowledge of the declarant.*

Objections
> ➤ *This statement contains inadmissible hearsay within hearsay.*
> ➤ *I move to strike the answer because it contains hearsay within hearsay.*

Response
> ➤ *Both statements are admissible because each either comes within a hearsay exception or is non-hearsay.*

IMPEACHMENT – BIAS, PREJUDICE, INTEREST, AND IMPROPER MOTIVE 607, 611

Objections
> ➤ (To questions posed on cross examination) *Counsel is attempting to impeach the witness on improper grounds. The testimony attempted to be elicited is irrelevant.*
> ➤ (To extrinsic evidence) *Counsel has not laid the proper foundation for use of extrinsic evidence to impeach. The witness whom counsel is attempting to impeach:*
> > (a) *has not yet been called as a witness,* or
> > (b) *was not confronted with the alleged bias, interest, or improper motive on cross examination.*

Response
> ➤ (To an objection posed on cross examination) *I am attempting to show that the witness is biased, is prejudiced, has an interest in the outcome of the case, or has an improper motive for giving testimony.*
>
> (To an objection posed to extrinsic evidence)
> > (a) (Where the witness with the alleged bias, prejudice, interest, or improper motive has not yet been called to testify) *The witness has been listed as a witness by my opponent and I offer this evidence conditionally to avoid re-calling the witness later.*
> > (b) (Where the witness with the alleged bias, prejudice, interest, or improper motive has already testified) *I confronted* (insert name of witness) *with his* (bias, prejudice, interest, or improper motive) *during cross examination when I asked him _____, and he denied it.*

IMPEACHMENT – CHARACTER EVIDENCE 608

Objections
> ➤ *The character witness has insufficient knowledge of the witness' character to give an opinion.*
> ➤ *The character witness has insufficient knowledge of the witness' reputation for dishonesty to report that reputation to the court.*

Response

➤ *A sufficient foundation has been laid to demonstrate the character witness' sufficient familiarity with:*

   (a) *the witness' character for dishonesty, or*

   (b) *the witness' reputation for honesty in the community.*

IMPEACHMENT – MEMORY   607
Objection

➤ *The question seeks to elicit irrelevant information. The question involves improper impeachment.*

Response

➤ *The question calls for an answer that will show the witness' inability to remember the events about which he has testified.*

IMPEACHMENT – PERCEPTION   607
Objection

➤ *The question seeks to elicit irrelevant information. The question involves improper impeachment.*

Response

➤ *The question calls for an answer which will show the witness' inability to perceive.*

IMPEACHMENT – PRIOR INCONSISTENT STATEMENTS   613
Objections

➤ *The proffered statement is not inconsistent with the witness' testimony and is irrelevant.*

➤ (For impeachment by extrinsic evidence of a prior inconsistent statement) *A proper foundation has not been laid for introduction of extrinsic evidence of a prior inconsistent statement in that the witness has not been given an opportunity to explain or deny the alleged inconsistent statement.*

Responses

(For impeachment by a prior inconsistent statement on cross examination)

➤ *The witness testified on direct examination that _____ and this statement is inconsistent with the thrust of his direct testimony.*

➤ *The witness testified on direct examination that _____ and this statement is inconsistent in that it omits facts testified to on direct examination.*

(For impeachment by extrinsic evidence of a prior inconsistent statement)

➤ *The witness denied making a prior inconsistent statement during cross examination.*

> ► *This prior inconsistent statement is an admission of a party opponent pursuant to Rule 801(d)(2) and therefore the witness need not be given an opportunity to explain or deny the prior inconsistent statement.*

IMPEACHMENT – PRIOR CONVICTIONS (Civil Cases) 609

Objections

> ► *The proffered conviction is neither for a crime which carries a potential sentence of at least one year in prison nor is it a conviction for a crime involving dishonesty or false statement.*

> ► *The date of the conviction and the witness' release date from sentence for the conviction occurred more than ten years ago and written notice has not been given and/or the probative value of the conviction on the issue of credibility does not substantially outweigh the prejudice to a party of admitting such conviction.*

> ► *The prejudicial effect of the conviction substantially outweighs the probative value of the evidence on the issue of credibility and/or the admission of the evidence will lead to confusion of the issue or will mislead the jury.*

Responses

> ► *The proffered conviction is for a felony or a crime involving dishonesty or false statement.*

> ► *Though the proffered conviction and the witness' release date occurred longer than ten years ago, written notice has been given and the probative value of the conviction on the issue of credibility substantially outweighs the prejudice to the opposing party.*

> ► *The prejudice to the opposing party does not substantially outweigh the probative value of the conviction on the issue of the witness' credibility. The jury will not be misled or confused as to the import of the evidence of conviction as it is limited solely to the issue of the witness' credibility.*

IMPEACHMENT – PRIOR CONVICTIONS (Criminal Cases) 609

Objections

> ► *The conviction offered to impeach the witness is neither for a crime of dishonesty or false statement, nor is it for a crime which carries a penalty of at least a year in prison or death. Even if the conviction offered to impeach is for a felony, the probative value of the conviction is outweighed by the danger of prejudice.*

> ► *The date of the proffered conviction and the witness' release date from his sentence occurred more than ten years ago, written notice has not been given, and/or the probative value of the conviction on the issue of credibility does not substantially outweigh the prejudice of admitting such a conviction.*

- ➤ (Where offered against the criminal defendant-witness) *The probative value of the conviction on the issue of credibility does not outweigh the prejudice to the defendant.*

Responses

- ➤ *The proffered conviction is for a felony, and its probative value is not substantially outweighed by any prejudice to any party in the case.*
- ➤ *The proffered conviction is for activity involving dishonesty or false statement.*
- ➤ *Though the proffered conviction and the defendant's release date occurred longer than ten years ago, written notice has been given and the probative value of the conviction on the issue of the defendant's credibility substantially outweighs any purported prejudice to the defendant.*

IMPEACHMENT – SPECIFIC INSTANCES OF MISCONDUCT 608
Objections

- ➤ (On cross examination) *The specific instance of conduct does not show lack of truth-telling ability.*
- ➤ (To extrinsic evidence, written or oral) *Extrinsic evidence of specific instances of conduct relating to truthfulness is inadmissible.*

Response

- ➤ *The specific instance of conduct shows lack of truth-telling ability in that* _____.

INSURANCE AGAINST LIABILITY 411
Objection

- ➤ *The proponent is offering evidence of liability insurance on the issue of negligence or other wrongful conduct. I move for a mistrial.*

Response

- ➤ *This evidence of liability insurance is not offered on the issue of negligence, but to show ownership, agency, control, bias, or some other purpose other than liability.*

JUDICIAL NOTICE 201
Objection

- ➤ *I object to the court judicially noticing* (insert fact offered by opponent) *in that:*
    - (a) *it is not generally known in this jurisdiction,* and/or
    - (b) *it is open to dispute and not capable of ready and certain verification.*

Response

> *Judicial notice of* (insert fact) *is appropriate because:*
> > (a) *the fact is generally known by people in this local jurisdiction,* or
> > (b) *it is capable of ready and certain verification by resort to authoritative sources which have been provided to the court.*

LAY OPINION EVIDENCE   701, 704

Objections

> *The question calls for an opinion.*
> *I move to strike the answer because it is stated in the form of an opinion.*

Response

> *This is permissible opinion from a lay witness because it is rationally based on the perception of the witness and would help the trier of fact to understand his testimony and to determine a fact in issue.*

LEADING QUESTIONS   611

Objection

> *I object to the question as leading.*

Responses

> *The question does not suggest the answer to the witness.*
> *Leading questions are permitted:*
> > (a) *on preliminary matters,* or
> > (b) *when necessary to develop the witness' testimony,* or
> > (c) *because the witness is hostile, is an adverse party, or is identified with an adverse party.*

MEDICAL AND SIMILAR EXPENSES – PAYMENT   409

Objection

> *This evidence is inadmissible as an offer to pay medical expenses.*

Response

> *This statement is admissible because it is not offered on the issue of liability.*

MISQUOTING THE WITNESS   611

Objection

> *Counsel is misquoting the witness. The witness has not testified to _____.*

Response

> *The witness previously testified to _____.*

NARRATIVES

611

Objections

> ➤ *That question calls for a narrative response.*
> ➤ *The witness is testifying in the form of a narrative.*

Response

> ➤ *The witness is testifying to relevant and admissible matters.*

NON-RESPONSIVE ANSWERS

611

Objections

> ➤ *I move to strike the answer of the witness as non-responsive.*

Responses

> ➤ (If the objection is made by questioning counsel) *The answer of the witness is responsive to the question. The question put to the witness was _____.*
> ➤ (If the objection is made by opposing counsel) *I accept the answer.*

OBJECTIONS GENERALLY

103

Objections

> ➤ *I object on the ground that _____.*
> ➤ *I move to strike the witness' answer on the ground that _____.*

Response

> ➤ *The evidence is admissible because _____.*

OFFERS OF PROOF

103

Offers

> ➤ By asking the witness to state, outside the hearing of the jury, what the testimony would have been if the judge had not excluded it, **or**
> ➤ By a written or oral statement by counsel which provides the substance of what the witness' testimony would have been, but for the adverse ruling.

PRESUMPTIONS

301–2

Motion

> ➤ *I move for a directed verdict on* (the fact presumed) *because my opponent failed to come forward with sufficient evidence to rebut it.*

Response

> ➤ *A directed verdict is inappropriate because we have produced sufficient evidence to rebut the presumption.*

PRIVILEGES 501

Objection

> ➤ *This evidence is privileged pursuant to the _____ privilege.*

Response

> ➤ *This evidence is admissible because:*
>   (a) *it does not fall within the privilege, or*
>   (b) *if privileged, such privilege has been waived.*

REFRESHING PRESENT RECOLLECTION 612

Objections

> ➤ *I object to the attempt to refresh the witness' recollection in the absence of a demonstrated failure of memory.*
> ➤ *I object to the witness' reading from the exhibit used to refresh his recollection because it is not in evidence and because it is hearsay.*

Responses

> ➤ *The witness has shown a failure of memory and I am attempting to refresh his recollection pursuant to Rule 612.*
> ➤ *The exhibit used to refresh the witness' recollection is already in evidence and is either:*
>   (a) *not hearsay, or*
>   (b) *meets an exception to the hearsay rule.*

RELEVANCE – CONDITIONAL ADMISSIBILITY 104

Objections

> ➤ *The proffered evidence is not relevant and admissible unless other facts are proved.*
> ➤ *I move to strike the conditionally admitted evidence of _____. Counsel has failed to prove the additional facts necessary to show relevance.*

Responses

> ➤ *I will show the relevance of the proffered evidence by proof of the following additional facts through the testimony of* (insert name of witness).
> ➤ *The relevance of the conditionally admitted facts has been shown through the additional evidence given by* (insert name of witness).

RELEVANCE – EXCLUSION ON GROUNDS OF PREJUDICE, 403
CONFUSION, OR WASTE OF TIME

Objections

> ➤ *The probative value is substantially outweighed by the prejudicial effect of the evidence.*

- *The introduction of this evidence will confuse the issue before the jury.*
- *The evidence is merely cumulative.*

Response

- *The evidence is admissible because it is logically relevant under Rule 401 and:*
  - (a) *its probative value is not substantially outweighed by the danger of unfair prejudice, or*
  - (b) *any potential for confusion of issues is easily cured by an instruction by the court, or*
  - (c) *the evidence is corroborative of an issue central to the case.*

RELEVANCE GENERALLY 401–2

Objections

- *The question calls for an irrelevant answer.*
- *I move to strike the answer as irrelevant.*

Response

- *The evidence has some tendency to make more likely a fact which is material to either a claim or defense in the lawsuit, or bears on the weight or credibility of the evidence.*

RELEVANCE – LIMITED ADMISSIBILITY 105

Objections

- *The question calls for irrelevant information on the issue of _____.*
- *I move that the court instruct the jury that the answer is irrelevant and inadmissible on the issue of _____ and I request a limiting instruction.*
- *The question calls for irrelevant information as against my client.*
- *I move that the court instruct the jury that the answer is irrelevant and inadmissible as to my client and I request a limiting instruction.*

Responses

- *The evidence offered is relevant and admissible for all purposes and a limiting instruction is inappropriate.*
- *The evidence is relevant and admissible against all parties and a limiting instruction is inappropriate.*

RELEVANCE – RULE OF COMPLETENESS 106

Objection

- *I object to the admissibility of the proffered writing (or recording) unless other portions of the writing (or recording), or related writings (or recordings), are also admitted. This other material is necessary to explain or to put in context the proffered writing (or recording).*

Response

> ➤ *The proffered statement (or recording) does not need explanation or context. Other portions of the statement (or recording), or additional writings (or recordings), are not necessary to a fair understanding of the proffered statement (or recording).*

SUBSEQUENT REMEDIAL MEASURES 407

Objection

> ➤ *This is evidence of a subsequent remedial measure.*

Responses

> ➤ *This evidence is not offered on a prohibited issue, but is offered to show:*
>   (a) *notice,* or
>   (b) *ownership,* or
>   (c) *control,* or
>   (d) *feasibility of precautionary measures,* or
>   (e) *impeachment.*
> ➤ *My opponent has "opened the door" to this evidence by its pleadings or the questioning of* (insert name of witness).

NITA EVIDENCE PRODUCTS AND PROGRAMS

NITA offers many evidence related products and programs. The following pages describe a few of these items. Call NITA Customer Support at (800) 225-6482 to order these products, or for more details.

Federal Rules of Evidence

This guide presents the Federal Rules of Evidence in a pocket-size, 4-by-6 inch format.

Federal Rules of Evidence with Objections

Anthony J. Bocchino and David A. Sonenshein

NITA's pocket-size volume of the Federal Rules of Evidence is combined with pattern objections and responses for each rule of evidence.

Explanatory paragraphs alert you to practice tips and legal inter-pretations crucial to understanding the rules. Key phrases for objections are listed alphabetically, with thumb tabs for quick reference.

State Rules of Evidence with Objections

These texts are modeled after the best-selling *Federal Rules of Evidence with Objections*. NITA offers state rules books for:

- California
- Colorado
- Florida
- Illinois
- Indiana
- Michigan
- North Carolina
- Ohio
- Pennsylvania

Call for details about other state books.

National Institute for Trial Advocacy
Phone: (800) 225-6482 ◆ Fax: (219) 282-1263
E-mail: nita.1@nd.edu ◆ Website: www.nita.org

TANGIBLE EVIDENCE: HOW TO USE EXHIBITS AT DEPOSITION AND TRIAL

Deanne C. Siemer

Book and CD-ROM available

Leading trial attorney Deanne C. Siemer gives you the up-to-date, practical information you need to get all types of exhibits admitted into evidence. In a clear, user-friendly format, this text divides exhibits into seven categories and gives foundation questions and answers for each. Use this information to create a solid trial outline and notes that will lead you to ask the right questions—and get the right answers—so your exhibits will be admitted into evidence. Each chapter covers:

- The foundation required to obtain admission for each type of exhibit

- Objections available to your opponent and how to counter those objections

- Technical information about creating exhibits

- Tactical considerations for using each exhibit type

From e-mail, workgroup documents, and faxes to sound recordings, computer animations, and simulations, you'll understand how to get cutting-edge exhibits admitted smoothly into evidence. And you'll see how to display them for maximum impact.

CD-ROM users can excerpt examples from the CD and edit them in their own word processing program to fit the case at hand. The CD-ROM also offers space savings and portability, condensing a 644-page text into a single compact disk.

The appendices offer vital lists of suppliers for equipment and technical assistance, forms for using exhibits at deposition and trial, and selected published sources on tangible evidence.

National Institute for Trial Advocacy
Phone: (800) 225-6482 ◆ Fax: (219) 282-1263
E-mail: nita.1@nd.edu ◆ Website: www.nita.org

Trial Evidence—
Making and Meeting Objections

Anthony J. Bocchino, David A. Sonenshein, and
JoAnne A. Epps

Trial Evidence is a series of 62 vignettes designed to
develop proper objection procedure through example and
argument. Each vignette gives a brief background description of the case and is followed by a short direct examina-
tion/cross-examination segment. The vignettes cover a wide
variety of evidence topics—from subsequent remedial
measures and character, to expert opinions and hearsay.

The series encourages discussion and helps you master the
complex skill of making and meeting objections.

The complete series includes four videotapes or audiotapes
and one *Trial Evidence—Making and Meeting Objections*
book. Individual tapes are not for sale.

National Institute for Trial Advocacy
Phone: (800) .225-6482 ◆ Fax: (219) 282-1263
E-mail: nita.1@nd.edu ◆ Website: www.nita.org

Basic Concepts in the Law of Evidence
with Irving Younger

The late Professor Younger's experience as a trial judge, law professor, and outstanding trial attorney, along with his flair for storytelling, make this series fascinating. The tapes cover:

- Introduction to evidence

- Basic concepts in evidence

- Failure of recollection, best evidence rule, and perception

- Expert witnesses

- Cross-examination, impeachment, and rehabilitation

- Hearsay (four tapes)

- Burdens of proof and presumptions

- Hearsay and the right to confrontation (two tapes)

- The Ten Commandments of cross-examination

Complete series includes 15 videotapes or audiotapes and support materials.

National Institute for Trial Advocacy
Phone: (800) 225-6482 ◆ Fax: (219) 282-1263
E-mail: nita.1@nd.edu ◆ Website: www.nita.org

Courtroom Evidence:
A Teaching Commentary

Michael H. Graham and Edward D. Ohlbaum

Courtroom Evidence and its *Supplement* provide a hands-on method of teaching evidence from a courtroom perspective. Using the text and supplement, students learn evidentiary rules and policies by applying them in the adversarial context for which they were formulated.

Courtroom Evidence opens with a general description of a trial's structure and addresses the admissibility of evidence at trial in a logical order. Throughout the commentary, short and crisp illustrations, examples, sample foundations, and examinations bring concepts and rules to life. Special reference is made to key evidence cases such as *Hillmon, Shepard, Michaelson, Huddleston, Bourjaily*, and *Tatham*.

The *Supplement* augments the main text and helps students apply theory through real-world courtroom vignettes, practice cases and problems, and review problems. Each vignette is a mock transcript of a witness examination directed at the text's primary topics.

A helpful *Teacher's Manual*, with annotated courtroom vignettes and answers to each problem, is also available.

National Institute for Trial Advocacy
Phone: (800) 225-6482 ◆ Fax: (219) 282-1263
E-mail: nita.1@nd.edu ◆ Website: www.nita.org

Mastering Federal Evidence
One-Day Workshops

Knowing the rules of evidence at trial is not enough. You also need to know when to object and how to respond—consistent with a winning case theory. Mastering trial evidence typically takes years of courtroom experience. NITA offers you a shortcut to this mastery in this special One-Day Workshop. In a single day, you will master the critical evidence skills you need to compete in the courtroom.

Through video trial vignettes, demonstrations, and interactive discussions, you'll master the skills of trial evidence on:

- Relevance
- Form of the question
- Lay opinions
- Limited admissibility
- Offers of proof
- Original writings
- Preliminary questions
- Expert testimony
- Hearsay and its exceptions
- Personal knowledge requirement

Contact NITA's Customer Support Department to learn about the dates and locations of upcoming Federal Evidence One-Day Workshops.

National Institute for Trial Advocacy
Phone: (800) 225-6482 ◆ Fax: (219) 282-1263
E-mail: nita.1@nd.edu ◆ Website: www.nita.org